Astride the Dawn

Tales of a Chautauqua Boyhood

written and illustrated by

Don Skinner

Copyright © 2005 by Don Skinner

Cover photos by Heather Munro. All rights reserved.
Interior and cover designed by Masha Shubin

All rights reserved. No part of this book may be reproduced or transmitted in any form or by any means whatsoever, including photocopying, recording or by any information storage and retrieval system, without written permission from the publisher and/or author. Contact Inkwater Press at 6750 SW Franklin Street, Suite A, Portland, OR 97223-2542.

www.inkwaterpress.com

ISBN 1-59299-130-0

Publisher: Inkwater Press

Printed in the U.S.A.

*To the people of Chautauqua—
because they—as much as the place—
make it uniquely what it is;
and especially to
Daniel L. Bratton,
classmate, colleague, and friend,
Chautauqua Institution President from 1984-2000:
his irenic spirit,
appreciation of history,
and focus on essentials
left Chautauqua stronger
when he was taken from us than when he came.
Vincent and Miller would be proud.*

Also by Don Skinner:

Prayers for the Gathered Community

A Passage through Sacred History

In a Valley Surrounded by Hills:
Stories of Growing Up in a Pennsylvania Town

Table of Contents

Acknowledgments xi
Introduction xvii

In the Beginning 1
    A Sacred Conspiracy 3
    Baptism by Immersion 9
    Clearing the Decks for a New Season 18

Cottages 29
    Our Own Bit of Brigadoon 31
    Culture Run Amok 42
    The Perfect Lakefront Cottage 51
    Chautauqua's Premier Community Dock 60

Boys' and Girls' Club 69
    If You're Red or Blue 71
    The Real Power of Teamwork 79
    How to Empty the Lake Out of a Swamped Boat 89

Lee 101
    A Geek by His Third Birthday 103
    The End of a Romantic Era 116

Hank 127
    Westfield Station 129
    Nantucket Sleigh Ride 137
    A Stroll on the Bottom of Chautauqua Lake 145

Sunday 153
    Bordering on Mid-Adolescent Glossolalia 155
    Awash in a Flood of Protestant Christian Piety 163
    Scared Song Service 172

A Succession of Boats 179
    An Exponential Leap into Uncharted Waters 181
    Boiling Mahogany over a Driftwood Fire 190
    God Saved the Shadow 205
    Supper in the Lee of Long Point 216

Around the Grounds 223
    Riding the Lightning 225
    Incidental Witnesses 236
    A Handsome Stranger Named Dominic 243
    The Valued Possession of the Many 256

On the Lakefront 267
    Learning the Hard Way What They didn't Know 269
    A Pretty Good Definition of Successful Fishing 280
    The Long Swim 288
    "What's the Course?" 294

Coming of Age 305
    Grubbing out a Living 307
    A Posterior of Granite 319
    High School Club 331
    College Club 343

Closing Up Shop 351
    Ben Hur and Messala on Wicker 353

Afterword 365

Acknowledgments

It would be flattering to believe that I get to take all the credit for this book. I keep trying, but the thought won't hold. Too many generous people are owed too much.

First and foremost, I owe an enormous debt of gratitude to Heather Munro, who is arguably the best thing that every happened to Steve Skinner, who just happens to be her husband and our son. When I approached Heather with the proposition that she serve as copy editor for this book, she didn't even blanch, which just goes to prove that great courage is sometimes wrapped in very petite packages. Her steady and painstaking assessment of her father-in-law's manuscript, including the pluck to write notes in the margin like, "I'd cut out this entire paragraph: it doesn't further your purpose any, and will just confuse the reader," earns her a measurable share of the credit for whatever quality the writing has attained. I won't go on to add the obligatory bunkum about "whatever faults the book possesses are mine alone." I mean, she *was* the copy editor. Besides, she wouldn't stand for it. One way she demonstrates her far-above-average integrity is her unwillingness to stand back while someone else takes the blame. If there's blame to be passed out along with the praise, she's right there to shoulder her share. Boy, that's rare. See why I admire her so? You can't buy that kind of loyalty.

My sister Ruth Ann, and my brothers Cliff and Frank, deserve a special word of thanks for the way that they joined me in communally scrounging through the attic of recollection, with no promise of reward. Indeed, they might fairly have asked whether the whole effort wasn't a waste of time. There was always the possibility that the book would never make it to the printers. Readers will not be able to discern their fingerprints, but trust me: they're all over this book.

I am also grateful for the resources that were available to me because of the disciplined professional labor of others.

Pauline Fancher's *Chautauqua: Its Architecture and Its People* (Miami: Banyon Books, 1978) opens an enchanted door to Chautauqua's architectural past and provides a fascinating record of the ownership of many historic structures.

Alfreda L. Irwin, for many years Chautauqua's devoted historian and archivist—and a warm friend—did Chautauqua an invaluable service with her history of Chautauqua, *Three Taps of the Gavel: Pledge to the Future*, published by Chautauqua Institution (Third Edition, 1987). It is an archive in its own right, critical not just to trace the Institution's history, but to refresh personal memory about the voluminous detail of the place.

Jeffrey Simpson, who undertook the well-nigh impossible task of capturing the history and character of Chautauqua in narrative form, succeeded in *Chautauqua: An American Utopia* (New York: Harry N. Abrams, Inc., 1999, in cooperation with Chautauqua Institution). It is arguably the most readable account of the Institution's history yet written.

The Fenton Historical Society of Jamestown, New York preserved a remarkable piece of Chautauqua Lake history in *Chautauqua Lake Steamboats* (Harold J. Alstrom, Ed., 1971). It records the growth and decline of a vital industry without which Chautauqua might never have flourished, now vanished and largely unknown to modern visitors. Too bad.

I owe a special word of thanks to the members of the (unofficial) North Shore Community—bounded roughly by North Lake Drive, Miller Park and Whitfield Avenue—our family's friends and neighbors for half a century. In 1995 and 1996, Priscilla Patton, with the help of Judy Jones McMillan, compiled and published our reminiscences in a booklet titled "Memories of Our Neighborhood." It may not be sophisticated writing; but to those who, to one degree or another, were privileged to be part of that neighborhood for over a century, it captures the core of our Chautauqua memories.

Finally, I must say a word of thanks to my wife, Patricia. She really wishes I wouldn't. She is given to shyness, and does not like being in the spotlight. And this is the third time I've done this to her. But the quiet way that she waits through the months it takes to bring a project like this to completion, offering encouragement and cautionary advice, should not go unnoticed. So herewith I notice her—with bells and whistles. Actually, she's easy. She doesn't care what I do, as long as I take her to Chautauqua at every conceivable opportunity. Why, just last week....

Map of Chautauqua

Introduction

Breathes there a Chautauquan who has not asked the one question that must be asked there whenever strangers introduce themselves: "How long have you been coming to Chautauqua?"

I have come to believe that the query is so dependably put because Chautauqua is a place at which—for all practical purposes—all of us arrive as strangers. And that is true no matter how often we come. It is not our hometown, nor is it the place where, as a community, we are bound together (or divided) by common history, and agree (or disagree) on political, economic, and religious concerns.

For all but a few year-round residents, Chautauqua is momentary, and a bit mysterious. It claims us at least as much as we claim it. We go there because we love it so, that is true. But inescapably, some of those present, who love the place just as much as we do, are strangers to us, and we to them. So we ask each other: "How long have you been coming to Chautauqua?"

What we seek, I think, is not the precise answer that we are likely to receive—"A couple of years" or "Since 1974" or "Oh, this is my first visit." What we want to do is to establish a kind of social matrix, a substitute for that intricate connectedness that defines us when we are among the citizens of our home communities. Whether we fully realize it or not, that connectedness is what gives us our sense of place. It tells us who we are and how we fit in. Of necessity, those kinds of links are missing at Chautauqua. They are the victims of our universal itinerancy. Even those of us who are there all summer are together only briefly. Then we return to the places where the bulk of our lives are lived. So we create a substitute for hometown connections by asking, "How long have you been coming to Chautauqua?"

Is there a hint of one-upmanship in all this? Of course there is. That's forgivable. Human beings require some sense of hierarchy. But enjoying status and worshipping it are not the same thing. I put the question: after you asked the Chautauqua question, did it ever change how you treated this latest stranger now become your newest friend? Did you ever respond by saying, "Oh, you haven't been here long enough," and turn away? Did you not greet each other as warmly the next time your paths crossed as if you had known each other for years?

That, you see, is fundamental to the Chautauqua experience. It is a place, to be sure. But so are tens of thousands of other villages across the country; and we don't rush off to any of them each summer and ask every new face we meet, "How long have you been coming here?"

In the end, what matters to Chautauquans is other Chautauquans. Do we love its unique physical character? Obviously. Do we pour our energy and resources into preserving and enhancing it? Absolutely. But would any of us think twice about spending our time there if we were not surrounded by the rest of us who thrive on intellectual challenge and artistic achievement and spiritual grappling? And do we not feel exactly the same way toward those who, this summer or next, will walk as strangers through the gate for the very first time?

Writing a book about Chautauqua subjects an author to the seduction of name-dropping. The reason is obvious enough. Which of us who grew up summers in that remarkable community did not at one time or another rub elbows with some famous personage, or several? I certainly did.

(Arguably my most unusual brush with fame came on July 4, 1961. I was asked to read the opening segment of the Declaration of Independence at the 10:45 a.m. lecture in the Amphitheater, and found myself alone on stage with Chautauqua President J. William Carothers and featured speaker U.S. Senator Barry Goldwater, Republican of Arizona and candidate for the United States presidency.)

See, at Chautauqua, you may bump into a famous person around any corner, which is precisely why it is so not-unique. This book mentions a few; but at Chautauqua, they're all over the place.

On the other hand, a number of "average" Chautauquans are named in this book, but many are not. There is a reason for this. If I started dropping names, where would I stop? The problem with listing Chautauquans who are gifted or friendly or helpful or generous is that you'd better be prepared to publish the phone book. So I set myself this guideline: if knowing a name was helpful to tell a story, I included it; if knowing it added nothing to the story, I didn't.

Beyond that, I make only this plea: that friends not named will recognize it as a concession to the constraints of publishing, and nothing more. The same may be said for the selection of stories I have chosen to include. There are many more that are not here. I can only tell so many stories before the book grows so large that no one in their right mind would want to read it.

So many stories, so little room.

I have learned by long exposure that members of a class or audience are likely to rate a session as exciting or helpful or successful in proportion to how much talking they do themselves. The more they contribute, the better they judge the event to have been.

So with this book of stories. My purpose has not been to write a history of Chautauqua, but to stimulate the memory of Chautauquans. These are my recollections of growing up there over half-a-lifetime of summers; but it is the stories that matter, not the story-teller.

I try to tell my stories in a way that will help resurrect the lost or dimly remembered facets of your own stories, and flood them with light. I hope you will find fragments of memory, forgotten half a lifetime ago, popping out of the subconscious archive of your mind. When you stop hearing my story and begin to retell your own, we will have met.

Oh, I almost forgot to ask: how long *have* you been coming to Chautauqua?

Meadville, Pennsylvania
February 2005

Astride the Dawn

PART 1

In the Beginning

CHAPTER 1

A Sacred Conspiracy

C hautauqua was founded by a pair of geniuses: John Heyl Vincent, a minister of the Methodist Episcopal Church soon to be sanctified bishop; and Lewis Miller, an industrialist and inventor. Vincent, a native of Tuscaloosa, Alabama, started to preach at the age of 18 and never looked back. Miller lived in Akron, Ohio, where he developed and marketed his Buckeye mower—the first that allowed the cutting bar to pivot up and down to accommodate shifts in topography—and became a millionaire. Neither attended college. This does not imply that they devalued education. Indeed, they thought it among the holiest of human endeavors—and it brought them together.

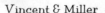

Vincent & Miller

They were, to a peculiar degree, men of their time—evidence of a providential serendipity that places just the right human beings with just the right resources in the right place at the right moment. The thought had gotten abroad in the land that the maintenance of democratic society depended on an educated electorate. It was an idea that resonated with particular force among Methodists, who viewed education of the masses as a primary obligation, and adopted it with missionary zeal. During one period the denomination (or some subdivision or member of it) was founding or adopting schools, colleges, or seminaries at an astonishing rate, and on a global scale. I suppose we should be relieved that most of them did not survive, else we'd have been buried in schools. But I will not gainsay the blessings bestowed by those that survived. I benefited from higher learning or employment—sometimes both—at three of them: Allegheny College in Pennsylvania, Syracuse University in New York, and Hamline University in Minnesota. And I'm not even a Methodist.

That, too, was a quality shared by Chautauqua's co-founders: they were men of ecumenical spirit, and so infected their peers that it remains one of Chautauqua's characteristic traits 120 years after the first Chautauqua Assembly gathered on the shore of the lake from which it took its name.

The immediate stimulus for Miller and Vincent's energy was the international Sunday School movement, which was exciting Protestant Christians all over the world. I recognize the skepticism that such a statement arouses today, when many rank the very idea of Sunday School somewhere between spelling class and appendicitis: if the boredom doesn't get you, the pain surely will.

Not so in the late 19th Century, when education beyond simple reading and figuring was out of reach for all but a privileged fraction of our people. The opportunity not only interested average folk, it enthralled them, and became a driving force behind their lives and the values they taught to their children. Those among them who were people of faith had a special, one wants to say ravenous, interest: to study biblical and moral theology. But who was there to teach them? Most Sunday School teachers, indeed most clergy, were abysmally ignorant of their topic.

It was this hunger that brought Miller and Vincent together, and to Chautauqua. As Sunday School superintendent in Akron and an ordained minister in a denomination struggling to broaden access to education, the two men shared an acute awareness of the deficiencies of their peers. Drawing on the burgeoning new model of education of public school teachers, they entered into a sacred conspiracy: to found a "Normal School"—a school of education—for Sunday School teachers. But where, and how? Both men were suspicious of the camp meeting model, believing that the orchestrated emotionalism typical of those venues was a poor substitute for true learning and intellectual growth. They were not averse to using such a facility, however, and Miller already held the key. He was a trustee of a "camp meeting" at Fair Point, a jut of land on the western side of a fourteen-mile basin of sparkling cobalt called Chautauqua Lake.

Oriented forty-five degrees off compass north, it was as if one of New York's sublime Finger Lakes had slipped its moorings and migrated west 150 miles in search of a new valley in which to stretch out in the sun. And there it lay, atop a rolling plateau near the crest of a continental water divide, ten miles south and 570 feet above the shore of Lake Erie. A drop of rain falling north of the divide flows to Lake Erie, hence to Niagara Falls, Lake Ontario, the St. Lawrence River, eventually to reach the North Atlantic. Only feet away, a companion drop tumbles south into Chautauqua Lake, which drains to the Gulf of Mexico by way of Chatequoin Creek, the Allegheny River, the Ohio, and finally the Mississippi.

In 1873, accompanied by Vincent's nine-year-old son George, the two men traveled there, surveyed the setting, and made a decision. It was, they concluded, perfect, and the announcement went forth: on August 4, 1874 a School Assembly would convene at the Fair Point campground.

I wonder whether either Vincent or Miller fully appreciated where their conspiracy would lead, or how far it would go. The assembly was a smashing success. People drew in not only from the northeastern states, which in itself would have been a significant achievement; they came from twenty-five states and were enriched by a salt-and-pepper sprinkling of folk from four foreign countries. Their sheer numbers overwhelmed the steamboat fleet that then provided most visitors passage to Fair Point.

And that was only the beginning. It would grow, that year and every year for more than a century. Renamed Chautauqua in 1879, the assembly was incorporated as Chautauqua Institution in 1902. The inaugural two-week assembly was expanded in 1876 to three weeks, and eventually reached nine. Lectures on religious and biblical issues went global, and Chautauqua's lecture platform soon acquired stature as one of the world's premier forums for debate of the salient issues of the day, ranging from political-economy to social morality to science and medicine. Literature of every form found a ready home and audience. People who had never painted anything but a shed took up artist's brushes and created pictures. Opera, theater, symphony and dance took their places as staples of the summer program. Physical education was encouraged, among which field games and water sports predominated, but none so universally enjoyed as simple walking. And by means of it all, Vincent and Miller bequeathed to America and the world a new idea about education: that it must not only serve the masses, it must last a lifetime. The very notion of adult education first found expression at Chautauqua.

One thing can be said with certainty: among all the places you can think of, Chautauqua is unique. Finer music can be heard in metropolitan concert halls, great universities maintain better art schools, and grander opera thrills at the Met. But no place offers it all, in a setting of such tranquil beauty, to a community composed almost entirely of active participants. No one stated it better, perhaps, than author and historian David McCullough, Chautauqua Lecturer for 1993: "Chautauqua is part of the American imagination. It belongs with Concord, Massachusetts or Hannibal, Missouri or Springfield, Illinois, as one of those places that defines who we are and what we believe in."

It would certainly be so for me.

The saga of Chautauqua needs no further elaboration here. Several encompassing and insightful histories have already been cited in the Acknowledgements preceding this chapter. The foregoing is offered simply to set the stage for the stories that follow. It was to this place, as its contours were taking shape toward the middle of the 20th Century, that my family came almost every summer of my youth. It was our mother's fault. In spite of the fact that Clifford Skinner, our father, grew up in the small crossroads village of Ashville, only ten miles down-lake and a mile inland, it was our mother's childhood passion that bonded us to the place. Traveling north by train from turn-of-the-century Pittsburgh with her parents and older brother, Ruth McCafferty boarded one of the "great white fleet" of lake steamers at Mayville for the three-mile cruise to Fair Point, there to disembark at the ornate Victorian pier building. (The pristine label given those boats was a misnomer, actually: the plumes of coal smoke they belched had to be visible from any tall building in Cleveland.)

To the end of her life, Mother spoke with impish delight of climbing with her playmates to the second floor porch of the pier building where they leaned over the railing with wooden paddles to which hard rubber balls were affixed by rubber bands, welcoming successive waves of arriving guests by bopping them on the head.

I was taken aback by that story the first time I heard it. I was about 12, as I recall, and could not imagine my mother doing such a thing—or much else, for that matter. The older I got, and the better I came to understand her, the less any of it surprised me.

By the time she was a young mother of four, married to a medical doctor on the faculty of Allegheny College (a comfortable 65-mile drive southwest at Meadville, Pennsylvania), she was determined to do everything in her power to ensure that her children benefited as fully from Chautauqua as she had. She and Dad introduced us to the place early in our lives, but none earlier than me, their youngest. In my case, however, it was not your usual introduction. More like a baptism.

CHAPTER 2

Baptism by Immersion

My introduction to Chautauqua occurred when I was two. It must have been during the off-season, because we drove down to Miller Bell Tower (a forbidden act during the summer "assembly") parked the car, and walked out to the tip of "Fair Point" to watch the waves lap at the shore. I was spellbound. It might have been the first time, but surely would not be the last, that I perched at the edge of that splendid water, gaze glued on the line where lake and land converged. Born where the leeward air riffled the surface at the far shore, and driven across two miles of open water, the ripples piled up into waves that continued to grow until their tops were knocked off in "whitecaps," and the lake was polka-dotted with froth. Concluding their landward march almost at our feet, the waves tripped on the rising lake bottom and fell face-down onto the gravelly beach. So consistent was their rhythm that the Chautauqua music school might have used it as a metronome.

My transfixation resulted in a baptism by immersion, of sorts. This was not spiritually necessary—at least by the tenets of reformed theology that my parents embraced. I was already baptized. And if the sprinkle of water that dribbled from the slender fingertips of the Rev. Dr. Crawford of Meadville's First Presbyterian Church did not satisfy the protests of those who held that only a whole-body soaking truly confers grace, Mother and Dad didn't much care. Nor, they were persuaded, did God. Taking seriously the teaching that a sacrament is "an outward and visible sign of an inward and spiritual grace," they preferred to focus on the inward part, satisfied that their intentions compensated for any deficiency of outward form.

Still (and long before anyone would anticipate my ordination to Christian ministry a quarter-century later), events conspired that day to ensure that I would receive whatever extra measure of inward and spiritual grace immersion might confer.

Modern-day visitors to the wave-lapped point of land over which Miller Bell Tower looms walk around the Casto Garden, ignorant of its history. It appears as an oval, rock-bordered flower bed halfway between the foot of the tower and the point beyond. A bronze plaque mounted on a stone half-cloaked by shrubbery declares it a memorial honoring Kirk David Casto. In my childhood, it was an eight-by-fourteen-foot pool bounded by a well-laid rock wall (the top rank of which still delineates the garden), its two feet of water barely visible beneath water hyacinth leaves that shrouded its surface. My friends and I called it the frog pond. Some bullfrog or other, migrating in search of a summer home, always managed to find it. There it passed the summer afloat on the lily-pad raft, gathering the warming rays of the morning sun or snatching delectable insects out of the air with its faster-than-the-eye tongue, ready at the loom of a threatening shadow to plunge through the water to the concealing mud below.

Frog Pond

"Don... C'mon, Don! We're leaving."

The voice penetrated my infant consciousness, still bonded to the mesmerizing waves, and it dawned on me that it had already announced the family's departure several times. My dreamy imagination did not readily assent to invasion in those days (some would say that seven intervening decades have not materially altered that characteristic). But at two, I already understood the limits of my parents' patience. Spinning about, my gaze still fixed over my shoulder at the ordered tumult of the shoreline, I broke into a run toward the sound of the summons, took three bounding steps and landed squarely in the frog pond, raising waves of my own sufficient to wash over the wall and onto the surrounding grass. There I stood, bits of flotsam and jetsam dripping from my hair and nose, my Sunday-go-to-meeting clothes saturated, my good shoes sodden with bottom muck. For two nanoseconds the shock held, as my siblings—Ruth Ann, Cliff and Frank—looked first at me, then at our parents, pie-eyes searching for some clue as to how they should react to this entirely irregular development. Then their faces relaxed into grins as I opened my dripping mouth and bellowed, and Mother and Dad burst into laughter.

Dad reached down, hauled me up out of the pond and set me on *terra firma*. Back at the car, Mother stripped me out of my sopping clothing and, from somewhere, produced something with which to dry me off and dress me for the ride back to Meadville.

I don't really suppose that my startled plunge caused any advance in my spiritual development. But it was a full-fledged baptism into the spirit of Chautauqua. No child who failed, at least once, to take an unanticipated bath in some collection of water, whether the frog pond, the brook that bisects the woods at the south end of the grounds, or the replica of the Dead Sea in the half-acre model of Palestine conceived by co-founder John Heyl Vincent—if not Chautauqua Lake itself—may truly claim to be a descendant of the genius of Vincent and Miller. And I, at one time or another, fell into all four. So I am a true child of Chautauqua.

My adoption into the Chautauqua family was not immediately decisive, however. It started out promisingly enough, in 1938, when Ernest and Florence McCafferty (Mother's parents) rented the lakefront cottage at 8 South Lake—on the Promenade, actually, a few yards south of Miller Park and directly behind the Sports Club bowling green. They didn't rent it for themselves, however, but for two generations of their offspring. The fathers weren't there much, actually. Dad's duties as the only anesthetist in Crawford County kept him constantly on call at both of Meadville's hospitals and precluded his being with us during the week, so he commuted, driving up on Friday afternoon and back on Sunday. And Uncle Tom McCafferty, Mother's only brother, was kept in Pittsburgh by his duties as treasurer at H.J. Heinz Co.

Which left Mother and her sister-in-law, Helen Thoburn McCafferty, youngest daughter of the first Methodist Episcopal bishop of India, sharing supervision of five grandchildren—four Skinners and Betty Jane. The presence of BJ (as we knew her) was a special treat. Our only McCafferty cousin, she was also our favorite because, loving though they were, all our Skinner cousins were much older than we. For Ruth Ann, BJ's presence was a double delight: the same age, the two "only" daughters were inseparable companions whenever circumstances put them within shouting distance of each another. Being at the transitional age of twelve, they were free to explore the grounds, and did, disappearing for hours at a stretch. What no one realized at the time was that during some of those disappearances they weren't out exploring the grounds at all. They were up in the attic, snooping in several trunks packed with possessions belonging to the cottage's owners. Finding a quantity of clothing among the effects, they sorted through them and played dress-up. One has to wonder why the owners never caught on, or if they did, why they never said anything.

That summer brought me my first brush with fame on a Chautauqua platform. BJ and my older siblings were enrolled in the Boys' and Girls' Clubs at the south end of the grounds—Chautauqua's ingenious system of communal child-care. Formed into supervised groups by age, children were kept productively busy from 9:00 a.m. to noon and 2:00 to 4:00 p.m., freeing their parents to participate in adult programs and classes. Still too young for Club, I was enrolled in the Children's Center at the north end of the grounds, where my musical genius was first recognized. "Youth Day" was coming up, when the whole Chautauqua community (or so it seemed to my impressionable young brain) poured into the Amphitheater to pay tribute to its children.

Admittedly, there was only so much that a gang of 3-to-5 year olds could be persuaded to do in such a situation, beyond standing in pigeon-toed self-consciousness, thumbs flying to mouths as they anxiously scanned 5,000 faces in search of at least one they recognized. So, numbers engendering security, it was decided that the entire Children's Center would perform in unison, as a rhythm band. And I was selected to conduct. Just why the honor fell to me I am unable to say, although my congenital audacity comes to mind. I was not in the least flustered by the thought of mounting that celebrated stage, where a thousand artists and lecturers, women and men of global renown, had faced one of America's most discriminating audiences, there to wave my midget baton while forty-five infant musicians rubbed and grated and pounded and blew on a collection of "instruments" found only in nursery schools—to which a less adoring audience would wish them returned as soon as possible.

My memory of the performance is confused—rather like the racket that we produced. One fragment remains vividly in mind, however. As we exited the stage to generous applause (mostly, I'm sure, because we'd finished) a woman gestured for me to come to the edge of the platform. She was a reporter, assigned to cover the event for the *Chautauquan Daily*, the Institution's newspaper. Could she please have my name for her report? Next morning, sure enough, the Chautauqua Institution Children's Center Rhythm Band, Don Skinner, conductor, was included in her account of Youth Day festivities.

As was so with everything else that her children did (insofar as she actually approved, that is) Mother clipped the story and pasted it into my scrap book. There it remains, yellowed and fragile, to remind me of my first brush with Chautauqua fame.

I asked Mother whether she thought my Youth Day performance might earn me an invitation to guest conduct the Chautauqua Symphony, but she didn't appear to consider the query worth answering.

As quickly as my Chautauqua connection was forged, it was nearly broken. In the summer of 1938, for reasons I never understood, our parents rented a cottage for several weeks at Van Buren Point on the bluff shore of Lake Erie a few miles west of Dunkirk, NY, and we never made it to Chautauqua. I remember it as a time of warm air, brilliant sun, and skinned knees. Bicycles were rented for each of us children from a shop in Van Buren Point's small village center, such as it was. Denied the opportunity as a child either to learn to ride a bike or to swim, Mother insisted that her children have the chance to do both, just as soon as the family could afford them.

The shortcoming of the plan was that I had barely learned to ride a bike by the time we arrived at Van Buren Point, and had never ridden outside the confines of our Meadville yard and driveway. Such instruction as I was given did not include the aid of training wheels. The way to learn to do something, in our parents' opinion, was to go out and do it—taking your lumps as they came. Ruth Ann and Cliff, being the eldest, were to instruct me. Taking turns, they ran alongside the bike, steadying me for a few yards before turning me loose to lurch on alone while my body's vertical plane shifted progressively toward the horizontal. When balance lost out to gravity, I went sprawling. Time after time, I got up, picked up the bike, and we did it again, until finally (Ruth Ann was mentor of my triumphal moment, as I recall) I went snaking across the lawn, front wheel jerking right and left as I struggled frantically to maintain my balance—and succeeded.

"I'm riding!" I shrieked exultantly over my shoulder, "I'm riding!"

Then I went sprawling. But this time, when I got up and was able to resume the ride without help, I thought I was really something.

The feeling lasted as long as it took us to pack up and drive to Van Buren Point, where I discovered—in about four seconds—that traversing our hardpan yard and riding on a dirt road were not the same thing. The erratic swerving by which I managed to keep my balance became downright dangerous as the bike's balloon tires bounced and skittered across the road's loose and ubiquitous gravel. Half-way around the block that Mother declared was the limit for our first-day wandering, I also discovered that psychological confidence is vital to safe bike riding. A three foot drainage ditch beside the right-hand berm yawned with the seductive appeal of the sirens summoning Odysseus. Helpless to do otherwise (or so I imagined) I rode right into it.

Once again in water—this time, fortunately, only to my ankles—I untangled myself from my bike and stood up to discover that my eyes were about level with the roadway. Looking right and left and realizing that no one was in sight in either direction, I didn't even bother to blubber, but summoned the whole of my strength and scrambled up the steep side of the ditch, dragging the bike up behind me. Over the next few days, my skinned knees provided a painful reminder to be more careful—and not to panic at the prospect of losing control, thereby assuring that I would!

Dad died in April of 1940, felled at 47 by two cerebral embolisms—clots thrown off by a heart mortally wounded during a childhood bout with scarlet fever. His death left Mother with four children aged 13 to 7 and a family budget stretched to the consistency of tissue paper. Of necessity, that summer was spent in Meadville. But Mother's life-long passion for Chautauqua beckoned. We would go again, if it meant scrimping on every penny and foregoing not only the luxuries, but some of the basics. And scrimp we did. The woman was the soul of determination. By the following June she was ready, and we would spend the first of many summers in the one place on earth that, to her mind, came closest to paradise.

That we were privileged goes without saying. We were one of a relatively small number of families whose stay at Chautauqua lasted for the entire season at a time when the average visitor stayed for two to four weeks, and many remained only one. Indeed, our privilege would, eventually, extend beyond that. Mother would never truly be content, or even willing to travel much of anywhere at all, until she sold our Meadville home and became a year-round Chautauqua resident. It just seemed that when she finally went someplace and returned home again, she wanted home to be Chautauqua.

But that's fifteen years ahead of my story. Until a permanent move became possible, she would have us there each summer for as long as she could manage. Compared even to our full-season Chautauqua friends, our stay was extraordinary: Mother got us there a month before the season opened. Admittedly, there was more at work here than her passion for the place. The reason behind her resolve was at least as much economic as cultural. We got the first pick of the odd jobs by which Chautauquans cleared the decks for a new season, and buttoned up for winter after it was over.

CHAPTER 3

Clearing the Decks for a New Season

Not all Chautauquans observed the opening and closing of the season on the same date. For some—mainly those able to attend the entire season—it started with the 10:45 a.m. community worship service in the Amphitheater on the first Sunday of the announced calendar. Among short-term visitors, those who spent only a week or two, the "season" was largely psychological: it opened the day they arrived and closed the day they left. We were ahead of them all. Our season got under way the evening before Pennsylvania's schools dismissed for summer vacation. It happened first in 1941.

Owning neither home nor cottage in those early years, Mother arranged to rent the main floor of the Eau Claire annex, at 14 North Terrace, that belonged to the Gibbses, an elderly and sweet couple who lived in the main building next door. That meant that everything required for a three-month stay by one adult and four children had to be stuffed into the car for the one and only drive to Chautauqua. Mother had no intention of returning to Meadville for second loads of anything. She said we couldn't afford it anyway. Whoever packed carelessly would just have to do without.

Mother also made it clear that, when our departure date arrived, the Chevy's fuel tank would be full, no matter what sacrifice that might entail. With luck, she didn't plan to stop at a gas station again until September—a realistic option when everything we needed was lined up right there on the main floor of the Colonnade, Chautauqua's administration building. They included a well-stocked grocery store, a drug store, a dairy market and a hardware store—in short, everything needed to survive a motor-less summer while the Chevy sat, nose to the fence, outside the grounds by state highway 394. (We didn't yet know it, but 1941 was only a test. By 1942, World War II gasoline rationing restricted families like ours—folks holding no job essential to the war effort—to three gallons a week. The less we drove at Chautauqua, the more fuel we would qualify to purchase on our return to Meadville, where driving was more essential.)

So, last-minute washing and ironing of summer clothes completed, and overloaded suitcases sat upon until the latches could be snapped shut, all hands turned out to load the car. Under Mother's experienced supervision, our effort put a sardine packing factory to shame. Not a cubic centimeter of trunk was left unfilled; bed pillows and sundries were jammed into the shelf of the back window or assembled, like a three-dimensional jigsaw puzzle, on the front seat between driver and passenger. Sheets and blankets were folded into precise rectangles and piled on the back seat until the whole thing gained a foot in elevation. Boxes of canned and dried foods were squeezed onto the floor of the back seat.

It should be no surprise that the last day of school was our favorite of the year, for reasons that were partly anticipatory, partly pretense. In our imaginations, we already saw the shimmer of sun-sparkles on the lake, felt the on-shore breeze tousle our hair and rustle the crowns of a thousand ancient trees and—if the wind were right—heard the strike of Miller Bell Tower's clock all the way up at the Main Gate. More to the point, the last day of school was largely a subterfuge. It began at 8:30 sharp with the obligatory taking of attendance, reading a verse or two from the Holy Bible (King James Version), and recitation of the pledge of allegiance to the flag of the United States of America and to the republic for which it stands; proceeded to the handing out of final report cards, and ended ten minutes after it began when the most welcome bell of the entire year ripped through the halls and sent the captive wards of Meadville's schools careening into the streets for three months of delicious freedom.

For the Skinner children, however, that final-day routine was different than it was for our friends. They got up, had breakfast, and walked to school only to wander home again a half-hour later. We engaged in the kind of high-speed getaway that a veteran bank robber would envy. As dawn of The Glorious Day convened over the eastern hills, we were up and at it, tidying up our rooms to stand vacant for three months and helping Mother with last-minute chores. Then, everything in readiness, we walked to school so excited that we were in jeopardy of coming unstrung. By the time the dismissal bell rang, Mother sat at curbside in front of North End School, the car's engine running, to gather up Frank and me. Aflame by then with Chautauqua fever, we shot out the door so fast that I, for one, nearly made it from school door to car door without touching ground. Three minutes later and a mile down North Main Street hill, Mother pulled up in front of First District School to collect Ruth Ann and Cliff, equally excited, but more decorous in their expression of it. Her family reassembled, Mother turned east on North Street and steered the straining Chevy up State Road Hill and out Pennsylvania 77 northeast toward the New York line.

I suppose that Ruth Ann's perennial claim to the front seat was another privilege of being both the eldest and the only girl, though she and Mother could hardly see each other over the stack of stuff resting on the seat between them. In the back seat, Cliff, Frank, and I commanded a view of uncustomary loft from our perch atop the aggregate bedding, our heads scraping the ceiling and our feet resting on the food boxes on the floor.

Barely seventy miles long, the trip might as well have been a thousand. To enter Chautauqua's Victorian village was less like arriving in another place than in another time. Was it turning the clock back a century? Or had we stumbled into Brigadoon just as it stirred from its hundred-year slumber? No matter: our spirits seemed suddenly to be astride the dawn. By lunchtime, we were settled into our rented quarters and the car had already been driven out of the grounds. Even the beds were made. We would hardly think of Meadville again until September.

And with that, we set out to make money by clearing the decks for a new season.

Those whose visits were confined to July and August had no idea what a mess the place was in June, before porches were furnished with freshly painted rocking chairs or sparkled with rainbow sprays of gladiolas, walkways were swept as clean as an Amsterdam street, and the mature bloom of summer mantled the land. It always strained credulity, wandering about a month before the season, to think that it could ever be transformed in time for opening day.

Walking about Chautauqua was a bit like hiking in a forest, among random ranks of maple and beech, shagbark hickory and tulip poplar—each of which grew a whole lot of leaves. In late October, after summer visitors had filed out the gates for home, porch furniture had been moved into basements or living rooms, docks had been stacked in ordered piles along the lakefront, and the streets were empty, those leaves came down—and they made a ponderous pile. (The season is not called "fall" for nothing.)

No one bothered to rake them up, or to dispose of them by fire or compost, because no one was there to do it. Its summer population having gone home to Pittsburgh or Cleveland or a thousand other places across America, taking the vibrancy with them, Chautauqua was left with fewer than 200 people. Many were institution employees, or families whose wage-earners worked in Mayville or Jamestown, at opposing ends of the lake. Others were elderly folk, mostly frail widows granted leave to reside, pretty much at cost, in the three-story, wood-frame St. Elmo Hotel overlooking the Plaza. They sat and read or worked jigsaw or crossword puzzles in the parlor and sun porch through the quiet months, or simply dozed or stared their way through winter, taking their meals in the hotel dining room. And they were not (take my word for it) in any condition to grab rakes and go outdoors to attack 700 acres of leaves.

No, Mother Nature was left to her own devices, and wanted no second invitation. Driven before the gales of November, unruly battalions of leaves stormed through the streets, piled up in windrows, and shoved into the sheltered corners of porches. In the weeks that followed, in obedience to the primeval choreography by which trees mysteriously die and are reborn year by year, the grooming winds of winter stripped away dead branches and twigs and dropped them atop the long-fallen and colorless leaves. Soaked, pummeled, and compacted by storm and squall, the whole was reduced to a gooey mass that clung everywhere as if glued. And there it waited, an inexhaustible opportunity for the child laborers of spring.

It would be difficult to overstate how much I detested that job. By June, even leaves jammed into sheltered porch corners were rapidly decomposing, aided by the tireless toil of an astonishing array of worms and centipedes and beetles that ran and wriggled and waddled out of each pile the instant it was disturbed. Painted floorboards were stained by leeching acids wherever leaves had settled, and no amount of scrubbing could entirely remove the blemishes. There were chairs to be hauled out of basements or living rooms and addressed with sopping rags and soapy water, swishing away the accumulated webs of over-wintering spiders and whatever dirt had escaped last summer's

Spring Sweep

dustings. Windows had to be washed with nostril-nipping ammonia water, and kitchen floors and bathroom fixtures scrubbed and disinfected.

Nor did we lack opportunities. Mother's large and growing list of friends, all with winter-soiled cottages and leaf-laden porches, saw to that. It went on for days, as Chautauqua woke from its long winter's nap, yawned, stretched, and put its summer house in order. By the time the gates closed and institution President Arthur Bestor rapped the Amphitheater lectern three times with the ceremonial gavel, inaugurating that first of our all-summer-residencies at the Eau Claire, the sparkle was back and the Skinner children's labors had been rewarded at the rate of ten cents an hour. It wasn't much; but to a family on the back side of the Great Depression and a meager year beyond the loss of its bread-winning husband and father, those dimes helped. In aggregate, they comprised more than enough allowance to get us through.

To this day, I am dumbfounded by how rapidly our earning power grew over the next few years. Improvement in the post-depression economy corresponded nicely with our advancing age and proficiency. Even the onset of World War II did not hinder our growing prosperity. With what now seems blinding speed, the hourly wage rose to twenty-five cents, then fifty. I still remember the thrill of sitting down at the kitchen table in our Eau Claire apartment as the 1945 season opened, to count my accumulated earnings: $85.00! I could hardly believe it. I had only seen that much money, all in one pile, a couple of times in my life. But there it was, in cool cash. I grinned at Mother, who stood at the stove across the room preparing supper. She had to be as pleased as I was. "I have enough here to get me through the whole summer!" I gloated, visualizing glazed donuts and vanilla malted milkshakes at the Pergola, or half-pint cartons of orange drink at the Dairylea store (the abbreviated trade name for The Dairyman's League, a milk co-operative), and movie tickets at Chautauqua's old church-turned-cinema up the hill at the north end of the grounds. Ruth Ann, Cliff and Frank each had their own hoard to tide them over until our return to Meadville, too. It must have been Mother's easiest summer in four years.

Still, no June brought home the earning power of work like that of 1947; and it wouldn't have been possible without Joe Witkowski. Joe was a regular visitor in our cottage. In his mid-twenties and the son of a poor Polish widow from Erie, Pennsylvania, Joe was born with a splendid tenor voice. Like many young musicians, he came to Mother's door in search of an accompanist and found a mentor. She never turned any of them away. Joe was also a devout Roman Catholic—and I do not use the adjective simply for traditional effect: he never missed Mass on a day when one could be found. Nor was the prevailing prohibition against eating meat on Fridays sufficient to satisfy Joe's focused piety: he refused it on Mondays and Wednesdays as well. Mother's congenital compulsion to feed anyone who crossed her threshold hungry, especially the young, played in Joe's favor. Joe was <u>always</u> hungry. Any afternoon that he appeared on our porch at an hour remotely proximate to dinnertime, which happened about twice a week (especially when he was broke—which Joe usually was), he was seated at the table and served a platter so laden with bread, mashed potatoes, peas, corn, beans, and whatever else of vegetable origin happened to be in Mother's pantry that day, that he was hard put not to spill it all over the table. Mother adored Joe, and he her.

Not only could Joe sing, he may well have been the strongest man I ever knew. Six feet tall, he weighed 270 pounds and not a smidgeon of it fat. The classic story of Joe's strength involved a Greyhound bus driver and twin foot lockers. Joe had received a scholarship, and was off to music school to study voice. Thinking he might need it, he packed all his music to take with him. Indeed, he packed more music than clothing. Rolling to the curb and stepping out to take tickets and supervise the loading, the bus driver eyed Joe's foot lockers and said cheerfully, "Here, I'll help you get those aboard." Grabbing the handle of one, he tried to pick it up. It might as well have been bolted to the pavement. Heaving a second time with no greater success, he realized that a third attempt might lead to irreparable injury. Brow furrowing, he muttered regretfully, "I guess we can't take them." Then he almost fell over as Joe, bubbling laughter, gripped one locker in each hand and stepped aboard the bus.

It was that strength that came to our aid when, in 1947, Frank and I stood at the shore of the lake, looking with some dismay at a large pile of horses and platforms that, properly unwound and assembled, would form a neighbor's dock. We weren't so concerned about the narrower sections that made up the runway. It was the flats used to form the large tee at the end that caused us to exchange doubtful glances. I sized them up to be about a quarter-acre, but that was probably an exaggeration. Amplified or not, it wasn't clear that we possessed the necessary manpower. At sixteen and fifteen, the best we could bring to the job was teenager power.

Mother instantly saw the solution. Next time Joe dropped by, she broached the subject: "How'd you like a job for a few hours, Joe? Frank and Don have been offered $120.00 to put in a dock. Could you help them?"

Never one to look a gift job in the mouth, Joe grinned in gratitude. Early next morning, clad in shorts, tee shirts, and "lake shoes"—ragged sneakers reserved for working in the lake, to grip the algae-clad rocks and protect our feet from razor-sharp clamshells that littered the bottom—we convened on the shoreline. It took only minutes to establish a routine. Standing a horse atop one of the 12-foot-long runway sections, we hauled the pair of them off the pile and floated them into position. While one of us set the horse up and kept it from floating away, the other two lifted the landward end of the platform into place against the previous section. Then, working together, we hoisted the lakeward end aloft, slid the horse underneath it, and shoved the whole assembly landward to close the joint.

That much Frank and I could have handled ourselves, if a bit less expeditiously. But the third man's arms were a boon; and when it came to the Tee at the dock's end, they were mandatory. Thank God they were Joe's. Our suspicions were confirmed when we lifted the first of the oversized platforms; it weighed a ton. Frank and I, about at the limit of our strength, grappled with one end; Joe, barely showing the strain, lifted the other. Getting them up and into place at the end of the dock was the greater challenge. We were, by then, working in five feet of water; and I was only 5'6" tall with no freeboard to spare. Closer to six feet, Frank at least had snorkel clearance. But we never would have made it without Joe. Somehow we got the platforms up and into place, though I am at a loss to say precisely how: submerged about half the time, I really wasn't in a position to see what was going on. I only know that, to that point in my life, it was the hardest work I had ever attempted.

By noon—gravity to the contrary notwithstanding—the dock was in and we divided the reward: $60.00 for Joe and $30.00 each for Frank and me. All for a single morning's work! It was a great—if totally exhausted—feeling; and I'm sure that the money meant even more to Joe than it did to us. Still, for the first time in my life, I felt like I was actually capable of earning a living. One thing

I can tell you without equivocation, though: it took only that first day to convince me that I didn't want to earn it by putting in docks.

Nor will I attempt to inventory the lunch that was consumed at Mother's dining room table that noon.

PART 2

Cottages

CHAPTER 4

Our Own Bit of Brigadoon

For as long as I can remember, it was foregone that Mother wanted to spend every summer at Chautauqua. But it never occurred to me that we might own a cottage someday. Dad's death at the tail end of the Great Depression, and during the build-up to World War II, left us living on the short end of frugality. Not that we were burdened with thoughts about "being poor." Ernest McCafferty, who was not only our maternal grandfather but also vice-president of H. J. Heinz Company in Pittsburgh, was not about to see his family in want. Unknown to us until years later, he began immediately to give Mother a monthly allowance sufficiently generous to be sure that our basic needs would be met. But the grandparents on both sides of our family understood the distinction between "need" and "want" more clearly than just about anyone I ever knew. The prospect of owning a Chautauqua cottage just wasn't part of our thinking.

Which is why 1944 was such a surprise. Out of the blue, Mother announced that she had bought a cottage. We children recall no discussion, only an announcement. On the other hand, we didn't complain about being left out of the deliberation, especially when we saw the cottage. It was at 14 McClintock, three houses down-slope from Pratt Avenue and a measly 30-second sprint from the lakefront. After our quaint but restricted quarters at the Eau Claire, it felt like we had just been given title to our own bit of Brigadoon.

14 McClintock
circa 1945

I recall Mother telling us that it had been built soon after the turn of the century—a boxy two-story-with-attic frame structure. It featured front and back porches both up- and downstairs and plumbing that hung on the outside walls. When we arrived that June and stepped in for the first time, it smelled like it hadn't been opened in two years. Lo, Brigadoon had an olfactory burden!

Opening doors and windows soon corrected that, but Mother as quickly undid it. She determined that while the exterior was in satisfactory shape, the inside had to be painted. Every room of it. It was the era of Kemtone, the world's first commercially produced water-based house paint that came in any color you wanted as long as it was pastel pink, yellow, green or blue. Mother allowed us to pick the color for our own bedrooms, but reserved to herself decisions about the rest of the house. Pressed to the work, we soon shoved such furniture as had been left in the cottage to the center of each room, and were busy transforming the place into a replica of butter mints at an Easter banquet.

The visual result was okay, but the aroma was determinedly unpleasant. In developing their product, the paint chemists either neglected to remedy the smell issue, or couldn't. The whole house smelled like Palestine Park when the Dead Sea was drained in the spring, exposing the previous October's leaf-fall as a six-inch layer of stinking black slime. The bouquet was penetrating.

I can't speak for Mother or Ruth Ann, who remained inside through the whole ordeal. But we boys quickly moved out onto the upstairs porches and slept on folding metal cots—Cliff out back, Frank and me out front overlooking McClintock. The arrangement proved so satisfactory that we stayed out there for the eight years that we owned the cottage. It periodically made for interesting nights, in particular when we were started awake by a burst of wind, lightning and thunder that warned of an oncoming storm. Then we scuttled out of bed, pulled our cots to the middle of the porch in hopes of avoiding a drenching, climbed back into them and went back to sleep. It never occurred to us to move indoors; and often as not we woke to find our outer covers saturated. Then blankets had to be hung over the railings or draped over indoor furniture in hopes they'd dry enough to return to our beds that evening.

I recall only one exception to our outdoor allegiance: the time Cliff and several of his friends borrowed canoes, went camping across the lake, and slept all night in a patch of poison ivy. By the time they got home, Cliff was a walking blister. Had his case been less severe, it might have been funny; but he was seriously ill for several days, requiring injections to neutralize a massive allergic reaction. Among the shared memories of our teenage years was seeing Cliff lying on his indoor bed, clad in nothing but briefs and head-to-toe calamine lotion. Pink never was his best color.

Being the only girl, Ruth Ann often enjoyed privileges denied to us boys—like being assigned the largest bedroom in the house with not one, but two, double beds in it while Frank and I shared a room less than half as large, and Cliff was assigned to a nook sandwiched between the stairwell and the back porch. Cliff did enjoy one amenity the rest of us lacked: his room had access to a half-bath built onto one end of the porch, presumably added sometime after the cottage was completed.

Because she got the dormitory, Ruth Ann was further privileged to invite friends to Chautauqua—for entire summers. And she didn't waste the opportunity. The Kemtone was barely dry when BJ, our McCafferty cousin, joined us again. She and Ruth Ann had gotten jobs waiting on tables at the Eau Claire dining room. The Gibbses by then had reduced their dining service to two meals a day—breakfast and lunch. So the girls were done for the day by 2:00 p.m., leaving ample time to indulge those opportunities, both social and cultural, that Chautauqua copiously provided middle teenagers. I watched with ill-disguised envy one day as they dumped their tip money out on their beds to count it. I have no idea how much was there, because so much of it was nickels and dimes and quarters. But, as a youngster unaccustomed to handling cash, I was more impressed by volume than value. And to my jealous eyes, there was a lot of volume. It was my introduction to a fact of life about waiting table at Chautauqua: tips generally exceeded wages by several orders of magnitude.

The next summer, when BJ's family began to vacation on Nantucket Island, Mother allowed Ruth Ann "Skinny" Skinner to double her guest list by welcoming two Meadville High School classmates, Marilyn "Tootie" Muckinhoupt and Willodean "Willie" VanKeuren, who arrived bag and baggage for the season with jobs promised in one of the cafeterias. I never learned what Willie thought; but years later Tootie did not hesitate to pronounce it "the very best summer of my life."

Whatever else might be said about Ruth Skinner, she steadfastly tried to raise her children according to high standards of conduct, and that included pulling our share of the load when it came to household routine. In the process, however, she succeeded in raising four children who would never pass up a chance to extract a price from her for it. With a bit of imagination, every lesson could be turned into a good-natured—if risky—challenge. In our McClintock cottage, we discovered a truly tempting opportunity.

It was the kitchen's fault. Nearly barren of conveniences, it was long and narrow, its length shortened at the east end by a set of steps that led up to a stair landing shared with the living room. The kitchen sink, a shallow cast-iron basin with a single built-in drain board and no cabinet beneath, was bolted to the tongue-and-groove bead-board railing for those stairs. There was otherwise a stove, but no cabinets. A wooden table served as a counter, and a pantry off the west end of the room held canned and dried goods. The only place suitable to store dishes was a small closet, also at the west end beside the door to the dining room. And therein lay our opportunity to torture Mother.

Washing dishes had always been a family affair for us, even as toddlers. Everyone who benefited from the meal was obligated to help clean up after it. But there wasn't room on the drain board to hold all the dishes once they were washed and rinsed, or anywhere to stack them once dried. And it was tedious to dry a dish, walk to the closet to put it away, and return for the next one. It took no great planning to develop a team approach: while one person washed dishes, a second dried and threw them the length of the kitchen to a third, who was stationed at the closet door to catch them and put them away.

If our purpose was to get Mother's goat, we failed. Long accustomed to our antics, she just skewed her lips to one side and rolled her eyes like she did the first time we went shopping, soon after World War II, at one of the newfangled "super markets" with shopping carts that began to displace neighborhood grocery stores. As Mother took items off the shelves, she handed them to the nearest boy to put into the cart. But the cart wasn't there. It was in the next aisle with another boy, who waited to catch the articles, one by one, as they flew over the intervening shelf unit. We went on that way until one day I put a bit too much oomph into a weighty product and Frank grabbed it out of the air inches before it collided with a six-foot stack of canned vegetables.

"Now that's enough!" Mother said sternly. She was right, as always.

The pantry was the technological nerve center of the house. It contained two "modern" devices. The first was cold—or at least was supposed to be. The second was hot—sometimes more-so than we wished—and was nearly our undoing.

The icebox was just that: an oak case three feet wide and four tall. The top foot of it, accessed by a hinged lid, was the ice chest. Food was stored below, in a larger compartment served by twin doors. A thick layer of cork sandwiched between the oak exterior and an interior of galvanized sheet metal provided insulation.

The ice chest was capable of holding a 100-pound block of ice. Like most Chautauqua cottages at the time, ours came with a diamond-shaped card with a hole punched in each corner, hung from a small nail in a front window where it was visible from the street. Large numerals were printed around the four corners of the card—25, 50, 75 and 100—in reference to the weight of blocks stored in the dirt-berm, sway-backed ice house on Massey Avenue, across from the top of Cookman. Three days a week, a wreck of a truck with a slat-wood cargo hold rumbled through the grounds, stopping to deliver a block of ice to each house with a card in its window. The hotter the weather, the larger were the numbers facing upward on the cards, and the weightier the ice man's labor.

Stopping right in the middle of McClintock and setting the emergency brake, the ice man jumped out. (My brothers and I once speculated on how far into the lake his truck might roll if that brake failed.) Stepping to the back end, he grabbed a wicked-looking pair of tongs that resembled badly warped scissors with ring handles at one end and sharp tines at the other, bent to point at each other. Like Santa Claus, he said not a word but went straight to his work. Clamping the tines around a block of ice, he jerked on the handle, simultaneously driving the tines into the ice and pulling the block out of the truck. Up the walk he trotted, onto the porch and through the front door without so much as a knock (the man knew the shortest route between his truck and every ice box on the grounds). Straightway across the living room he went, through the dining room and into the kitchen, where he hung a sharp left into the panty. He raised the ice chest lid with a clatter, dropped the ice onto the grating with a bang, slammed the lid, nodded to Mother on his way back through the kitchen, hung up his tongs, slid into the seat and coasted to the next cottage. Cost was by the pound, paid weekly.

Under normal conditions, 25 pounds would last us from Monday to Wednesday and 50 from Friday to Monday. An ice pick—like a large knitting needle with a wooden handle—was kept near at hand in case we wanted chopped ice to chill a glass of tea or pitcher of lemonade, as Mother determined.

But woe to the child who carelessly left one of the front doors ajar, allowing the inside, and everything in it, to warm up, hastening the melting of the frigid block that alone stood between "fresh" and "spoiled." Once the ice was gone, we had to wait until the next delivery; and by that time everything inside was so thawed out that Mother had to pay for a larger block of ice to chill it all down again. And Mother detested few things more than wasting money.

Unlike most ice boxes (or modern refrigerators, for that matter) one entire shelf of ours was devoted to milk. Most customers purchased milk by the quart bottle at the Dairylea store on the main floor of the Colonnade facing the Plaza. But a few families, of which ours was one, went around to the back door, downstairs on the alley across from the water purification plant. Dairylea had a deal that, even then, sounded too good to be true: if we provided our own large container, we could buy milk at a serious discount. Learning of it (and mindful that her entire food budget was barely sufficient to buy enough milk to satiate her dairy-addicted children—and surely not when purchased by the quart), Mother went out one day and came home with a two-gallon stainless steel can—a perfect miniature of the much larger ones used by dairy farms and distributors to transport bulk milk.

Arriving at Dairylea's alley door, we were met by a clerk who, using a half-gallon dipper, lifted milk from a twenty-gallon can in the walk-in cooler and filled ours. The cost: $1.21. When milk sold upstairs for .25¢ a quart, that was a 40% savings.

We boys soon concluded that the math was defective. What was saved in the buying was soon lost by the presence, in our oak ice box, of a seemingly endless supply of milk; and we did not hesitate to consume it as if it were. Mother's bulk-purchase saving was quickly neutralized by her gluttonous sons. We never said anything to her about it, however. And maybe we didn't need to. Though she frequently encouraged us to "Drink water if you're thirsty!," she knew full well that the only thing that would satisfy our craving for milk was more milk, and the size of the container was irrelevant. So she might just as well save what she could at the point of purchase; she surely wouldn't save anything at the point of consumption.

Accustomed to the electric refrigerator in our Meadville kitchen, one feature of the ice box took us children by surprise. Of course we knew that when ice melted, it turned to water. It's just that we didn't care for the manufacturer's solution to the problem: a tube attached to the bottom of the ice chest drained the water into a tray that slid underneath the ice box. The meltwater produced by a 25-pound block of ice is impressive, and it took only twenty-four hours to discover that the reward for our inattention was a mess. Coming downstairs the next morning, we found a modest brook flowing across the pantry floor and out into the kitchen. Cliff soon solved that with a modern invention of his own. It was called a hole, and he drilled it through the pantry floor. Our cottage was erected on brick piers, with no basement, and six inches of hose added to the drain tube thereafter conducted the melt water directly onto the ground beneath the house, where it quickly vanished.

The water heater was less benign. It's a wonder we didn't blow our cottage to splinters. We surely came close enough. The tank was iron with riveted seams, and had a "side-winder" heater attached to it. Moved by gravity, cold water flowed out a pipe at the bottom of the tank into a coil suspended over a gas burner in the side-winder. As the temperature of the water increased, it pushed its way up through the coil and flowed back into the tank. The thing worked like gangbusters. But it had neither thermostat nor pressure-relief vent. A thumb-valve controlled the fire, anywhere from candle-flame to blow-torch. Otherwise, it heated water if it was on and didn't if it was off. Only an imbecile would let the thing run all night, so it was someone's job to go down each morning and light the side-winder. That was the easy part. The hard part was remembering to turn it off before we all left for the morning. Early on, we forgot a couple of times.

Returning from a trip to the store one day, we were greeted by the odor of scorched metal, as if a pot had boiled dry on the stove, but more intense. Way more intense. The kitchen was palpably warm, in a way that didn't feel healthy.

"Oh mercy!" Mother cried, almost knocked over backward by the heat when she stepped through the pantry door. "The water heater was left on."

By that time, the whole assembly was so hot that touching any part of it—including the gas valve—would have cost her a layer of skin.

"Hand me a hot pad, quick!" she demanded, and turned off the gas.

We had no way of knowing to what extent the tank was emptied, as the rising pressure pushed its overheated contents back into the town water main, or whether any of our neighbors turned on their cold water taps that morning and got warm water. But opening the hot-water faucet in the kitchen sink to release some of the backed-up pressure came close to clearing the kitchen. What water was left in the pipe exploded all over the room, followed by a jet of superheated vapor that roared like waste steam from a locomotive. Oh, it was an admirable show.

It was a full three minutes before the faucet again ran a steady stream of water.

God only knows what might have happened if we were a half hour later returning home. My appreciation for how tough that old water heater was, indeed the whole plumbing system, rose dramatically. But so did my appreciation for the thermostatically controlled, safety-vented gas water heater in the basement of our Meadville home. We loved our bit of Brigadoon, but a few of its early conveniences might better have been left in the "good old days" where they originated.

CHAPTER 5

Culture Run Amok

It never occurred to me, as a child, that there was anything unusual about having two pianos in our Meadville living room. They were there before I knew music from meat loaf—and they got a lot of use. It would later sink into my slow brain that music was to Mother's soul as milk was to her children's bones: a source of nourishment without which she would shrivel up and waste away. If she was not accompanying a vocal or instrumental soloist, she was playing duo-piano or anchoring a string trio or mixed ensemble, or practicing her score for the next performance of the Meadville Orchestral Society, or for an upcoming wedding or next Sunday's service at Meadville's Grace Methodist Church where she was organist for the eight years following Dad's death. Whether all this was helping her to put food on the table, or building a nest-egg for Chautauqua, we'll never know. She never talked about such things, and we didn't ask because, as children, family finances were not our business.

So it was no surprise when a truck stopped in front of our McClintock cottage soon after we moved in, and several burly men hauled an old upright piano into the living room alcove. Just as it earlier surprised me to discover that ours was the only living room in Meadville with two pianos in it, it struck me as odd that so few of our Chautauqua friends' cottages had none. Never mind that Institution regulations stated that practicing on musical instruments would be confined to the practice-shack village at the northwest corner of the grounds, where Chautauqua's fence bounded state road 394. Mother ignored the rule. It was an odd departure for a woman who made it crystal clear that her children would respect every law, without question. That none of our neighbors ever complained was, I suspect, a testament to the fact that many of them appreciated good music when they heard it. Even Chautauqua President Sam Hazlett and his family, who lived across the street and up one, never protested. Nor was there a complaint from the Wiggins family, directly across the street, mostly because Alfred Wiggins couldn't get enough music as it was. Hardly a week passed that he did not press one or more of us to come over to his living room while some duo or trio played chamber music. We never understood where he got all those people. It was a clear case of culture run amok. Having all we cared for on our side of the street, my sib-

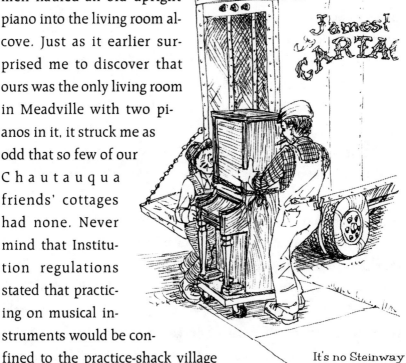

It's no Steinway

lings and I became adept at sneaking by without being caught in an invitation; or, if taken off guard, at conjuring up a plausible-sounding prior obligation—even when none existed.

In any event, the music on both sides of the street really was good stuff. You see, Mother was a musician-magnet, and had been for most of her life. The pattern had been established in our Meadville home, where anywhere from one to five musicians might show up at any time. We had barely moved into our McClintock cottage when the pattern began to repeat itself, and it only intensified when Mother became registrar of the schools program. Responsible to register students desiring to study in the school of music, the faculty of which consisted largely of members of the Chautauqua Symphony, she was soon on a first-name basis with most of the orchestra. At the same time, she drew others not officially part of anything—talented, mostly younger musicians, themselves drawn to Chautauqua by the rich cultural environment and in need of an accompanist because they had been invited to perform at a denominational house service or wedding reception or gathering of the Women's Club.

Nor did we children escape. Of the four of us, three became accomplished instrumental musicians. (I will not name which of us failed to make the grade in order not to embarrass myself.) After Dad died, Mother formed the Skinner Ensemble, consisting of herself, piano; Ruth Ann, violin; Cliff, flute; and Frank, cello. The only thing that permitted me to participate at all was my garrulous mouth. Mother arranged a twenty-minute medley of classical pieces by the likes of Schubert, Mendelssohn, Beethoven, Chopin and Mozart, none of whom, I suspect, realized that they were composing music for a young—and very determined—widow and three of her children. Even less did they realize that their compositions would be announced by a boy whose primary musical achievement to that point was a failure to learn how to play three musical instruments in a row. But I could pronounce their names and those of their compositions correctly. I hadn't the foggiest idea what the words meant, but that never seemed to matter.

The ensemble was soon playing all over Meadville, before every community group and civic club the town owned, and there were a number. And when the ensemble itself could not perform, Mother could be counted upon to cobble together some arrangement suitable for herself and whoever was available, often recruiting friends to enlarge the ranks. Nor did the pace slow down when we came to Chautauqua, where the musician roster was even longer and the opportunities more plentiful.

I'm not making this up; documentation is available for any desiring to peruse it. Mother was an inveterate (one wants to say compulsive) keeper of memorabilia and compiler of scrapbooks. She adopted the custom as a little girl, and never quit. I really think she started a scrap book for each of us about ten minutes after she emerged from the delivery room at one of our births, and was still enlarging them—and her own—when she died at age 90. Each of us inherited about fifteen of the things, a multi-volume vignette of our lives from the moment we drew breath until we were ourselves on the point of retirement. (A word of warning to those who suffer from allergies, however: in aggregate, our scrapbooks constitute one of the largest extant collections of allergens in the western world, and should be avoided lest they result in a terminal reaction.)

Among the items pasted to the pages—wretched examples of kindergarten art, report cards (which I really could have done without) certificates of perfect attendance at church school, graduation and marriage announcements, notice of the births of our children—is a mind-boggling array of newspaper clippings reporting on performances by anywhere from one to four-and-a-half Skinners.

Too, Mother kept things moving for her children. Ruth Ann had by then laid down her violin in favor of developing a bright coloratura soprano voice. At Chautauqua, she connected with one of the best professional coaches around, the elegant Elizabeth Wheeler of Cleveland whose husband, William, was on the music faculty of Western Reserve University. One such heady experience convinced Ruth Ann: at the end of her sophomore year, she withdrew from Allegheny College (which did not yet have a music major) and transferred to Flora Stone Mather, the women's division of Western Reserve, where she could continue to study with the Wheelers year-round.

About the same time, Mother arranged for Cliff to study with Ruth Freeman, principal flautist of the Chautauqua Symphony. Ruth was arguably among the most diminutive musicians ever to perform on that platform, and one of the first women to hold a first chair. Problem was the chair was too large. Cliff loved to watch her because, seated on it, her legs wouldn't reach the floor and she had to prop her feet on the cross strut. But make no mistake; the woman played a mean flute. Even though we seldom could see her (nor comprehend how *she* could see the conductor) the authority with which she addressed a score was never in doubt.

Likewise, Frank studied under cellist Ardath Walker from New York City, a stimulating and demanding teacher. The most demanding part was not that she became irritated when Frank did not practice as much as she would like; it was when she asked him to set aside his music and "just play." For Frank—the only member of the family to excel in mathematics (he would later enroll in MIT and become a computer engineer)—improvising was not simply uncomfortable, it was a congenital impossibility.

Recalling it later, he observed dryly, "It's probably a good thing I didn't plan a career in jazz." He was, however, awarded the third chair in the cello section of Chautauqua's student symphony.

Looking through those scrapbooks, it is hard to avoid the impression that, for a time, it seemed that half the preludes, offertories and postludes played in some of Chautauqua's denominational houses involved at least one Skinner, if not the whole ensemble. *Chautauquan Daily* notices list half-a-dozen such performances in a single summer. Nor were such appearances confined to the summer season. The fall that Mother moved to Chautauqua year-round, she joined Hurlbut Memorial Church (the only parish congregation on the grounds) and supported it faithfully for forty years. Glued in among those *Daily* notices are dozens from Hurlbut, because Mother's sense of commitment never ended with herself. She had a knack for "volunteering" her children in ways we couldn't refuse. Every time one or several of us was home on vacation, we could count on being pressed into service.

None, however, quite equaled the Friday evening that Mother almost bolted out the door to meet me when I came home for a weekend. I hadn't put my suitcase down yet when she blurted, "Frank Laundry was rushed to the hospital this morning for emergency surgery. Could you preach Sunday morning?" The Rev. Mr. Laundry, Hurlbut's beloved pastor, had been stricken with a clogged blood vessel to his brain. He would fully recover—but not in time for Sunday worship! My "Yeah, no problem" response wasn't quite what Mother expected. I think she would have found a larger display of anxiety reassuring. But she was on my turf now. I might have been the family's instrumental black sheep (as well as in a few other endeavors best left unspecified). But when it came to garrulousness of mouth, I was without peer. Mother told her friends, "Don has a gift of gab." I never quite knew whether she meant it as a compliment.

Then there was 1955. Following the death of George W. Volkel (Chautauqua's official organist since 1932), Robert V. Woodside succeeded him. It was a case of losing one friend while affirming another. Our relationship with George started soon after we began to spend the full season at Chautauqua and grew to the point that I could walk up on the platform during a postlude and climb up on the bench beside him, and did. We still watch his over-six-foot frame emerge from an amphitheater ramp (though George was more likely to "erupt" than to "emerge"), grinning at being caught by surprise on Mother's 16-millimeter home movie camera. His death did not go down easily in our house. But it prompted mother to nominate Bob to take his place. Growing up in the village of Cambridge Springs, Pennsylvania, fifteen miles north of our Meadville home, Bob was one of the company of students Mother mentored. Few, certainly, were better able to appraise his considerable skill.

I can't say it was payback time, but four Skinners—Ruth Ann, soprano; Mother, alto; me, tenor; and Frank, bass—sang in the Motet choir for Monday-thru-Friday Amphitheater worship that summer. Indeed, it came closer to being a family affair than that: also on board were sisters Hester and Edith Fleck from Philadelphia and their brother Harold, a grade school principal in Meadville and double bassist in Meadville's Orchestral Society. In aggregate, we comprised half of that summer's Motet. But all of us together were barely a match for soprano anchor Marge Prescott, perennial soloist for Amphitheater services both Sunday and weekday, blessed with enough lung-power to be heard on the third tee of the golf course across state road 394. All of them (like George Volkel before them), were "family," as much at home in our living room or on our front porch as we were in their choral company. There was kindred wealth there, and those were wonderful years to grow up summers at Chautauqua.

Most summer visitors assumed—with some justification—that with the close of the season in August, cultural events evaporated faster than Chautauqua's population. And it plummeted from about 10,000 to 250 in a weekend. Gone home to communities scattered across the country, they were not aware of how often the year-round residents gathered in Smith Memorial Library or the lobby of the St. Elmo Hotel or at Hurlbut Church for events sponsored by, and for, themselves. These events often drew nearby county residents who, being unable to afford the gate fees, came into the grounds more often in the winter than during the summer. Mother was soon in the middle of it. As long as she had anything to say about it, the music would never quit. Nor would the appreciation of that miniscule population.

And, after her manner, she added a new twist. The Institution's plethora of pianos had to be stored somewhere. The quarters they inhabited during the season—unheated, poorly ventilated practice shacks and warm-weather performance studios—were hardly suitable for New York Januaries. But heated space was at a premium, so the best of it—the large room at the south end of the Port Office that housed temporary staff during the summer but was unoccupied during the off-season—was reserved for the best instruments: the Steinway concert grands. There they stood, quilt-covered and ignored through the harsh months—until Mother discovered them, and they became a seduction not to be resisted. Never willingly without a piano, and with hers locked up in our McClintock cottage, as brittle and inaccessible as everything else in the house, her covetous eye was soon attracted to the Steinways. It took little effort to convince Ralph McCallister that it would be better for them to be played than to sit idle while their moving parts stiffened and froze in place like arthritic knee joints.

She found a ready ally in Helen Brock, a wry-mouthed stringbean who was chief receptionist and secretary to the Institution in an era when the off-season administrative staff numbered a baker's dozen. Helen occupied one of several third-floor apartments in the Colonnade until the building's upper half was consumed by fire on a sub-zero January day in 1961. The next morning, Mother stood on Ames Avenue—atop a foot of iron-hard water from the firemen's hoses that got that far but would go no farther until spring thaw—and took a picture of the sky through what had been the ceilings of the portico and second floor offices. The third floor was never rebuilt, forcing the residents to find new quarters.

Helen also played piano.

The two of them soon wrestled the Steinways into position and began to spend a noon break each week playing extemporaneous duo-piano music. Word of their concerts soon spread among Chautauqua's all-season mavens via the tried-and-true medium of gossip. Thereafter, as the appointed noon hour approached and Mother and Helen made their way across the snow-clad Plaza to the Post Office, the lobby filled with winter residents, many nestled into folding lawn chairs carried from home. Some brought lunch, and most waited until the noon hour that day to check their mailboxes, then sat, sorting and reading their mail to nimble strains of classical music scored for two pianos and played on the very same concert grands that thrilled them every July and August in the Amphitheater.

And they didn't even have to buy gate tickets.

CHAPTER 6

The Perfect Lakefront Cottage

In 1950, Mother made another of her quiet decisions and set us on a course that changed everything—although it did take her a while to pull the whole thing off. It started that spring when Ralph McCallister, Chautauqua's vice-president for program and education, hired her as registrar of the summer schools—a position she held for eleven years. For Mother, it was the answer to a petition half-a-century in the praying: to live at Chautauqua year-round.

The first two years were difficult. Our McClintock cottage—the only home we owned by then—lacked even the rudiments of winterization. Other than the overzealous sidewinder in the pantry, the only source of warmth was a small fireplace that radiated three percent of its heat into the living room and sucked the other ninety-seven per cent right up the chimney. And, of course, there was that plumbing hanging on the outside of the house where it would freeze solid ten minutes after the thermometer dipped below 32° Fahrenheit.

Not that Mother gave up easily. She closed the unused rooms, made do with what she had, and hung on through October. At first snow, she rented a room from Mr. and Mrs. Baker, regulars among Chautauqua's 250 winter residents and friends at Hurlbut Church. The Bakers had several spare rooms that they rented out during the season, so there were places for the three of us still in need of a home during vacation—Cliff and me from Allegheny, Frank from MIT.

I can't speak for my brothers (nor would I for the world fault the Baker's hospitality); but my Christmas vacation was vividly etched into memory by frost. When I stepped into my room and saw my breath, it dawned on me that while the Bakers might rent it out during the summer, they didn't bother to heat it during the winter. I don't know just why they put a thermometer in it. They were much too kind simply to rub it in. But one morning, when so much frost laced the window that it resembled etched Victorian glass and unremitting winter held Chautauqua in thrall, the thermometer read 34°. I may, on some morning of my life, have dressed faster than I did that day, though I can't recall just when it might have been. Remember those stories about how your great-grandparents woke in unheated prairie lofts, jumped into their clothes, and scrambled down ladders to huddle against their mothers' wood stoves before rigor mortis set in? They're true. If I could know that crossing heaven's threshold was anything like stepping into Mrs. Baker's kitchen that morning, I'd make the trip right now.

In late March, when remnants of plow spoils still bordered a few streets and melting drifts still lay sheltered on the north sides of a few cottages, Mother was back in ours, toughing it out as the vagaries of weather dictated.

She hung on through one more fall, then rented a winterized house at the corner of Clark and Foster, between the Baptist House and the Episcopal Cottage; and while it was more to her liking, and gave us a whole house to share during vacations—including heated bedrooms—her mind was made up before she even moved in: before winter snows flew again, she meant to have a year-round home of her own. Unbeknownst to us, she had set aside the proceeds from selling our Meadville home against just such an eventuality. Before we even realized that she could afford it, she had. And what a home it would be.

It was not evident at first that Mother could pull it off—at least not in the way she had hoped. What she wanted was a home overlooking the lake. But lakefront cottages seldom came on the market; they passed down to the next generation of the family that owned them. When they were put up for sale, they didn't last long, and few were winterized to begin with. Nonetheless, she would try. Retaining the services of Charles E. Pierce, secretary of the Institution and dabbler in real estate, she learned that a house had just come available. It was substantial—not simply a cottage—and well suited to our needs. It was also one of the shortest real estate ventures of the decade. When Mother made an offer the following day, the owner pulled the property off the market.

It was a blessing in disguise. Charlie knew a cottage-owner who no longer came to Chautauqua. He had rented his place out for several summers. Approached with an offer, he agreed to sell, and Mother had her lakefront home. Well, after a manner of speaking. It was neither substantial nor a house in the usual sense. It was a vintage Chautauqua cottage. It had no basement, but stood on brick piers—not a good bet for winters at that latitude. Inside walls consisted of boards nailed to one side of the studs with wallpaper pasted over them. On the other side, the wallpaper was glued to the backs of the same boards, but went in and out around the studs. The stairs ran up from the kitchen—covering two windows that faced the lake—and ended on a second floor platform leading to four different levels. Unfazed, Mother retained contractor Fay Flanders to renovate and winterize it. When his crew jacked it up to dig a basement under it, the house fell apart in the middle. The two halves had been erected at different times, and had barely been fastened together.

All of which freed Mother to turn it into whatever she wanted. As fall yielded to winter, Fay and his crew transformed a disaster into a jewel. The separated halves were re-secured and set down on a spacious basement equipped with a gas furnace and automatic(!) water heater. The kitchen was enlarged and the stairs relocated. Space was reordered to accommodate one and a half baths up and a powder room down, and the interior finished with unpretentious charm, including pre-finished hardwood maple floors throughout the house. By June of 1952, it was ready for occupancy.

9 North Lake Drive
circa 1985

From the day she moved in, it always seemed to Mother—and to us—the perfect lakefront cottage in the nicest neighborhood of the most wonderful community in America. In no small part, that was because it served our family so well. It was rather like an English cottage on the outside, so well nestled onto its lot and in among its neighboring houses that it seemed almost to have grown there, like one of the sentinel maple, oak and shagbark hickory trees that sheltered it. But it was amazingly flexible inside. I well recall occasions when two or three of us, by then married and with young families of our own, returned home to visit at the same time. The house never seemed to strain to accommodate us.

True, Mother had by then gotten into the habit of moving out on an upstairs screened porch in late March and staying out there until October's first snow sent her indoors for the winter. But we had a new family member to accommodate, too. After twenty-seven years of widowhood, Mother married—and we happily adopted—retired career Army officer Carroll R. Hutchins, a.k.a. "Uncle Hutch," into our family. (They wed right there in the living room, with the pastor of Hurlbut Church presiding and their best friends—a Presbyterian minister and his wife—as witnesses.) And no one even hinted that Hutch, in his eighties and not given to porch sleeping, should vacate his room for our comfort. So the rest of us adults drew straws for what was left and lined our children up like cord wood on the front porch floor in sleeping bags. They liked it so well that they tried to persuade Grandma that it should be the standard venue for visiting grandchildren. Grandma smiled indulgently—but the porch furniture stayed put.

There was even room under the switchback basement stairs for a large compressor, because Mother's new living room no longer housed two upright pianos like our Meadville home, nor even a single one like our McClintock cottage: it housed a baby grand piano and a two-manual, four-rank Moeller pipe organ. The organ was a steal, actually. By chance (or grace or serendipity, depending on your theological perspective) the organ builder she contacted happened to have a "used" instrument available, although calling it "used" was a stretch. It had been installed in the Syria Mosque in Pittsburgh the year before for the Jewish High Holy Days, played four times, and taken out again. Mother could have it for three thousand dollars, but was advised to insure it for forty. She didn't need to have it explained to her twice.

Thus began a new chapter of her musical mentoring. When her father died that year, Mother received an inheritance that made her financially independent for the first time in her life. By season's end, she had established a fund in the Chautauqua Foundation to provide a music scholarship each summer, and periodically added to its principle. The ink was not yet dry on the first award notice before the winner was invited down to the house for tea and cookies on the front porch. And with that, a tradition was established: every recipient for 35 years received the same invitation, and every one came.

Others followed as word of her living-room organ got around. Students had access to two instruments (not including the Amphitheater's Massey Organ, for which "practice instrument" never seemed an appropriate designation). Both were in public buildings, however, where scheduled events limited their availability.

"Never mind," Mother told one or two students every summer thereafter. "I'll leave my front door unlocked and you can go down and practice on my organ."

She did, they did, and household routine adapted. We soon learned to ignore total strangers who walked in, powered up the organ, practiced an hour, and left, as if they really belonged there.

It went on for years, and I never once recall that a student abused the privilege. Only at Chautauqua.

But don't assume that life at 9 North Lake was all sober-sided. If I have failed along the way to convey how social an animal our Mother was, my writing is remiss. The only thing she loved better than a gathering of friends was a boat ride; and whenever the two could be combined, she felt herself to be on the pinnacle of the good life.

An essential if unsettling disclaimer needs here to be stated. Gatherings of Mother's friends were an amalgamation of rich desserts, verbal combat, and raucous laughter. Those unable to endure the three in concert without throwing up or passing out were better advised to stay away.

The favorite hour to gather was on an evening when none of her circle of friends had tickets to Norton Hall, and the Amphitheater program was a take-it-or-leave-it affair. Put another way, they only occurred on evenings when no opera, play or symphony concert was scheduled. The sole exception to that rule was Sunday evening. Sacred Song Services began and ended earlier than most evening events, leaving ample time to disrupt the neighborhood after "Day is Dying in the West" and Handel's *Largo* had filtered off into the night.

When that crowd did gather, however, they took every seat in the living room plus extras dragged in from the dining room, razzed each other without mercy, and indulged in gastronomical excess without a discernible twinge of guilt. The summer that still comes most clearly to mind was the year of the chocolate chip torte. It wasn't that the torte itself was so exceptional (although it certainly was popular). It was because, for some reason,

Mother decided that I executed the recipe especially well. She asked me to make one practically every week of the entire season—if not for a gathering at home, then to celebrate the birthday of one of her staff in Kellogg Hall, or as dessert on a boat picnic on our family boat, *Shadow II*. I haven't made another in the intervening half a century, but could almost do it without consulting the recipe—which I still have. It was a flat cake, really, nine-by-thirteen inches in spread and two inches thick. But it more than made up in calories what it lacked in loft. Beyond the obligatory eggs and sugar and melted butter, the underlying flavor ingredient was cocoa; but it was so riddled with chopped dates that the batter resembled terrazzo. Before it went into the oven, a dense coat of chocolate chips and chopped nuts was layered on top. But the crowning blow was saved for last: each piece left the kitchen with a great glob of freshly whipped cream on top. Or a scoop of ice cream on the side. Or—what the heck—both.

Ten to a dozen people attended those gatherings, and there never was enough torte left over in the pan to bother scraping it out before dropping it into the dish water.

It was about that time of the evening that things usually got out of hand, though there was an odd feature to it. Mother possessed a responsive sense of humor, by which I mean that she immensely enjoyed other people's wit, but she seldom contributed a funny remark of her own. She embodied, rather, the virtues of a "straight-man," feeding out lines that the nuttiest of her friends would grab and run with. And they'd carry on for an hour without allowing enough of a pause for the rest of us to draw breath, until those of us who hadn't fallen off our chairs in hysteria were in danger of passing out for lack of oxygen. As I reflect back, it was probably a good thing that we lived on the lakefront. There were, fortunately, no windows on the back of our living room, the wall of which was mere feet away from the backs of our neighbors' cottages that faced onto Miller Park. They were great neighbors, and we had no wish to force them to participate in our parties from across the alley.

However, we did leave the front doors open. There had to be some escape valve for the noise, else the structural integrity of our home might have been severely compromised. I truly believe that crowd could have blown the top deck off a parking garage. In any event, such decibels as escaped—and there were many—were unlikely to disturb anyone short of Dewittville Bay on the other side of the lake.

CHAPTER 7

Chautauqua's Premier Community Dock

The Skinner family was not often accused of subversion, but in at least one case we were guilty of challenging a long-standing Chautauqua policy—and of succeeding. For generations, docks almost entirely belonged to single families, and largely to families privileged to live on the lakefront. Some were generous, and allowed friends to share them; others were less so. It was a natural consequence of the way Chautauqua developed, but not one that would stand the test of time. As more and more people joined the Chautauqua family, the proportion of them who might ever hope to own lakefront property shrank, so fewer and fewer had access to the lake except by way of the Institution boat dock and the public bathing beaches.

The first breach occurred during our McClintock years. Several families up and down the street were interested in gaining access to a dock. Given how jealously the Institution guarded the business of granting dock permits, it was not at all certain that we would succeed. However, we had a secret weapon in the form of one of our neighbors. That would be Dr. Samuel M. Hazlett, who earned the acclaim and gratitude of a whole generation of Chautauquans by reorganizing the Institution's debt to avoid receivership during the down days of the Great Depression; and went on to serve Chautauqua as its president for the decade begun in 1946. Sam did not often frequent the waterfront, but he had children and grandchildren who did. So, during casual conversation, Mother raised the question: why could we not bring several families together to build a dock? There was, at the time, nothing between the Peters dock at the bottom of McClintock Avenue and the new Shaw home in the recently opened north section. Sam liked the idea. It would relieve the pressure of having to decide which single family was awarded the privilege.

Five families—the DeWiesses, Feltebergers, Hazletts, Jacobs, and Skinners—signed on and pooled their resources. That winter, Sam exercised his executive authority by inveigling the Institution's carpenters into building the thing. So it was that Chautauqua's first multi-family dock was born out of a combination of neighborly cooperation and petite graft. Next spring, a fine new dock, crafted of wormy chestnut and likely to endure for fifty years, lay neatly stacked on the waterfront. All that was left was to put into the lake, and take it out that fall, and put it in again the next spring, and.... For some strange reason, the task fell to the Skinner brothers—most likely because we were among the first to arrive in June and last to leave in September.

When, several years later, Mother bought our home at 9 North Lake, we again found ourselves dockless. On the other hand, we stood on the porch looking out toward the lake at a two-hundred foot gap between the Miller-Babcox dock to the south and the

Muncie Hotel dock to the north, more than sufficient room to accommodate another, and we smack in the middle of it. Nor were we alone. A number of neighborhood families, most with several children and at least one boat, and all eager for a way to enjoy the lake nearer home, were interested.

By 1955, the conversation had evolved into a plan. Mother, an "insider" by virtue of her position as registrar of the summer schools, took the lead in notifying Gerald Lynch, Institution treasurer, that five or six families were interested in having a dock, pointing out the space available and seeking Institution sanction. Several weeks later, Gerry suggested that, since it would probably be the last dock to be approved along that stretch of waterfront, some of us should meet to discuss a precise location before everyone went home for the winter.

Enter J. Paul, a.k.a. "Dick," grizzled patriarch of a Jones family and, with his wife Julia, parents of a spirited female foursome, Nancy, Betty, Shirley, and Judy. (Shirley and I were Allegheny College classmates.) Dick and I were assigned to meet with Gerry and reach an agreement. That required a bit of preliminary fence-mending. We did not realize, when we bought 9 North Lake, that we had mightily offended the Jones family through no fault of our own; they were the ones who had rented it, and were consequently dispossessed. Indeed, had they known that the owner was willing to part with it, they would have snatched it up so fast that we would never even have heard of it. Fortunately for the Jones family—and for our friendship, which survived both the loss of their rental cottage and the intervening years—they were able to purchase the home at 16 Miller Park, and transformed it, too, into a jewel.

Some time earlier, Dick had launched a project that, over several years, grew to be a central feature of community life on the north shore: he created a beach. Realizing that sand and gravel were constantly washed down lake by littoral currents and waves, he built a small rock groin out into the lake directly in front of our house, causing the water to drop its burden and the shoreline to extend further into the lake. As beach accumulated, more rocks were added. Periodically, one or two truckloads of washed sand were purchased and spread across the lake's deposits, providing a softer surface for sunbathing and play. By the time we moved into 9 North Lake, several hundred square feet of beach lay on the shore, appropriately (if tongue in cheek) dubbed "Jones Beach." When Dick and I called on Gerry Lynch in late August, we had no problem convincing him that Dick's stonework was the perfect take-off point for a dock, and we were officially granted the permit to erect Dock No. 36. By that time "we," included the Arnolds, Brandons, Fleeks, Jonses, Lawsons, Pattons and Skinners.

Lacking Sam Hazlett's intervention this time around, we had to arrange to have the dock built ourselves. A flurry of correspondence during early fall resulted in agreement concerning the thing's vitals—length, composition, color—and a local contractor was retained to build it for $1,038.00. But we still had to put it in and take it out ourselves—under the watchful supervision of the neighborhood's patriarchal triumvirate, Dick Jones, Campbell Brandon and Don Patton.

Community Dock

Other families were soon invited to become part of the Jones Beach Dock Association, and Chautauqua's second community dock soon had eighteen member families. Over time, some inevitably withdrew as older family members passed on and cottages changed hands. But the association endured, and over thirty families were members for varying lengths of time. Each new family was asked to contribute $100.00 to a revolving fund to be used to repair and maintain the dock or, if necessary—and as has happened once already—to replace it. It remains Chautauqua's premier community dock and a source of pride for those of us who enjoy a periodic sally into subversion.

It was not possible, however, for so much community spirit to confine itself to dock maintenance. There must be other outlets, and the most enduring was not long in being identified. It began innocently enough: several neighbors who were around for the Memorial Day weekend and bumped into each other as Chautauqua neighbors must, decided to throw themselves a potluck supper. The weather was dismal that weekend, cold and sodden, so Dyke and Millie Underwood—proprietors of the Muncie Hotel (Dyke had once been a pilot aboard several of the old lake steamers)—invited the group to come on over and use their dining room.

It was so much fun that everyone promptly agreed to do it again in the fall, on Labor Day, and did. Which led to a Memorial Day reprise the following spring. By then, however, word was out, and a chance gathering of a few neighbors was well on the road to ritualization. Memorial Day was dropped from the schedule a few years later: the weather was dependably undependable, the Muncie had been sold and was razed to make way for a private cottage, and the gathering had grown so large that it no longer fit into anyone's living room. But it didn't end there; it simply shifted emphasis, and the Annual North Shore Community Labor Day Picnic was born.

Things got under way soon after noon, when the Institution erected barriers blocking off North lake Drive from its Whitfield intersection to Miller Park. Card tables and folding chairs and park benches were hauled out, and a long serving table was set up right in the middle of the road above Jones Beach. When, for sheer numbers, the potluck approach grew too unwieldy, the menu was unified. Early afternoon, the young people (faultlessly supervised by the paternal troika) erected a huge beach fire of scrap and drift wood and an occasional discarded section of dock or an old boat, while dozens of ears of sweet corn, purchased fresh from a nearby farmer, were tied into burlap bags and thrown into the lake to soak. Half the afternoon the fire burned, until it settled down to a deep bed of white-hot coals on which an old iron steam radiator was laid to absorb heat until it nearly glowed itself.

Mid-afternoon, a professional barbecue crew arrived, set fire to a dozen bags of charcoal, and soon had a hundred half-chickens sizzling and dripping while smoke filtered into nearby cottages and raised people's appetites to somewhere between famished and ravenous. Late afternoon, bags of fresh rolls, relish trays, and potato salad arrived in sufficient quantity to bury the serving table, leaving just enough room for the large coffee thermoses at the end, while soda pop coolers filled with ice were set on the ground nearby. At the last, families made their ways piecemeal to the beach and greetings and banter and laughter grew so loud that people up on the Plaza must surely have wondered what all the fuss was about. Then the bags of corn came out of the lake and the ears, still in their water-soaked shucks, were lined up in the slots between the radiator sections until the outsides were charred black and the insides were steaming golden sugar. And when all was in readiness, and everyone stopped where they were and quit talking and laughing for a moment while one of the community's elders, priest of the moment, thanked God for all of it—including the inexpressible privilege of being Chautauqua neighbors—we knew that we really were blessed beyond measure. We honestly couldn't imagine how it could get any better.

North Lake Drive Footnote: In late winter of 1987, then in his 98th year, Uncle Hutch settled his accounts and took his leave. In failing health, he had been confined to Jamestown's WCA Hospital for several weeks. But it was evident that his mainspring was simply running down and there would be no rewinding it. He asked to go home. A hospital bed had been set up for him some weeks earlier in the living room where, twenty years before, he and Mother had exchanged their vows. That afternoon, as Mother fed him some soup, he quietly slipped away.

A month later, arrangements made and family gathered, Hutch was buried with full military honors just as Arlington National Cemetery burst into bloom. When Mother and Hutch first talked of marrying, they hesitated for fear that, "at their age," something might happen to either of them at any time. The impetus to get on with it came largely from their five children—Mother's four and Marjorie "Hutch" Taylor, Hutch's only daughter and nick-namesake in New England. As evidence that old age should never be determinative in matters of the heart, I offer this simple irony: Mother and Hutch had six more years together than she and Dad did.

In October 1991, approaching her own 91st birthday, Mother also died quietly in her beloved lakefront home. Pat and I had driven up from Meadville earlier that day to visit her. She lived alone, kept her own house, cooked her own meals, and drove her own car—and would have it no other way. Anyone who finds that somehow regrettable never knew Mother. Her steely determination was the last thing to abandon her. When friends missed her at church and at a china painting class, and went looking for her, they found her peacefully curled up and gone away, and we were called to drive up again. As we went about the grounds on the essential but oddly comforting errands that her departure made our responsibility, we encountered several of her friends who had not yet heard the news.

"Ruth Hutchins? It can't be. Why, she'll live to be a hundred!" they cried. Then emphatically, when we explained what must have happened: "Oh, that's *just* the way Ruth would have wanted it!"

Sometimes still, when we are at Chautauqua, we walk out to the end of the community dock late in the evening after a concert or ballet performance, sit down on the old chairs that for years spent winters in our basement, and look out over the lake. At such moments, we feel as if our old home is still there behind us, its windows aglow, beckoning reassuringly for us to come settle into bed for the night in the perfect lakefront cottage in the nicest neighborhood of the most wonderful community in America.

PART 3

Boys' and Girls' Club

CHAPTER 8

If You're Red or Blue

Grabbing mostly-dried bathing suits off the line in the sun porch of our Eau Claire Annex apartment, Ruth Ann, Cliff, Frank and I folded them into our towels, rolled them into tight drums, called "See ya!" to Mother and banged the screen on our race to be first out the runway to the street.

"Have fun today," she called back, already preparing to walk out the door to whatever fun she had in mind for herself that morning. That was Chautauqua: parents could turn young children loose to head off for Boys' and Girls' Club—or simply to wander the town with a friend or a mob—with never a worry. Every child seemed mysteriously to have acquired several hundred aunts and uncles, total strangers who'd dry a tyke's tears and brush the dust off, the while speaking in gentle tones of reassurance and encouragement. How many children were rescued through the years by grown-ups they didn't know and would never see again, their own parents neither aware nor the wiser, is an unrecorded Chautauqua datum.

Mother, who couldn't ride a bike, swim a stroke, or catch a ball if her life had depended on any of them, nonetheless let us go knowing that we'd be doing all the above and more, every day of the summer, and never gave it a second thought.

Bicycles were the preferred mode of transport for children—and many adults. With automobiles largely barred from the grounds during the season, pedestrians were in undisputed possession of Chautauqua's streets. So, most traffic problems resulted from fast-wheeled children tangling with slow-footed adults. The fastest-wheeled part of the Skinner children's preferred route to Club during our North Terrace summers was the second block of it, when we stormed down Vincent hill. "Storming" wasn't the wisest way to take that precipitous grade, but it was the most fun.

Well, usually. There was the time that Frank raced down it with his friend Harry "Doc" Pollock balanced on the crossbar, belatedly to discover that his bike had no brakes. A 90-degree turn onto Simpson might have neutralized the danger—assuming they didn't turn squarely into a gaggle of elderly ladies. Who knows how many undeserving pedestrians might have been knocked flat then? Fortunately for the hypothetical gaggle, but unhappily for Frank and Doc, inertial law was against them: Frank managed a quarter-turn, barely avoided a large tree at the edge of Miller Park, but caught his front wheel on a piece of curb that curved in behind the tree. Like a brace of clowns in training, Doc flew through the air and landed on his reverse end and Frank did a somersault right over him. In keeping with Mother's dictum that children grow up by the grace of God not the ability of parents, both boys walked away with nothing more serious than some colorful contusions and abrasions. But ever after, Frank checked his brakes before starting down that, or any other, Chautauqua hill.

Fortunately for our survival, that sort of ride was the exception. More generally, we hooked right onto Simpson and (resisting the temptation to continue up the walk at the end of it, through the huge double door and right on into the Athenaeum lobby) turned downhill at Bowman. Angling across the hotel's front lawn to the Promenade that paralleled South Lake Drive, we fell into "Indian file" (a necessity imposed by the narrow dirt-and-gravel pathway) merged with other children coming along the lakefront, and pedaled past the Women's Club and the Methodist Missionary Home, and the cottages of friends whose families lived along South Lake—Brahams, Karslakes, and Heinzes. As a brook gathers a dozen tributaries on its run to the sea, swelling into a river, streams of biking children converged on us from ten directions. We were in full flood by the time we skidded to a dust-kicking stop under the ball field's weathered wooden bleachers and dropped our bikes among the hundreds lying in the dirt.

Girls raced up the steps to the Girls' Club porch and disappeared into the building, where chatter and giggle soon gave way to song. The girls, it seemed to me, started every day with singing. Beyond that, I cannot tell further their part of this story. No slight is intended. It's just that Club was gender-separate in most things, and I wasn't privy to the distaff side of it. It's just the way we were raised, and that's all that can be said for it.

In contrast, our day—as befitted children of the male gender—began with military calls played on a bugle so battered and tarnished that it may well have endured a war or two of its own. "Assembly" sounded first, ranging along the waterfront and up the side streets to urge latecomers to get a move on, and ordering us into rows of wooden benches set on the grass in front of the Boys' Club building. First order of the day was to stand for "Raising the Flag"—several hundred young boys assuming a posture close enough to call it attention, while the flag was run up the pole at water's edge. The most somber moment of the day followed—never more restrained than during World War II, when each of us likely knew someone who was in harm's way, perhaps a member of our own family. We were not inclined to take lightly the Pledge of Allegiance to the breeze-stirred banner that symbolized everything about our country that we loved and depended on.

But that was about it for orderliness. Morning announcements behind us, organized chaos ensued as four boisterous groups headed off in as many directions to engage in three hours of hyperactivity. The problem for me and my friends (and I suspect for every other generation of Club children, before and after) was having too many favorites. Were we scheduled for field games, where teams weighed in against each other at softball or running races or tugs-of-war using a rope that stretched from first to third base and was as big around as my arm and so heavy that it took half our effort simply to get it up off the ground? Alright! Were we to divide the woods behind the Girls' Club into "territories," with the Thunder Bridge the Mason-Dixon Line, and launch a game of Capture the Flag that ranged from Hawthorne to the Hall of Christ and from the back of the Girls' Club to Massey Avenue? Great! (And when we weren't busy chasing each other or skulking around in dense woods trying to sneak up on the other team's flag to steal it, or to free captured teammates from their picnic-table prison, we mucked around in the stream catching water spiders and crayfish or turned over slabs of sedimentary rock looking for shellfish fossils.) Were we scheduled for shop or arts and crafts, where we made actually useful stuff like a milk-bottle carrier or a lanyard? Terrific! Those were the best rainy-day activities in the world. I would happily have stayed in the shop all day, until the last slat was nailed to my carrier or the paint dried on my totally-original, made-from-scraps paddle-wheel boat model that, when launched, listed fifteen degrees to port and traveled about seven inches before it ran out of rubber-band power. Nor can I ever forget sitting on the end of a dock or sipping a soda in the pillared Pergola at the northeast corner of the Plaza as a friend's finger patiently served as a hook while I braided four strands of lanyard and we endlessly mulled every bit of weighty trivia we could conjure.

"Alright boys, we're going to count off again," said Mr. Llewelyn, senior counselor of Group 1 my first year in Club. He was, I thought, one of the handsomest men I had ever known. Neither brawny nor frail, his skin tanned to soft leather, he retained most of his sandy-brown hair just becoming edged with gray. As a child, however, I was mostly drawn to his no-nonsense but kind gray eyes, wrinkled about by so many years of smiling that if you laid the creases end-to-end they'd reach from here to next weekend.

But why take roll again? We'd just finished.

(An aside for readers never privileged to attend Club: roll was taken every hour, at the start or finish of each activity. It was the Club's way of making sure that no child got left behind when a group moved from one venue to another. If one did by chance come up missing, the staff turned the whole south end of the grounds on its head until the lost lamb was returned to its fold. It was one of the reasons that Mother—and every parent like her—did not hesitate to see her children head off to Club, or worry about us when we were there.)

"This time," Mr. Llewelyn explained, "instead of calling your number, you're to call out either 'red' or 'blue.' The first boy will be red, the second blue, and so forth. From now on, when we do anything that requires teams, like softball or races, the teams will already be chosen. It will be the reds against the blues."

Oh, how I wanted to be a blue! It was my favorite color. What would I do if I got stuck being a red? What if Ruth Ann and Cliff and Frank were blues, and I was the only red in the house? (It didn't initially occur to me that it might just be the other way around.) Anxiety mounted as the count-off started, the boys in the first row dutifully assigning themselves to one team or the other. As the count-off progressed up the second row in front of me (having a last name that started with S, I spent my entire life in third rows), finger conspicuously pointing at each boy's back in turn—red blue red blue—I tried to get ahead of the count to see where the tally would be by the time it got to me. But I lost track. Boys bobbed and weaved as boys will, and threw my calculation off. Before I could catch up, the voices were coming down my own row, and I had completely lost track when, suddenly, the boy to my left said "Red."

"BLUE!" I shouted. At least it seemed like a shout. I was that eager—and that relieved.

The significance of it did not begin to dawn on me until that Friday's field-meet, the first in a series of contests that alternated between field games and water sports. Every child enrolled in Boys' and Girls' Club competed. The two Groups 1, being the youngest, led off. It was our first taste of the larger spirit of it: children of all ages and both genders cheered for us—half urging the reds on, half the blues. It dawned on us for the first time that we weren't team members just within our own group; our team was half the Club.

We never had to ask, after that, about the twin score cards hanging on the front of the Boys' Club facing South Lake Drive, one red, the other blue. The numbers changed at the end of each week of the passing summer, a cumulative record of all the effort of all the children in Club, competing against one another.

At the time, that was as deep as I saw into it. I thrilled when the blues soared ahead, felt ill when it was the reds. I took only partial satisfaction from Group 1 blue victories when they were erased by red triumphs in older groups. It was not until years later that it dawned on me that the division did not signify a simplistic belief that competition is inherently good. Sometimes it is, sometime it isn't. But for boys and girls at Club, it served a larger purpose: to profit from the real and valuable lessons of athletic and social competition, we had first to agree to compete. There were both oppositional and cooperative aspects to it, and they were linked. Neither reds nor blues could "win" until both blues and reds were prepared to run the risk of "losing." Indeed, our satisfaction depended on it: a willingness by each of us to put ourselves on the line was necessary before any of us could have fun. So we stuck our necks out, and you know what? Cooperation always outweighed competition. I don't ever recall seeing the oppositional side of things last one minute longer than it took to tally the score. Then we linked arms with our usual friends—red or blue—and went off to have fun at something else. It wasn't that we did not play hard, or that we were not out to beat the pants off the other team by playing better than it did. It

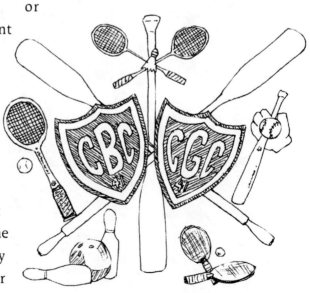

"...if you're red or blue."

was just that neither winning nor losing was as important as friendship.

I think it the main reason why, six decades later, I sit in the Amphitheater on Old First Night, my wife grinning and shaking her head in good-humored tolerance beside me as I join in—with gusto—when Chautauqua's Boys' and Girls' Clubbers hurtle down the aisles and fill the pit as the Massey Organ thunders their—and my, and our—theme song: "Onward Boys' Club, onward Girls' Club, full of life and pep!"

But the most important words in the song come in the fifth and sixth lines: "Onward Boys' Club, onward Girls' Club, if you're red or blue,

You'll win..."

Indeed, you can't help it.

CHAPTER 9

The Real Power of Teamwork

Tumbling into the boys' locker room, thirty small hearts leaped in unison at Mr. Llewelyn's words: "Get changed into your bathing suits and line up at the paddle rack on the porch of the Athletic Club building."

His words that morning could mean only one thing: we were going canoeing! I never knew anyone who didn't want to get into a canoe. Scrambling into our bathing suits, we ran to the canoe rack, bunching and jockeying for position, grabbing at everything in sight until our counselors stopped us and explained lesson 1 of canoeing: picking the right paddle. Anarchy evolved into order as we stood the blades of paddles on the ground at our toes and drew the handles in against our faces. The hand grips at the top should come just to our noses. Though essential to learning, it was an exercise largely wasted. No way could "Club" (our nickname for the Chautauqua Boys' and Girls' Clubs) afford enough paddles to meet the requirements of every child in a throng of five-hundred 5-to-14-year-olds. So we embraced the ideal but submitted to the reality, each of us walking away with a paddle that was as close to regulation as possible. It was a lesson relearned every summer, and became more pointed as I grew in stature: get to the rack first or get stuck with a paddle that barely reached my chest—an omen of dismal labor. But given the right paddle, a good friend as my buddy, and permission to shove off in one of the Club's Maine-built Old Town Canoes, it really didn't matter what activity was planned for our aquatic training: it would be simply splendid.

But enthusiasm pulls me ahead of my story. The day in question came during my first week of Club. That being so, I knew to expect only what my older brothers told me; and somehow it didn't occur to them to tell me that canoeing at Club began neither in a canoe nor on the lake. It began in dry dock.

Standing on the lawn in front of the Boys' Club building, our bare toes hooked into the brittle, sun-baked grass, we listened impatiently while Mr. Llewelyn and his "junior counselor" carefully (and tediously, I thought) taught us the basic stokes we would need to propel and control a canoe. We rehearsed them all, forestroke and back-stroke, J- and C-, while wet-wonderful waves splashed against the seawall and our over-heated bodies struggled awkwardly to master the hold and feel of a paddle. The while, our eyes looked yearningly toward the many-hued canoes resting on their pull-out ramps at the far side of the waterfront.

We never did make it into the boats that day. We got only as far as the gravelly shallows between the swimming docks, where we stood, lined up in ranks and rows in water to our knees while our counselors ordered us through the whole choreography again, and our corporate labor churned the lake into a seething caldron of muddy water. Then we lined up along the length of the dock, crouching on our knees (the correct bearing, we were instructed, when paddling a canoe) and did it all a third time. By then it was not only boring but painful: kneeling on the weathered wood, tender knees chafing where skin pressed into the gaps between the boards, reaching for water that was two feet too far below us, we fore-stroked and back-stroked and C-stroked and J-stroked until our backs ached from the strain. We grinned in triumph when, at last, Mr. Llewelyn pronounced his satisfaction that we had mastered the basics. We were ready to go! That expectation was among the briefest in history. "Okay, boys, the hour is up; put your paddles back in the racks and line up at the dock for swimming."

Our collective groan must have been audible on the porch of the Athenaeum.

Nor, a few days later, when the blessed word again appeared on our schedule, was it what we wanted. Aquatic training at the Boys' and Girls' Clubs was on a par with every other form of learning that Chautauqua underwrote: methodical and thorough—and for good reason. Hardly a summer of my youth passed that Chautauqua Lake did not claim the life of someone who, untrained or unprepared, ventured onto or into it. But never since the day of their founding had the Boys' and Girls' Clubs lost a child; and no one, from director Tom Moore to the youngest junior counselor, was prepared to bear the responsibility of having it happen for the first time. We would get to handle a canoe alone when we could manage it under every condition that Chautauqua Lake might throw at us; and Chautauqua Lake, in spite of a generally benign countenance, was capable of turning mean in a minute. That day and for the remainder of the summer, canoeing for us first groupers was a bulk enterprise: we were confined to the "war canoes."

The war canoes were outsized affairs that, at 24 feet long, were capable of carrying fifteen small clubbers and a counselor apiece. Still, they were genuine canoes and, used singly, required even greater skill than that needed to handle a standard 16-foot model, because fifteen children ensured enough shifting-about and disorganization to be dangerous. Accidentally swamping one of the things several hundred feet from shore would not be a trivial event. So twin, ten-foot two-by-fours were lashed between them, at the second and the next-to-last thwarts, so that each canoe served as an outrigger for the other. The result was a catamaran boat 24 feet long and 10 in the beam, rendering a tip-over not only difficult but impossible. Nor was control a problem: an experienced counselor in the stern of each easily retained steerage, the while belting out orders to us enthusiastic, if erratic, paddlers.

We even learned that we could turn the whole assembly on a dime: "Red canoe, forestroke! Blue canoe, backstroke! Ready, stroke! Stroke!" We didn't move. The bulky craft, burdened by 34 bodies—even small ones—and hampered by the resulting pressure of several tons of water pressed against its sides, wasn't going anywhere without serious persuasion. But we soon caught the spirit of it, our awkward but determined paddles sweeping as hard as our small bodies could make them, until water roiled forward from the blue canoe and sternward from the red: "Stroke! Stroke!" Increasingly responsive, the two canoes pivoted slowly on the axis of their two-by-four bridging until they faced about into the lake. "Blue canoe, forestroke! Stroke! Stroke!" rang Mr. Llewelyn's voice. With surprising agility the twin craft surged into open water, and we were under way, inscribing a slow arc that directed us north up the shore toward Miller Bell Tower a half-mile away.

We were admittedly a Raggedy-Andy lot. Wielding a paddle is an acquired art. Leaning out over the gunnels of a canoe, straining to push water with a flat piece of wood that extends eighteen inches below the surface, lacks the natural grace of movement one feels when pulling the oars of a rowboat. Nor was progress aided by our uncoordinated attempt to master a whole new array of movements, all of them strange. Focused on the rhythm set by our taskmaster in the stern ("Stroke! Stroke!") one boy reached his airborne paddle forward just as the boy in front of him swept his back, the paddles colliding with the muffled clack of wet wood. So we banged our way up the lake, our well-chewed paddles edg-

War Canoes

ing one degree closer to disintegration. Another boy, trying to lift a too-long paddle clear of the water to swing it forward for the next stroke, caught its tip in the lake and sent an icy spray across the hot, naked backs of three rows of boys in front of him. The penalty for such clumsiness was foregone: three aggrieved paddlers sent a wall of water aft into the offender's face—soaking not just him but his neighbors as well, who then felt compelled to retaliate. "No splashing!" rang the order from astern, and we returned to the labor of learning ("Stroke! Stroke!").

Actually, license to splash was at the discretion of our counselors. On especially harsh days, when no breeze tempered the assault of the sun, we were encouraged at least once each outing to indulge in a water fight, both canoes raising a torrent of spray to soak those across the way, and benefiting by a cooling shower in return. But not today. Today was for learning, and the learning was beginning to pay off. One by one, we caught both the knack of it and the urge to compete, each of us striving to outdo his peers in zealously shoving water. Chatter faded as boys leaned to their work, encouraging the forward surge of the great canoes until small arms burned from the effort. For the first time in my life, I was struck by the real power of teamwork; and while we were probably clipping along at a whole three miles an hour, it seemed to our immature brains like those great canoes might just get up and start to hydroplane.

It could only last a brief time, and did. Small boys are not conditioned to keep up so severe a pace for very long. After maybe ten minutes of churning, I was thankful to hear the call to "Rest!" from the stern, followed quickly by "Ship paddles!"

Relieved to be excused just as most of us were about to give up anyway, we slumped against the struts, panting for breath, and turned our paddle blades skyward, standing their hand grips on the bottom of the canoe. Cool water trickled off the blades and down the shafts, pooling up in the hollows between our thumbs and forefingers. I can't speak for the others, but it took all my powers of resistance not to yield to the temptation to lap it up (while Mother's emphatic "Don't drink the lake water!" echoed in my head). Unnoticed as we sat catching our breath, Mr. Llewelyn dragged his paddle through the water, the blade ruddering the stubborn craft around until we again found ourselves aimed south, back toward Club. We waited for the command to resume paddling, but it didn't come. Mr. Llewelyn had one more lesson to teach before the hour was up.

"Feel the breeze," he said. "Turn your paddles so that the blades are flat to the wind." After some brief disagreement about just where the wind was coming from, we arrived at a consensus, all paddles turned thirty degrees off the axis of the canoes, their flat sides facing in the general direction of Dewittville Bay across the lake. For a moment—but only for a moment—we wondered what this was about. Then, a gust born somewhere beyond the far shore riffled the face of the water and struck the lakeward side of the canoes. Each paddle pulled slightly, tilting forward at the bidding of the breeze. Instinctively, we gripped them more firmly, forcing them to remain upright, unwittingly transferring the power of the breeze to the canoes. At first, we barely sensed it. Then one boy, glancing at the shore, exclaimed "We're moving!" followed by another, then several more. We all looked. Sure enough, the big canoes were ghosting homeward, down the south shore past the Women's Club and the bathing beach. And we weren't doing a thing.

I glanced back at Mr. Llewelyn, and smiled to see the grin on his face. It was only the first of many lessons I would learn at Club—lessons learned so indelibly as never to be forgotten. In the hundreds of hours I have spent canoeing in the years since, I've never come ashore without resting, if only for a moment, to feel how much wind power can be harnessed by the blade of even a single canoe paddle.

Given my initial disappointment at being restricted to the war canoes while that rainbow of 16-foot Old Towns beckoned from the other end of the waterfront, it is interesting to recall that my absolutely most favorite experience at Club was an all-day war-canoe excursion. To be all-day anything was unusual for Boys' Club. Activities commenced at 9:00 a.m. sharp when the bugler sounded "Assembly," recessed at noon, reconvened at 2:00 p.m. and dismissed at 4:00. Somehow, during those years, we Chautauqua kids learned to run home, gobble lunch, join friends for an hour of horsing around (in spite of being urged to rest, even to lie down and take a nap) and—as if moved by herd instinct—to arrive back at the benches in front of the Boys' Club building at 2:00 sharp, without prompting from anyone. During that two-hour break, however, we were not just expected to be gone from Club, we were *required* to be gone. The break was assumed to be as important for the staff as for the kids.

So it was a surprise when Mr. Llewelyn passed out permission slips for us to carry home in anticipation of an all-day outing, including the provision that each boy bring lunch. With providential good fortune, we woke two days later to a clear sky and warming air, with the promise of a lovely day. Morning assembly barely behind us, we raced to the bathhouse, changed into swim suits, grabbed our lunch bags, piled aboard the war canoes, and were soon paddling furiously down lake on a direct line for Prendergast Point two miles away. A few of the boys whose families owned a power boat had probably been there before. But for most of us, either boatless or new to Chautauqua, the excitement was as fresh as it must have been for Columbus or Magellan when the first Atlantic swells lifted the prows of their squat vessels.

A light breeze out of the south, harbinger of good weather on Chautauqua Lake—so long as it does not continue past noon—barely slowed our progress southeast; by 10:30 we rounded the bluff tip of Prendergast, and fifteen minutes later Mr. Llewelyn called for shipped paddles as he nosed us in toward the shore. With a barely audible hiss, the twin prows sliced into pale, glistening sand that lifted the bows and brought the boats to a gently grinding halt. The beach spread a hundred yards inland and a half-mile north and south, punctuated only by tufts of beach grass and scattered driftwood. Neither cottage nor human being was in sight. Looking over the gunnels, it dawned on us that the same sand lay under the boats and extended as far into the lake as we could see bottom. I thought it the most beautiful beach I had ever seen. Piling out of the canoes, we stood staring dumbly, hardly knowing what to do with ourselves. That lasted about five seconds. Shoes flying in eighteen directions and shirts and towels dropped where we stood, we bounded for the water like a convention of otters. One giddy leap followed another as we discovered that, 20 yards off shore, the water was barely waist-deep. It was pure heaven, and no one was discounting the blessing. For an hour we leapt and screeched and splashed until we were exhausted and there was nothing to do for it but to flop down on the hot, dry sand and catch our collective breath.

Then began the scrambling search for our lunches, most of which were packaged in identical brown-paper bags that our mothers had carried home from Chautauqua's only grocery store. They littered the beach with the same abandon as our clothing, and might never have been sorted out had our mothers not had the good sense to write out names on them. Mine may only have been peanut butter and jelly on white, an apple, two oatmeal cookies and a half-pint of orangeade from the Dairylea store. To me, it was a feast that conformed perfectly to the day. Life just didn't get any better than that. Or if it did, I didn't care.

By the time we endured the half-hour wait required for swimming after eating, and were allowed into the lake for another hour of thrashing about in those delicious, sand-carpeted shallows, it was time to dry off, brush as much sand off ourselves as possible (it wasn't), gather our things into the canoes, and push off for the paddle home.

Then came the rude surprise. As we cleared the sheltered water of the bay and rounded the lea of Prendergast Point, we were hit full in the face by a spanking breeze. Had we been older, we would have expected it. Between noon and 2:00 p.m. of a good summer day, the gentle breeze that moved up Chautauqua Lake from the south hauled around to the northwest, filled the sky with brilliant balls of Cumulus cotton and churned the lake into heaving white-caps. It was that pattern that made Chautauqua one of the best sailing lakes in the nation. But that afternoon, for thirty small boys fresh from half-a-day of rollicking play, it was like rounding Cape Horn.

The going was both rough and cold as white caps, slapping the prows of the canoes, broke into sprays of chill water that the insistent wind blew clear to the stern seats where Mr. Llewelyn and our junior counselor urged us on with laughter and their own wet labor. We had, by then, mastered the skill of wielding our paddles in unison; and doing so had built the muscle and stamina needed to keep it up. Good thing, too: it took forty minutes of unremitting effort to bring the boats home, and we edged into the war-canoe slip at the Club dock just as the other groups were climbing out from afternoon free swim and heading for the bathhouse.

I was exhausted. But either I didn't care, or I got over it. Else why would I remember it as the very bestest day?

CHAPTER 10

How to Empty the Lake Out of a Swamped Boat

"How far are we allowed to go?" we yelled back to our counselors as they slid one of the Club's rowboats down the ramp and clambered aboard.

"As far as the lily pads," came the reply. "No farther."

That was all the encouragement we needed. Paddles splashed and clacked against each other and against the sides of canoes, and shouts of "Look out!" and "Watch it!" filled the air as boys nearly paddled right into each other. In spite of flap and flurry, a dozen brightly painted canoes got sorted out and moving in the same direction, paddles churning the lake as each crew strove to get there first. Sweeping around the barren point of ground below Club, we cut across a patch of milky and fetid-smelling water—the discharge from Chautauqua's sewage treatment plant that tarnished the lake and curled our noses. Immediately, then, we passed the end of the fence that demarked the southern extremity of the Institution grounds, slumping akimbo out over the water a few feet as if that would be enough to discourage someone from crawling around it, when they could just as easily climb over.

"Slow down, now," one boy cautioned.

"Everyone be quiet," shushed another.

"Ship your paddles," stage-whispered a third.

Two dozen paddles came out of the water, though our graceful Old Towne canoes kept right on going until they slipped in among stiff-leaved water hyacinths that covered a quarter-acre patch of water, rooted in pure sand twenty yards offshore of undeveloped acreage that stretched from Chautauqua almost to Prendergast Point. The water was two feet deep and as transparent as air. Whispering against the sides of the canoes, the stiff-edged leaves slowly dragged us to a halt. For a moment, no one said a word as our counselors' rowboat hissed in behind us.

"There's one!" The boy's words had the emotional spike of "Thar she blows!" shouted from the crow's nest of a Yankee whaler.

"There's another!" cried a second boy, lifting his paddle and pointing it toward our quarry like it was a huge finger. All eyes followed.

A dozen yards ahead, a pair of knitting needles lined with tiny dagger-like teeth poked up out of the water, then slipped back beneath the surface. Another pair followed, then a third. We called them gar-pike, but gar-fish was okay, or just plain gars. Fifteen to thirty inches long with a girth that barely exceeded a garden hose, they looked more vicious than they were because of all those teeth that lined their beaks from tip to tongue. They came almost daily to feed among the hyacinth pads, and as often as we were given leave, we formed an armada and went gar-hunting.

As quietly as we could manage, we moved out canoes toward the place where the beaks had protruded, spreading out as if to surround the unsuspecting fish. Up came the beaks again, as if probing the air, almost within reach now. The boys in the bows raised their paddles over their heads, poised and ready, striving to keep their excitement in check until the moment was right to strike.

"There!" cried one. His paddle arched over and struck the water edge-first several feet in front of his canoe, right where the silver-backed prey rested an inch below the surface. The paddle sliced into the water as clean as a knife cutting butter and struck... water. The odds always were long, and definitely favored the gars. Before our paddles even touched the water, the fish were gone. With single flicks of their tails, they flashed out of sight so fast that we couldn't even see them go.

Several other crews got to chop at the surface too; but we went home empty-handed, that day and every other day that we tried to club fish with canoe paddles. Gars were no brighter than any other fish, but their instincts were far quicker than our nine-year-old arms. Before the third paddle severed water, the whole school was halfway to Prendergast Point.

Knowing we'd lost another round, and not caring, we turned our attention to the water hyacinths that surrounded us. Thousands of bulbous and bright yellow blooms poked above the mat of flat leaves that mantled the lake. Reaching into the water, we popped them off six inches below the surface and stuck their stems into the rib slots in the gunnels of our canoes. Soon (even while we could discern no difference in the number of blossoms that still stippled that aquatic pasture) every canoe in the troupe was gilt-rimmed. We might paddle back to Club empty-handed of mighty gars, but we were as festive as a Polynesian water pageant.

"Center your weight," Paul warned. (Paul Arnold, waterfront director of the Boys' and Girls' Club, sat a few yards away in a rowboat, administering one of Club's most important aquatic tutorials.) "You're too far to this side. If you're not careful, you'll tip your own canoe. Then you'll have two of them swamped."

Jim and I shifted our weight over the keel of our craft and considered the swamped canoe resting in the lake beside us, water sloshing over its gunnels and its crew treading water next to it, waiting to be "rescued." Jim Braham and I were the same age, and shared the status of youngest brothers in our respective families: Cliff and Jim's older brother Walt were close friends through Club and beyond. (Their dad, W. Walter, known to family friends as "the Judge" because he was one in their home town of New Castle, Pennsylvania, served as Chautauqua's president from 1956 to 1960—one of nine whom I was personally privileged to know.)

But neither sibling rank nor paternal prominence was our concern at the moment. We were being taught how to empty the lake out of a swamped boat, and to save its occupants, without tipping over our own. To do so required us to pull the bow of the drowned vessel up over our gunnels, flushing as much water out its stern as possible. Then we had to bring it clear on board to drain out the rest of the water, right it, launch it back into the lake, and help the "victims" climb aboard without swamping it all over again.

"Don't try to rush it," Paul cautioned. "Be patient. Give the water time to drain." Gripping the bow of the wallowing boat, Jim and I heaved with all our might to lift it high enough to set it down on our gunnels. At first, it felt like the lake was sucking at the swamped boat more strongly than we could lift. Slowly, however the water moved to the back end and flowed over the edges. The more it flushed, the lighter the bow became, and soon, by stages, we had several feet of it resting atop our canoe. When it was clear that no more would drain on its own, Paul ordered us to roll it over and bring it the rest of the way on board, completing the dumping process. Jim and I eyed each other.

"Coming your way," Jim said. "Ready?"

"Yep," I answered. "Heave."

Working together, we rolled the canoe over and hauled on it at the same time, dragging it on board until, more of it over our boat than not, the bow—like the high end of a teeter-totter when the big kid gets on it—dropped with a thump and the stern lifted clear of the water. Jim and I shared a grin of triumph.

Rescue at Lake

"Good," Paul encouraged. "Now roll it over and slide it back into the lake—carefully. You don't want to gouge up your canoe with that keel."

Again we turned it over, Jim's way this time, lifted it by the bow to drop the stern into the water, and floated it away from us until we could set the bow back into the lake.

"Well done," said Paul. "Now," (to the two boys in the lake) "get into your canoe. And" (to Jim and me) "you boys swamp yours and we'll do it the other way around."

Gripping the gunnels on one side, we shifted our weight out over the other, tumbled into the water and pulled the canoe over with us. Now we got to play stupid and tread water while the other boys learned how to rescue us.

I had no way of knowing how many times I might be called on to employ that lesson in the ensuing years. There weren't many, but there were more than I would have expected; and a couple of times I might actually have saved someone's life.

Then, of course, there was the lesson about what to do when no second boat was anywhere to be seen. We learned that one on a different kind of day—the selection of which, I later concluded, was deliberate, even if not malicious.

A squally rain had come during the night, and we woke to a nor'easter. We seldom got more than one of those a summer. A mass of air circling counter-clockwise around a low-pressure center somewhere up in northeastern Canada came at Chautauqua from straight across the lake, hell-bent-for-leather. Those were the days on which boats moored along the south shore took a beating. Chautauqua's storms mostly came from the northwest, across Lake Erie, and barreled down-lake parallel to the north shore and right past the front door of our cottage. (On more than one occasion, some of the boats moored off our neighborhood dock heaved so hard that, if they didn't part their lines, they would surely drag anchor, and neither was an acceptable option. Then we'd fight our way out to them, one by one, and either run them up onto Jones Beach or take them around into the lee of Miller Bell Tower.)

When a nor'easter struck, roles were reversed. It was time for south shore boat owners to scramble to tend their craft lest they be swept up against the bluff shoreline and the rocks that lined it, together with a few sections of washed-out dock, just to make the mix interesting. It had happened more than once.

So we weren't expecting much waterfront activity that day. Were we ever in for a shock.

"Okay, boys," our counselor said after roll call. "Change into your swimsuits. We're going canoeing."

"*Canoeing*?!" We looked at him slack-jawed, like he just might have taken leave of his senses. Not so. He was in dead earnest. And there was clearly method to his madness. Not only were we going out on that whip-lashed lake in canoes, each of us was going out alone.

"Now, remember," he reminded us as we lined up next to the canoe ramp, "your canoe will float even if it swamps. What's the lesson there?"

"Never leave your boat!" we shot back. We had that lesson down cold. In a lake like Chautauqua, most people who drowned did so because they got separated—or separated themselves—from a boat that kept right on floating, and could have saved them.

"And where do you sit in a canoe on a lovely day like this?" he continued.

"In the windward end," we answered. The lighter end of a canoe or rowboat sticks up in the air, even if only slightly. But it's enough: the wind grabs is like a weathervane and spins it around. It can't be helped. So we learned to put the weight up front if we wanted to go upwind on a heavy day—the heavier person of a pair or the single boater if alone. By the same token, if we wanted to go downwind, we moved the weight to the back. If across the wind, to the middle.

"Okay, our counselor concluded. "Here's what you're going to do. We'll station a rowboat out in the lake. Each of you is to paddle out to it, swamp your canoe, and bring it in flooded. Got it? Okay," he gestured to the first few in line, "you boys get started."

One by one, boys climbed into the bows of their canoes and headed out into the lake, the wind keeping their high sterns aimed at the shore behind them. It still took a while; that much headwind is never a canoeist's friend. When my turn came, I stepped into the bow of my canoe—soaked from having been drenched twice already—reached out forward and started to paddle. It was harder than it looked. The constant whipping around required me to shift my paddle from side to side every three or four strokes. And the wind was so fierce that I was sure the boat would blow backward every time I lifted the paddle out of the water. It proved to be an illusion. Soon enough, I noticed that I was beyond the end of the dock, then past the diving platform. I was indeed making steady—if pokey—progress toward the rowboat 50 yards out. I was reassured to see that our junior counselor had to row almost as hard to keep on station as we had to paddle to get there.

"Okay," he said as I came next to him. "Swamp your canoe. And remember, when it fills with water, keep your weight as low as possible. If you try to sit on the seat or stand up, it'll sink under you. Just let yourself float inside it."

I dutifully shoved my paddle under the thwarts so it wouldn't take off by itself, stood up, and tilted the canoe onto its port beam until water flooded in and the canoe settled to the gunnels. Worming my way to the center, I leaned against the back thwart, hooked my legs over the middle one, pulled the paddle free, and began to make wide, sweeping strokes. I was amazed to discover how easy it was to move a canoe when I was up to my chin in lake inside it. I also discovered that, once under way, I could stop paddling without slowing down: when I got all the water in the canoe moving, inertia wanted to keep it going, shoving the boat along with it. The problem, I learned, was getting it to stop once I had it moving. As I approached the ramp and discovered that the canoe and its aquatic burden intended to keep right on going, I had to leap out and dig my feet into the gravel to stop it. It did not take appreciably more time to get the canoe back to shore submerged than it did to paddle it upwind in the first place.

I would never again doubt the ability of such a boat to save my life—or to get me back to shore—if I just used my head. I also made it one of the first lessons I taught my own children the first time I took them out in our family canoe twenty years later.

Not every training experience at Club was as practical as those canoe lessons, among which the bowling ball incident may have been the most questionable. Of course, it had nothing to do with bowling.

Swimming at Boys' and Girls' Club was taken with a degree of seriousness that was unqualified. Among the venues in which the Club had never lost a child—in spite of supervising more than a thousand of them every summer—was Chautauqua Lake. No one rested easy until everything had been done to preclude such a frightful loss. That was the reason for all that training and taking roll every hour and holding counselors responsible for knowing where every one of their charges was, every minute of the day.

I still feel the dread that spread through the staff when a child disappeared one day just before the noon break. Large boards, erected at the swim dock ramps with rows of numbered nails neatly pounded into them, were intended to serve as our failsafe device: children going onto the docks for any reason took metal washers from a bucket hung beneath the board and slipped them onto nails that corresponded to their group and number. At the close of the activity, the washers were removed and dropped back into the bucket. Theoretically, it was possible to tell at a glance how many children were on the waterfront, and whose responsibility they were. It was an essential device to keep track of several hundred children, especially during free swim when every one of them was jumping and diving off docks and thrashing around and swimming to and from the diving platform fifty feet further out in deep water.

The word that passed swiftly from one staff member to another that noon was like a jolt of electricity: a boy had never checked out with his counselor; but he was gone, and his washer hung alone on the otherwise empty board at the waterfront. For what seemed half-a-century, though it was barely half an hour, staff crisscrossed the waterfront, scouring the bottom of the lake. Their sense of despondency was almost unbearable by the time a messenger, dispatched by Club director Tom Moore to speak with the boy's parents, returned. Relief shuddered through the whole staff at the word: the boy was at home. He'd gotten cold swimming, so he just got dressed and left. His washer on the waterfront board? Oh, he forgot, just as he "forgot" to say anything to his counselor. You can take my word for it: that lad was given a heavy-handed re-education about his responsibilities as a group member.

It was to preclude that kind of heart-stopping crunch that the Club's rules were designed. Everyone learned to swim, starting from their first day, and progressed by stages through increasingly difficult requirements. By the time most children were 10, they were advanced swimmers. Many progressed on through Red Cross Junior Life Saving and Life Saving, and a few advanced to Water Safety Instructor.

For each of us, there was a practical as well as a safety consequence: how far we were allowed to venture from shore was determined by the level of ability we demonstrated; and achievement, not age, was the criterion. The better we swam, the further out we could go and the greater freedom we enjoyed. I still remember the swell of pride I felt when told I had passed the test permitting me to swim out to the diving dock; and the stomach-churning thrill that followed when I got my nerve up, climbed the eight-foot tower, and jumped into thin air, plunging so far through the ten-foot deep water that my feet punched into the lake bottom.

Then came the day (I think it was my tenth summer), when a group of us were horsing around out there and Paul Arnold picked up a scratched-up old bowling ball, carried it to the base of the tower, and dropped it into the lake.

"There," he said brightly, looking right at me. "Jump off the tower and bring that up."

I gawked at him, unsure whether to believe him or not. He didn't even blink.

"You can do it. Give it a try."

I had long since grown accustomed to diving off the tower. And the depth of the water no longer concerned me. But I'd have to hold my breath long enough to find the ball once I got to the bottom, with enough left over to get back to the surface with the thing weighing me down. But Paul had his good-natured smirk on his face, and my friends were looking at me. I'd have to try it, just to save my pride. I certainly couldn't think of any better reason.

I climbed the tower and looked down. The elevation seemed somehow greater than I remembered. Oh well. I took a couple of deep breaths, exhaled, took one more and stepped off the tower, aiming for the spot where I thought Paul had dropped the bowling ball. Trying to make like a stick, I hit the water feet first and plunged straight to the bottom. I opened my eyes, but it didn't help. It just made them burn; the water was so roiled that I couldn't see a thing. I'd have to resort to Braille. I was running out of air and about to give up when my hand landed on the ball, sunk about half its diameter into the mud. Gouging it out, I struggled with both hands to hang on to the slime that coated it, and kicked furiously for the surface. It took about two kicks to realize that I wasn't going to make it that way: I needed a hand. Happily, enough muck had flushed off the ball by then that the fingers of my left hand slipped into the holes. Gripping with everything I had, lungs about to burst, I reached up with my right arm and pulled frantically at the water, kicking as hard as I could. I wasn't even sure I was rising until I cleared the bottom murk and saw the algae-covered ladder only inches above me. With one final surge that finished off what was left of my oxygen supply, I grabbed the bottom rung, hoisted my head above water and gulped for air. When I looked up, ten faces, like wide-eyed gargoyles set on cathedral eaves, hung out over the edge of the dock looking down at me. With a triumphant grin, I struggled up the ladder one-handed and rolled the ball onto the dock.

"There, see?" said Paul with a grin. Then he leaned over, picked the ball up, and dropped it back into the water.

"You next," he said to another boy.

So if you ever lose your bowling ball in ten feet of water and need help....

PART 4

Lee

CHAPTER 11

A Geek by His Third Birthday

Bounding down the Wythe Avenue steps of his family's low-slung, stick-built cottage (the address was 22 Vincent, but I never saw anyone use the front steps) Lee Delasin and I turned down the brick walk, angled across the Plaza to the far corner of Smith Memorial Library, and veered right toward the Amphitheater. Early teenagers, our legs longer than our brains were able fully to control, we consumed ground like trotters pacing a track. Barely a minute from home, we stepped over the lip of the Amphitheater, surrendered to gravity, plunged to the pit, ricocheted off the back pew ends, and loped down the left aisle, stopping only when we reached the long desk bracketed to the front of the stage. On its far end rested a gray metal amplifier, maybe twice the size of a shoebox. Clicking the toggle switch, Lee waited until a warm glow shone through the ventilator holes, turned two of its four dials to the pre-marked numeral 4, and nodded his satisfaction: the Amphitheater's amplification system was up and running. When a speaker stepped to the lectern a few minutes later, his voice would magically emerge from six bull-horn speakers mounted, three each, twenty feet up on twin steel pillars flanking the stage and several rows up into the side-ramp seats. The whole assembly probably cost $300.00, and I never recall anyone complaining that they couldn't hear.

We shivered as we waited. Shorts and tee-shirts weren't sufficient to ward off the chill that settled into the Amphitheater pit every night of even the warmest summer. Still, being teen-aged boys preoccupied with our peer image, we eschewed the sweaters and jackets that adult Chautauquans had the good sense to wear to morning events. We distracted ourselves instead, by jabbering about things having nothing to do with why we were there until Ralph McCallister—Chautauqua's new vice-president for program and education—strode to the podium to introduce the morning speaker. Then even teenagers knew it was time to shut up. Lee loved that job, and didn't want to lose it because of an unbridled mouth.

Had Lee been born a half-century later, he would have been branded a geek by his third birthday. Slender of build, he was—in that less politically-correct era—labeled "skinny." But such bulk as his limbs and torso were missing appeared to have been redeployed to his head: he had enough brains for two of me. By the time he was eleven, he had built his own radio from pirated parts, a contraption the more absorbing because it had no case. Its wires and gizmos and whats'its were right out there in the open, where he could point to each and explain to his blockheaded friend how it worked and what it did—arcane wisdom known only to electronic engineers and Lee Delasin.

I thought it just a splendid little contraption—and I didn't understand a word he said.

I didn't often sit with Lee at his Amphitheater counter, because I was enrolled in Boys' Club—an activity he abandoned early. He preferred to wrap his brain around some new electronic challenge, or to find a job that put his passion to work, than to swim or play field games. And the jobs he got during the years of our friendship gave me entry to at least two places that most Chautauquans knew nothing about. By far the most impressive was the one 50 feet directly over his amplifier desk.

"I have to run a new speaker wire," he announced one day when I stepped up on his porch. "Want to help me?"

"Sure," I replied. "Where does it go?"

"Through the attic," he replied matter-of-factly.

That sounded a bit spooky. I didn't even know the Amphitheater *had* an attic. As it turned out, the thought wasn't half as spooky—or as delicious—as the reality.

Stepping through the door off the north end of the choir loft, we entered a small chamber up the right wall of which rose a rickety-looking wooden staircase.

"Up here," Lee directed, starting up the steep and narrow steps with a coil of wire hooked over his shoulder. "Bring that box of tools, will you?"

Clambering up behind him, all I could see above us was a narrow port opening into what appeared to be total darkness. Only when my head cleared the top did the impact of where we were hit me. It was like an enormous cavern, its air laden with mold so ancient that I could easily imagine that these very spores once tickled the noses of Lewis Miller and John Vincent (I wouldn't breathe freely for two days). I hesitated, unable to see in the feeble light of a few incredibly dirty bulbs that struggled to penetrate the murk. Stepping gingerly off the top stair tread, I was relieved to find myself on a platform easily as large as the stage beneath and equally solid—except for half-a-dozen rectangular holes amply large enough for a boy to fall through. Edging up to one and looking through it, I was momentarily disoriented by looking down on the tops of things that I was used to viewing laterally. Take my word for it: from straight up, the stage looked a lot bigger than it did from a seat in the audience. That small, box-like contraption at the edge had to be the lectern; so those smaller squares were chairs; and those creatures skittering about must be the stage crew—except all I could see were their shoulders and the tops of their heads. They looked like large beetles walking sideways.

Stepping back, I almost ran into a gangly, daddy-longlegs sort of contraption—a metal frame taller than me and twice as long, rigged with pulleys and cranks and wires. Beneath it, barely visible under several decades of dust and detritus, a long, narrow trap door was set into the Amphitheater ceiling. Clearly, it had not been opened for a generation. Squinting into the semi-darkness beyond, I spied what appeared to be several large panels leaning against some braces. Brushing the accumulated dust off one, I was curious to see an image emerge. It was a faded painting of a walled, turn-of-the-century garden, complete with fountain and gazebo. Suddenly it dawned on me: the crank-and-pulley assembly had been used to raise and lower scenery for use on the stage below. The once bright and pastel artwork, now wilted to a pallid wash, was the ghost of some long-ago operetta or play performed, no doubt, for an audience of women in frilly white blouses and full-bodied, tight-waisted skirts, and men in celluloid collars and everything from straw hats to bowlers.

Turning from the abandoned scenery, I looked beyond the edge of the platform. The more my eyes adjusted to the dark, the more my mouth gaped. I had never reflected on what held the massive Amphitheater roof up, and was astonished to see half-a-dozen enormous trusses spanning the breadth of the building, their members comprised of six or eight 2-by-16-inch boards ganged together by lag bolts as thick as my arm. Each would bridge a seventy-foot river; and two of them, set side by side with a deck between, would suffice for heavy traffic. The entire central ceiling, an arched array of narrow tongue-and-groove boards, was suspended beneath—little more than a false screen, yet central among the features that lent the hall its acoustical merit.

At first, I failed to notice the grimy catwalk that stretched from truss to truss until obscured by gloom. Having discovered it, though, I still hesitated to step onto it. Here and there, splinters of light pierced the tongue-and-groove ceiling from below, confirming that there was nothing under there but air. As uncomfortable as the Amphitheater's benches were to sit on, I was certain that landing on one after a fifty foot drop would be a whole lot worse! Summoning my courage and placing one foot onto the catwalk, I found it to be more solid than I had anticipated, and followed it all the way to its end—a stroll that seemed like it must reach halfway to the Main Gate.

"Are you going to help me with this or not?" For a moment, I couldn't tell where Lee spoke from. His voice, threading between the truss braces and bouncing off the broad underside of the roof, seemed to come from everywhere at once. I squinted back down the catwalk to see him, still crouched on the floor over the stage, half a mile away.

"Sorry," I called, retracing my steps. After that trip, the work area above the stage felt remarkably secure, holes and all.

Finishing the job we'd come to do, we made our way back down the narrow steps. Their steepness was more apparent going down than it had been coming up, making our descent seem even more perilous. But that didn't prevent me from making the climb several more times, or discourage me—once I accidentally discovered the access route—from climbing to the ridge of the roof. Being clear up there out-of-doors was less mysterious than being in the attic; but the view was demonstrably better!

After that first climb with Lee, however, I never again attended a lecture or concert without recalling that all there was keeping several hundred tons of roof off the audience's collective cranium were those immense trusses. That, in turn, enhanced my prayer life: more than once—especially during Sunday morning worship—I muttered a silent intercession for the Amphitheater's truss-work.

The other closed-to-the-public place to which Lee's employment gave me access, while a whole lot smaller and not nearly as dramatic as the amphitheater attic, was far more entertaining. When he was about fifteen, Lee was hired as projectionist for the movie theater in Higgins Hall, at the north end of the grounds. The job conferred on him the right to carry a key to the building; and I was his best friend.

The projection booth was a hot little hole built against the back wall of the balcony, close up under Higgins Hall's steep-pitched roof. Only inches from the last row of seats, it had to be as soundproof as possible; and in those days, "soundproof" equated with "lousy ventilation." Only the overhanging limbs of trees that fenced the building about, some practically sprouting from crevices between the foundation stones, kept the building from overheating and Lee from being parboiled.

Barren of frills, the booth was dominated by two massive projectors, each six feet tall and six long. Their front thirds comprised their mechanics, where reels of 35-millimeter film—endless ribbons of it—were loaded, threaded and run. I was mesmerized by the projection gates, where each frame of film paused for one nanosecond, bathed in brilliance too intense to endure.

In the same instant, the lens reassembled and focused the image-bearing light and sent it hurtling toward the screen on the stage below. So rapid was the process that an eye in the audience, delighting to be fooled, did not see discrete images striking the screen one after another, but a sequence of movement. It was close enough for reality.

The other two-thirds of each machine was the hot part, where incaution could result in a handful of blisters. No bulb yet invented generated the intensity of light that a commercial projector required. High-voltage electricity, concentrated by a large transformer that stood behind each projector, passed through twin carbon rods mounted in a barrel-shaped chamber, like pencils laid point-to-point. A minute before show time, Lee fired up the transformer for one of the projectors and turned a crank, moving the retractable rear rod into contact with its fixed mate in front. At their meeting, a discordant buzz filled the booth, smoke erupted from the rods, and sparks like molten metal dribbled from their tips. Peering into hell through the tinted window set in the side of the drum, Lee opened the gap between the rods until a brilliant arc of light hung suspended between them, light so intense that to look directly into it was to risk blindness.

And they required constant tending. The rod-tips receded as they burned, enlarging the gap until the high-voltage current was no longer able to bridge it. That fast, the projector went dark, and so did the screen. Then a great stomping and whistling arose from the folks downstairs, upset at losing the imitation of reality they had paid .50¢ apiece to enjoy; and Lee's attention, regardless of what had distracted it, returned straightway to the task at hand.

Corollary responsibilities were equally engaging, and Lee was soon training me as his assistant (though I don't recall that he ever formally cleared the arrangement with the manager—or that he ever paid me!). Two to three reels were required to hold a normal-length commercial film. Throw in cartoons and special features, and a single program might require shifting from one projector to the other three or four times. This demanded coordination. Moviegoers may have noticed the sequence of symbols, something like ¤, that periodically flashed in the upper corner of the screen during a show, but took them to be scratches on the film. I did, until Lee explained that they were cues used by projectionists when changing projectors. The first generally meant, "I'm running out of film; fire up the other projector." That accomplished, Lee stood at a window in the front of the booth, watching the screen, his hand on a wooden bar that controlled a pair of shutters positioned just in front of the projection lenses. At the second signal, he quickly slid the bar sideways, simultaneously covering the lens of one projector and exposing the other. So rapidly was the shift accomplished that the image from the

Reel Change Time

second projector reached the screen before that of the first faded. The audience didn't even notice.

But there were ways to botch the job. Shift the shutters early and a piece of story got chopped out, while the audience shifted in their seats and frowned at the discontinuity, and the boys in the booth could only hope that the action was so compelling that patrons would quickly become reabsorbed and forget. Shift them late, and a groan ascended from downstairs as the first reel expired and its trailer flared across the screen, something like, "Wizard of Oz, Reel 1, End Trailer." Funniest of all was when a new reel was racked up with too little of its leader threaded through the gate. Then a unison chorus interrupted the story line as the audience chanted the leader markers in reverse: "... SEVEN ... ¤ ... SIX ... ¤ ... FIVE ...¤...", and cheered lustily when the picture finally resumed.

There was one other duty that didn't affect the audience directly. But goofing it up sure caused excitement in the booth. Bolted to the wall was a rewinding device—two spindles set about four feet apart, one equipped with a crank. After it came off the projector, the loaded "take-up reel" was clamped onto the plain spindle, and the film's "home reel" mounted on the crank assembly. Hooking the film's trailer to the axle of the home reel, one of us began to turn the crank to rewind the film. Being teenagers, and therefore slow learners, we turned it into a running contest to see who could rewind a reel in the shortest time. That gizmo really worked, too. Its gear ratio caused the reel to turn about ten times for every turn of the crank. It didn't take much to get it up to ramming speed. With luck and a steady hand, forty-five minutes of film could be rewound in two or three minutes.

There was just one hitch: the faster the film flew, the greater the likelihood that the take-up reel would get to spinning faster than the home reel. Then we'd watch, consternation rising, as the span of film between the reels lost tension and began to flop around. Easing up on the crank didn't help: it merely slowed the home-reel while the take-up reel rotated merrily on, feeding even more film into the increasingly unstable gap. But slowing the take-up reel was painful: its only brake was a human hand placed against the rim—which usually resulted in a nasty brush-burn. And when things really got away from us, we watched helplessly as the ribbon of film became a serpent possessed and flew all over the room, dumping ten minutes of story-line onto the projection room floor like a huge mess of spaghetti. Oh, it was a magnificent snarl. God help us if the ensuing untangling party overlapped a projector change: it was not likely to be a smooth one.

But let me be candid: the reel [sic] reward for working with Lee, and for all those overheated hours in the projection booth, was getting into the movie for free—especially when the film was one that I just couldn't get enough of. It wasn't clear why the manager permitted it, but I suspect he realized that Lee would be happier if he had a friend to pass the time with—as long as we didn't totally foul things up. But for that kindness, I would never have been present to watch some of Hollywood's best (and worst) movies four or five times in a row.

Not that I always enjoyed the privilege. I was not, nor ever would be, a fan of romances that flowed like bunker oil; and I never liked the kind of ghost story that raised the hair on the back of my neck even as I knew that, on a reality scale, it ranked somewhere between "Fantasia" and the Keystone Cops. Nor was I ready to handle the harsh angst of "Snake Pit." But I got sweaty palms three days running watching Gary Cooper being shot at while clambering over the presidential faces carved into Mt. Rushmore in "West by Northwest." And I would be thirty-five and a father before I concluded that there were more important things to do than to witness another dust-up between "Tom and

Jerry;" or watch the accident-prone coyote execute another suicidal scheme trying to catch the "Road Runner"—although I no longer recall what those things were.

On the other hand, I might never have outgrown my disappointment had I missed the opportunity to sit in the balcony through six consecutive performances of "Singing in the Rain." Lee worked those shows alone; I wasn't about to miss a single minute of Debbie Reynolds. And if Gene Kelly got the girl, well, that was okay, because he was as handsome as she was pretty, and a swell guy to boot. I was content to play vicarious second fiddle alongside Donald O'Connor—just so long as I could run home after the matinee, gobble supper, get out of doing the dishes, and be back in the balcony for the 7:00 screening.

Lee and I lost touch during our college years, our boyhood yarns fading to disorderly reminiscence. I saw him only once, around 1965. Pursuing my doctorate at Syracuse University, I learned that he was an engineer at General Electric's sprawling facility in North Syracuse. A phone call brought us together briefly one Sunday afternoon to introduce our families to each other. I never saw him again.

Thirty-three years later, however, Patricia and I were blessed by a serendipitous Chautauqua moment. It was 1998—the last year that we supervised the United Church of Christ Society's program. Returning from an errand one day, we met a couple emerging from the Headquarters building, looking for us. (We were accustomed to that. I'd be hard put to list all the friends who surprised us during those summers. As compensation, they beat the salary all hollow.) I didn't recognize the woman, but the man's features set my brain bells to chiming. He had Delasin written all over him, and I thought it must be Lee. He replied no, that he was Bob, Lee's older brother, and introduced his wife, Dottie. Bob was enough older that, during the summers that Lee and I were exploring Chautauqua's restricted venues, he moved in a different orbit. I had known him only casually. The visit turned poignant when they informed us that Lee had died several years earlier.

We chatted for fifteen minutes before they left us and started down Bowman hill. Five minutes later, Bob bounded onto the porch and through the door again, out of breath from trotting back up the hill they had just walked down. Would we, he asked, help Dottie and him observe their fiftieth wedding anniversary? Two weeks before, he informed us, there had been a family celebration when everyone could make it home. Before those plans were finalized, however, they had reserved four places for dinner at the Athenaeum Hotel for the coming Friday night—the actual anniversary of their marriage. But they knew no one at Chautauqua to invite. Would we honor them?

What could we say? How many couples invite you on a double date on their golden wedding anniversary? A few minutes before seven that Friday, crisply bib-and-tuckered (as mandated by the Athenaeum's antique dress code—likely the only surviving remnant of what was once a near-universal dining tradition at Chautauqua), we walked down the hill and into the Athenaeum's capacious Victorian lobby where we found Dottie and Bob beaming their anticipation.

The hostess showed us to the front veranda, wide as a highway and half-a-county long, its scale accentuated by slender, widely-spaced pillars that soared two Victorian stories high to support the sheltering roof. We were seated at a table against the front railing, overlooking Chautauqua Lake at the close of a perfect, high-summer day. Having no interest in that evening's Amphitheater program (a high-decibel affair scheduled not to enhance cultural awareness but to enlarge the Institution's gate receipts) we savored our dinners, took full advantage of the Athenaeum's two-desserts-per-guest tradition, lingered over coffee—and didn't get up again until 10:30. During it all, the conversation never faltered longer than it took to draw the next breath. It was an exercise in mutual recall, as Bob and I tripped over each other spilling out stories that neither of our brides had ever heard, and some of which we hadn't heard ourselves. And through it all, we laughed so hard that we almost got sick.

The while, our waitress, displaying monumental patience, bustled about clearing and wiping other tables, but left us undisturbed far longer than could possibly be justified. When it finally dawned on us how close she already was to the hour at which she would have to report for work next morning, we apologized, (she brushed it aside—that woman deserved a serious tip, and received one) we reluctantly put the stopper to our conversation and gave our table up to the quiet of a Chautauqua night.

It was arguably the most rewarding evening of the summer.

CHAPTER 12

The End of a Romantic Era

"We'll have to leave early," Lee cautioned.
"How early?" I countered.
"Eight-o-clock."

Accustomed as I was to being awakened by the 8:00 a.m. ringing of the Miller Bell Tower chimes, that was a tad early. But to spend a day aboard Chautauqua Lake's only surviving steamer? Free of charge? That was worth getting up a lot earlier!

"I'll be here," I assured him.

For a 14-year-old, Lee Delasin had a disconcerting flair for making connections. He had somehow become acquainted with the chief engineer of the *City of Jamestown* who, as part-owner of the vessel, could invite anyone aboard. He had invited Lee for an all-day outing and told him to bring a friend. The single roadblock was getting to the Jamestown boat landing, seventeen road-miles south of Chautauqua, in time for a 9:00 a.m. sailing. And since the trip would end where it began (steamers hadn't stopped at the Chautauqua pier for a decade) we'd need a ride home, too.

The whole adventure might have run aground right there had not Lee's father offered round-trip taxi service. The Delasins appreciated an opportunity for their sons when they saw one.

Our *City of Jamestown* was the third steamer to bear the name of its patron community. The first, built in 1869, had an odd history. Laid down at 105 feet, it was lengthened to 156 in 1875. I can't even imagine what kind of cosmetic meddling that must have entailed. Nor do I know whether the remodel contributed to the conflagration that destroyed it, right there at the landing, the following October.

The second vessel to bear the name (and the earliest of only three stern wheelers to join the fleet) was originally called the *Nettie Fox*. That name survived only a year before a re-christening party changed it to *Jamestown*. At 175 feet, it was the biggest of the fifteen large and thirty-one small steamboats that operated for varying lengths of time between 1826, when the petite *Chautauque* was launched, and the late 1950s when the last boat to operate commercially—the vessel that Lee and I climbed early from bed that day to board—was retired from service.

And our steamer didn't acquire the Jamestown name until the year before my birth, by which time it was already forty years old. Its keel was laid in 1891, and it came down the ways as the *W. C. Rinearson*—another one-year moniker. In 1892 it was re-christened *City of Cleveland*, a regular carrier during the heyday of the fleet. It was a grand period, that, when Chautauqua Lake was serviced by two railroads. Daily trains of the Western New York and Pennsylvania Railroad, linking Pittsburgh and Buffalo, stopped at Mayville, while the Erie Railroad, connecting New York and Chicago, served Jamestown. Attended by trunks and mounds of luggage, summer visitors from all over the country stepped off the cars and boarded steamers for vacation spas like Bemus Point,

Sylvan Park, Maple Springs and Point Chautauqua—and Chautauqua Institution.

The boat was finally given the Jamestown name four decades after its behemoth predecessor, following the example of the first *Jamestown*, immolated itself at the end of its thirteenth season in 1892, also while lashed to the boat landing—precisely where we stood at ten-before-nine that morning, blissfully ignorant of all that history.

In the wheel house on the *City of Jamestown's* third deck, the pilot pulled the overhead cord that released steam to the massive whistle bracketed to the front of the smoke stack. It shook the whole basin, rattled windows in houses and buildings that overlooked the landing, and caused Lee and me—standing on the starboard stern quarter near the engine room—nearly to jump out of our skins. We looked at each other with grins that bordered on grimaces of pain, and shouted, "Wow!" No one heard us. For that matter, during those few seconds no one heard much of anything but the whistle.

After a second of comparative silence, a bell in the engine room clanged—the pilot's signal for Lee's friend the engineer to back the boat away from the dock. With an audible rush, steam coursed from the huge boiler into the twin cylinders below deck, and a slurry of muddy water surged out from under the boat. Slowly, as if reluctant to let go of the dock, the *Jamestown* backed into the river channel. It had barely cleared the dock when the pilot clanged the signal to cut the flow of steam and let the boat drift; and drift it did, clear across the basin. Seconds before the fantail tangled with tree limbs that overhung the far shore, the bell clanged again, the engineer released a new burst of steam, and the great propeller sprang to life so abruptly that all 120 feet of the vessel shuddered. While water lashed at the stream bank, Jamestown paused momentarily, then moved forward in a graceful sweep that swung the bow upstream. Again the whistle's sonorous bass sent a clear message to any boat that might happen to be upstream: "Whatever you are, I'm a lot bigger than you and I'm just around the bend, headed your way!"

Moving north from Jamestown, the pilot was required to thread the steamer through two miles of twisting slack-water river called "The Narrows." Seemingly only twice the width of the *Jamestown's* 21-foot beam and so densely wooded that branches periodically caught on the posts and railings, it gave Lee and me the feeling that we were embarked on a safari up the Amazon. Looking aft, the disconnection from home was intensified by a pall of smoke, entrained in the boat's draft and trapped in the corridor of trees, that blotted out all detail behind us. And when we looked ahead, we were dumbfounded to see the level of the river drop eighteen inches as water was drawn down the muddy bank by the suction of the approaching vessel. It didn't fully recover until it was behind us, piled up in the rush of stern waves that overwhelmed the banks and washed into the low-lying woods.

We also learned—courtesy of our unshaven and garrulous host, the engineer—that the pilot only partly steered the boat through The Narrows. The river did the rest. An experienced pilot didn't try to hug the inside corner of a bend; he curved toward the outside of it, almost as if he intended to run the boat aground at an angle. As the boat approached the outside of the bend, hydrologic pressure built between hull and river bank until the sheer force of it countered the boat's inertia and shoved it back into the channel.

Lee and I ran to the port rail as the boat rounded the last bend and slipped by Celeron. The amusement park, built so close to the water that several rides stood on small artificial islands joined to the land by foot bridges, rang with shouts and screams and laughter as people moved from one distraction to another.

Looming over it all, one of the world's largest Ferris wheels, so tall that a single circuit took ten minutes, labored through its rotations. On a clear day, riders at apogee could see right over the hills surrounding the lake and pick out Miller Bell Tower a dozen miles north.

The steamer found its stride as we entered open water and the engineer responded to the pilot's command to open her up.

"City of Jamestown"

To the steady throb of the pistons, the steel hull cut cleanly through the water, scarcely raising a wave from the time the prow split the surface until the passing water got chewed up in the disorderly wash of the propeller and tumbled rapidly astern.

"Want to see the engine?" the engineer asked, freed for a moment from immediate duties. The boat had veered west to cruise open water to Lakewood, where it would angle northwest, right up the center line of Chautauqua Lake's broadest stretch on a direct bearing for its narrowest, the passage between Bemus and Stow Points.

"Sure!" we said in unison. Who wouldn't?

"Come through here," he invited.

Giving the seething boiler as wide a berth as the restricted cabin allowed, we descended a narrow gangway to the steamy belly of the ship and a slatted catwalk. Over the din of machinery and the slosh of oily bilge beneath the catwalk, we could hear lake water gurgle swiftly along the flanks of the steel hull, and reminded each other that we had descended below the water line. A few yards ahead, illuminated by several naked light bulbs, a shining stand of well-oiled machinery half again taller than us filled the center of the boat. We stopped to admire its flawless machining, mesmerized by its melodic rhythm. Steam piped into giant cylinders at the bottom drove massive, gleaming twin piston rods that rose and fell in opposition to one another, turning an enormous camshaft. Then we stepped around the engine and found ourselves within touching distance of the propeller shaft. With a diameter like a telephone pole, it stretched a third of the length of the hull and vanished through the waterproof bearing that sealed the lake out. I was struck by how slowly the shaft rotated—not more than 30 or 40 revolutions per minute. It was difficult to imagine how such apparent lethargy could, with so little seeming effort, drive that much ship at fifteen knots.

Back up on deck and approaching the Stow-Bemus narrow, the engineer lowered his voice, as if to take us into his confidence: "There's a hot spring in the lake, you know, just north of Long Point."

Lee and I looked at each other. We were fascinated, and we loved hearing his explanations. But we weren't stupid, and we didn't believe him.

"No, really," he said. "I'll dip up some of the water when we get there."

"This I gotta see," Lee and I signaled each other without exchanging a word.

Just then the whistle sounded again, and we ran to the bow as the *Jamestown* moved smartly between Bemus Point to starboard and the hamlet of Stow to port. It was especially fun to be aboard just then. Wherever we looked, people on shore, or in boats forced in closer by the limited clearance, stared at the steamer or took its picture. We waved and basked in assumed importance.

Timing was important, however, in negotiating that constricted channel, so as not to tangle with the car ferry that crossed from Bemus to Stow and back, dozens of times a day, from early morning to late evening. Operated by Chautauqua County, it was part of the public highway. Seven months a year—give or take an early freeze or late thaw—it was the only crossing at the lake's midpoint. When the lake froze, people simply had to drive around—a detour that could add as many as ten miles to a simple errand.

A square barge, really (the one in use during my youth could hold a dozen automobiles, or eight cars and a truck), the ferry repeated its half-mile crossings for generations. A schedule of fees, framed and hanging between the rails on one side, illustrated how its patronage changed over the years: in addition to the toll for a motor vehicle, bicycle or pedestrian, it listed the fee per cow or pig. It had no helm, only a Chevrolet automobile engine with a friction clutch that enabled it to turn the paddle-wheels on each side in both directions; and was held on course by twin steel cables suspended some feet below the lake's surface. As the ferry approached, the cables rose to meet it, entered one end, traversed the hull, and exited the other end to settle again into the depths. Passing boats needed not just to avoid the body of the thing, but to avoid snagging a propeller or sailboat centerboard on one of the cables. And the steamers, requiring more berth than most, waited until the ferry was on one shore or the other before moving through.

"We're almost there now," the engineer insisted as the boat's two-story superstructure tilted precariously, first one way, then the other, as we negotiated the S curve that took us hard to port around Stow Point, then equally hard to starboard around Long Point. The latter was aptly named—a spit of land that curved out from the east shore of the lake, its tip hooked like a hawk's beak and so narrow that it seemed possible to straddle it with a foot in the water on each side. It also lay just south of the lake's deepest point. While Chautauqua's southern expanse averaged 15 to 18 feet in depth, and the northern 35 to 40, a hole between Long Point and Whitney's Bay, diagonally opposite on the west shore, had been plumbed to 90 feet. It was, for that reason, the final resting place of the hulks of several of the *Jamestown's* older siblings, remnants scuttled there after they had worn out or were destroyed by fire—in several cases deliberately. Two of the old steamers, the *City of New York* and the *City of Buffalo*, drew large crowds to Celoron Park on August 29, 1926 and Labor Day of 1929, respectively, when they were moored offshore and set ablaze as public spectacles.

"Here we are," the engineer said, carrying a bucket from the engine room to the port rail.

Leaning out and peering up-lake as if in diligent search for some tell-tale wisp of steam, he shortly nodded, climbed outside the rail, and leaned down to scoop up a bucket of lake water. Clutching the handle triumphantly, he clambered inboard again and held out the steaming bucket for our inspection. The water was indeed hot. In deference to his earnest effort to entertain and fool us (and because he was, after all, our host for a free day on a lake steamer), Lee and I reached into the bucket and felt the warmth of the water. Satisfied, he turned the bucket back into the lake and went in the engine room to hang it up, while we sidled over to the rail, leaned out to observe the jet of cooling water that steamed out of the exhaust pipe in the hull just below the deck, and grinned at each other. The engineer knew perfectly well that we weren't fooled. But it was fun anyway.

The day was far gone by the time the *Jamestown* completed its loop, making only one brief stop at Midway Park to discharge and pick up a handful of passengers and allow us all-day riders a moment to buy a hot dog and bottle of soda. The sun was touching the tree tops when the engineer, on the authority of the engine room bell, slackened speed and the *City of Jamestown* nosed into the narrow confines of the outlet. The river's mood was different now, somber, as if saddened by the waning of the day. The trees seemed to stretch farther out over the water, like children anxious to caress the boat as it passed. The engines went to a dead stop as we coasted into the open patch of water surrounding the boat landing. As the pilot hauled the wheel to starboard and the boat curled in toward the dock, the bell called for reverse power, and our forward progress stopped inches before the bow touched the wharf. It was Teamwork with a capital T. When a dockhand had cinched the bowline around a massive piling, the bell commanded forward steam just long enough to move the boat ahead, then rang dead stop. It was enough. Tethered by the bowline, the burst of energy brought the stern in against the dock where another line was quickly snubbed onto a second piling. In no time, the gate was lifted and the gangplank brought out and laid between deck and dock.

Thanking the engineer for his kindness, Lee and I stepped ashore where Mr. Delasin waited for us. We didn't know it, but we had just been privileged to take our last ride on the last vestige of the Great White Fleet. A decade later, saddled with rising expenses and declining revenues, the owners filed for bankruptcy and the *City of Jamestown* was sold at auction to settle part of the debt. It never returned to regular service, and ended its days miserably. Shuffled from one mooring to another, it suffered the ravages of weather, vandalism, and attempted arson. When a final effort to raise funds for its restoration failed, steamboat transit conclusively ended.

That still wasn't a bad record: steamboats survived three decades longer on Chautauqua Lake than on any comparable-sized body of water in the U.S. I was just glad that it lasted long enough for me to benefit by Lee Delasin's knack for making connections by getting us aboard. Better to ride out on the end of a romantic era than to miss it entirely.

PART 5

Hank

CHAPTER 13

Westfield Station

Lounging about on the Peters' spacious porch doing nothing in particular, Hank Suhr and I looked up respectfully as his father opened the screen door and stepped onto the porch. It was a great place to hang out, that porch. The house, a substantial structure that faced North Lake Drive at the corner of McClintock, was originally built for the Studebaker family of fleeting automotive fame. Even in drizzly weather, the porch was protected by an overhanging second floor and commanded a view of the entire north end of Chautauqua Lake. Dropping into a chair, Mr. Suhr spoke off-handedly.

"Boys, how'd you like to drive over to Westfield tonight and watch a couple of trains?" Henry Suhr, Sr., a.k.a. Heinie, was a boy's kind of dad—easy-going, athletic, and heart-breakingly handsome. And his brain was packed with the kind of information that boys pant after.

I never called him Heinie, however. While a joy to be with, and wonderfully accessible to us children, to be that familiar with him would be disrespectful. That degree of familiarity was a privilege reserved to Hank's mother and his friends around home in Oil City, Pennsylvania.

But there were ample other opportunities for familiarity. In Hank's family, nicknames were a cottage industry. I never knew a clan with so many, all memorable. His father affectionately addressed Hank's mother Elizabeth as Lee; and her only brother, Edward Peters, was for years Uncle Eedie—not just to Hank and his older brother, Charles, but to every kid in the neighborhood. When I first became acquainted with Henry Jr., who was a year older than me and demonstrably more athletic, he introduced himself as Emie (pronounced Ee-mee)—a nickname given him as a child. And Charles was Chotsie. (The family speedboat, a powerful 21-foot Chris Craft, was *Chotsie II*; and even at Chautauqua, to have a boat named after you was a signal honor.) Somewhere during the boys' teen transition, that all changed. Uncle Eedie assumed the more dignified Uncle Ed, and the boys simultaneously announced that they would thereafter answer to Chaz and Hank. Me, I was stuck with Don, start to finish. Some Christian names do not lend themselves to nicking.

Even though I never called him anything but Mr. Suhr, I felt a special attraction to Hank's father because he made a place in their family for me at a time when I, like my siblings, was struggling to find a way beyond the anguish of Dad's death. I was included in activities I otherwise might not even have dreamed of, because they seemed so far beyond my family's reach, like learning to use a giant swing crossbar (I never mastered it, actually) or diving off the *Chotsie* in the middle of the lake on boat picnics. And aquaplaning. I almost mastered that. The Suhr's aquaplane was homemade, a discarded two-by-five foot tongue-and-groove cabinet door equipped with a tow bridle of half-inch manila rope and hand reins to match. The object was to balance on the board's trailing edge, reins in hand, while being dragged at impossibly high speeds around the lake by the *Chotsie*.

Going up and over the fast-moving boat's wake and out across the undisturbed water beyond was a special challenge. It required tilting both body and board back toward the wake while maybe two square inches of the board remained in contact with the lake. If you put enough oomph behind the maneuver while keeping the bridle taut, the board inscribed an arc that almost brought it parallel to the boat. The trick was knowing when to quit. Stay out there too long and the tow rope went slack, the board lost headway, and board and rider began to settle. At that point, a wise aquaplaner would concede the point and jump off, because when the *Chotsie* regained the lead it jerked the tow bridle mercilessly, causing the board to leap nearly out of the water and the rider to execute a back flip. And even if the dynamic tension between board and boat was maintained, allowing the outside corner of the board to catch in the water sent board and rider tin cups over teakettles. I actually saw Hank turn one-and-a-half somersaults across the surface of the lake before penetrating it. Water skis would not make their advent on our lake for several more years. When they did, I thought them a noteworthy improvement.

All that aside, an invitation such as the one that Mr. Suhr now extended was so beyond the ordinary that it would require Mother's personal dispensation. It wasn't the character of the event that would lift her eyebrows, it was the time: it would bend her early-to-bed rule to the fracturing point. We wouldn't even leave home until well past the hour at which she wanted me tucked in and gone to nod. The only thing that saved me was her trust in Mr. Suhr. His simple assurance that he would be in charge was all she required to lay her anxiety at rest. But it was still more sacrifice than most casual observers might assume. Her entire life, Mother never truly slept until all her children were home and in bed. I was cognizant that letting me go would mean a long night for both of us.

So it was that we pulled into an empty parking lot at 11:30 that night, climbed out, and walked around the ebony bulk of the Westfield Station at trackside on the main line of the New York Central Railroad. And it was some piece of line: four tracks wide and stretched like a taut rubber band all the way from Ripley, ten miles to the southwest, to Fredonia, sixteen miles to the northeast. It was the heyday of the great steam trains, when those steel-ribbon roads were flawlessly maintained. No engineer worthy of his calling, entering the Westfield stretch astraddle several million pounds of steam-generated horsepower, could resist the temptation to haul the throttle open and let 'er rip.

Both station and platform were dark and deserted, for good reason: the next train actually scheduled to stop at Westfield wasn't due in until mid-morning the following day. That was alright with us. Mr. Suhr hadn't brought us to Westfield to see trains stop. He'd brought us because two of America's crack passenger trains, the Empire Express and the 20th Century Limited, where due through in the next two hours; and, thanks to the immaculate condition of that twenty-four-mile stretch of rail, they weren't even going to slow down. For us midnight visitors, alone on the platform, conditions were perfect: the glow of the single naked bulb over the locked station door imparted just the degree of mystery needed to lift our anticipation to fever pitch.

"Now, boys," Mr. Suhr began, "let's get ready," and launched into a tutorial on the vital statistics of the New York Central's rolling stock—locomotives and tenders, and mail, Pullman, passenger, dining, and lounge cars.

"So," he concluded, "if we count the number and type of cars as they go by, and clock the time it takes the train to get through the station, we can calculate the speed at which it was moving."

Wow. No one ever introduced a lesson that way in any school *I* ever attended! Or out of one, either. With little fuss, we divided the assignments: Hank would hold the stop watch, starting the count at the precise instant that the locomotive's nose passed his, and stopping it as the tail end of the lounge car went by. I'd count the units of the train, specifying the type and number of each. And Mr. Suhr would back up my count and do the math on a clipboard he brought with him from home, illuminated by flashlight.

Excitement got visceral when the first headlight appeared in the northeast, and we all got ready. But something was wrong. It was approaching too slowly. Sure enough, twin locomotives rumbled smartly through the station at a respectable but hardly remarkable speed, proving it to be a false alarm. We watched them tug their ninety-car load of freight with the level of enthusiasm that we might generate watching a team of draft horses drag a plow around a cornfield. Interesting to be sure, but hardly electrifying. Mr. Suhr had us clock the freight's passage anyway, just to be sure we had it right before the main event. Boredom was setting in by the time the boxy red caboose rattled by and we stood watching its twin taillights slip down the track and vanish in the midnight murk. (It was the only unit in the whole train that showed any sign of life, though we couldn't be certain: who knows how many knights of the road might be slumbering somewhere among all those rolling accommodations?)

Excitement recovered as fast as it had waned, however. Like a star just ascending above the eastern horizon, a twinkle appeared before the freight's tail lights fully faded from view. Studying it intently for a moment, Mr. Suhr called us to out posts.

"This will be the Limited," he asserted. "It's coming fast."

Indeed it was; even five miles away we could see how quickly it was eating up track. Grasping the physics of the thing, Mr. Suhr instructed us to move twenty feet back from the edge of the platform. And he used his no-arguments-you-guys tone of voice—the one reserved for occasions on which he meant business. Hank had learned to respect that authority before he was old enough to frame a reply; and I learned to follow his lead the very first time the issue came up. Mr. Suhr never teased when danger was involved, even when only theorizing. But there was nothing theoretical here. He knew, watching that monster coursing up the track toward us, that it was trailing a draft powerful enough to suck a young boy off the platform to be torn to pieces by the massive drive wheels. He wasn't taking any chances, and Hank and I weren't arguing.

Nothing, however, could fully have steeled us for the passage of that behemoth. It came on so swiftly that I, for one, almost lost track of my assignment. The wall of air being shoved out ahead of it smacked us like a body blow yards before the nose of the beast drew opposite us, throwing us back on our heels. And forget recovering. Before we could regain our balance we were run over by sound so visceral that we involuntarily cringed—the roar of high pressure steam churning out the funnel, not like a child's innocent "choo-choo" but like a tornado at touchdown; the painful hiss of spent steam exhausting from the massive pistons; the steel-on-steel ramming of twelve drive wheels, each taller than us, tearing at rails burnished silver by just such abuse.

As it flew past, the buffer of air pushed out in front of it turned negative, just as Mr. Suhr had promised—a violent sucking that clawed at our clothing and sought to drag us into the maelstrom of churning steel. In blinding succession came the tender, itself big as a house, trailing two mail cars, their windows opaque with smoke and road dirt. (Only the Pullman cars, where early-to-bed passengers had turned off their lights and lay blanketed behind plush, maroon privacy curtains, equaled them in gloom.) But the rest of the train was a blur of brilliance, a run of expansive glass that afforded us a voyeur's view into passenger and dining cars and the bring-up-the-rear lounge car. It all struck like lightning and was gone, leaving us with nothing but fragmentary images caught on the fly of people reading or talking or dining, dozing or smoking or drinking—a high-velocity tableau of American social intercourse.

Babbling in amazement as the train's roar faded in logarithmic proportion to its distance, we stood on the vacant platform and submitted our findings to Mr. Suhr. Watching him tally up the cumulative length of the train, divide it by the number of

Westfield Station at Midnight

seconds consumed in its passage, and translate the result into speed, we stood back and looked at each other, gape-mouthed and wide-eyed: the 20th Century Limited had passed through Westfield Station at between ninety-six and one hundred miles per hour.

We hoped for a repeat when the Limited's sister came by in the opposite direction, but were frustrated by the vagaries of railroad scheduling; another freight train was already opposite the station when the Empire Express came into view. The narrow gap between the monster in his charge and the lumbering freight he was passing required the Express engineer to amend his speed. Both trains passed without incident, but it just wasn't the same.

It was 2:30 by the time we arrived back at Chautauqua's main gate, long since closed for the night to automobile traffic. Finding an open slot among the myriad vehicles parked against the wire-mesh fence next to the highway, Mr. Suhr parked the car and we walked in. I don't recall ever seeing the grounds that dark, or that quiet. Of course, I had never been up at that hour of the night—and would regret it five hours later when called to drag my bones from bed and get dressed for Club. No flicker of sound marred the stillness of the streets or the somnolence of those resting in the cottages that lined them. We spoke little as we walked, and then in hushed tones, a dramatic contrast to the din and clamor that we'd witnessed only a short time before.

I was hard put to decide which I liked better. Certainly the tranquility of Chautauqua was easier to live with over the long haul. But I would be increasingly grateful in the coming years, as those magnificent trains withered one by one before the competitive advantage of private automobiles and airplanes, and new technologies stilled the rant and bellow of their incredible iron horses, that I had been privileged to be in Westfield Station that midnight. It was a chance I would never have again.

CHAPTER 14

Nantucket Sleigh Ride

Some days, more than others, it was clear that God got to take credit for our survival. Heading the list of such days was the afternoon of the Nantucket Sleigh Ride.

Hank's Uncle Ed owned a fourteen-foot dory called the *Empsie* (pronounced Eemp-see, taken from Hank's first childhood moniker—the one he was given as an infant). It was arguably the second-most-graceful small boat I knew of on Chautauqua Lake. Firstmost was the lap-strake, Adirondack Mountain guide boat that Campbell Brandon still rowed across the lake and back every morning, even when he reached his late eighties—<u>before</u> his morning swim off the end of our neighborhood dock. Rowed up to speed by an experienced oarsman, that double-ender would coast through calm water for a hundred yards leaving nothing but a ripple as evidence of its passage, inscribed in a line so straight that a yardstick could not improve upon it.

Uncle Ed's boat was almost as efficient. Close-ribbed and buttplanked with a narrow prow, its gracefully rounded sides rose clear of the water at the stern and converged on a transom barely a foot wide. It was seaworthy enough for salt water, and we put it to a supreme weather test.

Waking to a breezy day one morning and scanning about for a new adventure (he was always in search of a fresh challenge), Hank decided to convert the dory into a sailboat—without, of course, actually meddling with the structure of the boat, which Uncle Ed would not have tolerated. Cutting an old bed sheet corner-to-corner, he went searching for a mast in the stooped storage space beneath their front porch. Just about everything we needed to get ourselves in trouble could be found under that porch, and that day was no different. Finding a sturdy eight-foot pole, Hank tacked his sail to it and lashed it to the *Empsie's* front seat. Bracketing some scraps of plywood to a crossbar produced a workable set of leeboards to resist slippage in a cross-wind, keeping the boat more-or-less on course, although they would have to be held in place by hand. And he figured that one of the boat's oars would serve for tiller and rudder.

Everything in readiness to launch on a neck-risking adventure, he invited George Felteberger and me abroad. (George was our third musketeer. He lived at 10 McClintock, halfway between our cottage and Hank's.)

It seemed a perfect day for a sail. The air was bright and brisk, studded with fast moving clouds driven by an offshore breeze. A west wind like that barely riffled the surface of the water along Chautauqua's north shore; but pushed further out, the ripples grew and merged into increasingly respectable waves that ran for the far side. Were I more attentive to the weather clues that Chautauqua Lake dependably signaled to anyone prepared to receive them, I would have known that we were sailing into trouble. But I didn't, and Hank and George were being as oblivious as I was. But then, had better weather sense dissuaded us from going, we would have missed the exhilarating adventure that waited for us like an unseen waterfall around the next bend in the river.

So we pushed off from the Peters dock, blissful in our ignorance and expecting too little from Hank's small sail. It harnessed way more wind than we anticipated, and we were suddenly scrambling from one side of the dory to the other in a frantic effort to fend off boats lying at anchor in the mooring area. Gratefully, we surged into the clear without side-swiping or ramming some exquisitely expensive craft and getting all three of us dry-docked for the rest of the summer, and settled down to master Hank's unique rigging. We did so quickly. Almost before we realized it, we had put some serious distance between us and the shore.

We were, however, going in the wrong direction. Wise sailors, setting out on a blustery day, close-haul their sails and steer a windward course, because sailing into the wind requires a lot more work than sailing with it at your back; and tacking upwind puts sailors "above" their starting point. Later, after wearing themselves out on a windward leg, they need only come about and run home before the wind—a sailboat's course of least resistance. Unhappily for us, we got it backwards and sailed off downwind. It was a reasonable error. Uncle Ed's dory wasn't designed for sailing in the first place, and it was more comfortable just to give the boat its head. In the end, it made little difference: we were about to discover that Hank's Rube Goldberg rigging wasn't capable of taking the boat upwind anyway.

Cruising steadily east, prattling on about what a great boat it was and how much fun we were having, we looked back to see that Miller Bell Tower (a convenient landmark for anyone navigating Chautauqua Lake's northern end) had blended with the trees almost to the vanishing point. That didn't particularly trouble us; we knew where home was, although we sensed right off that we might have a long row getting there. It was the other thing we saw that wiped the grins off our faces and put us on notice that we were in for it. Preoccupied looking east toward the far shore, we failed to notice the mass of cloud, big as half the horizon, that had stealthily risen behind us. By the time we realized it was there, its leading edge was already overhead.

We all knew what that meant. Laying just ten miles south of Lake Erie, Chautauqua Lake was subject to sudden storms at any season of the year, the summer no exception. A developing storm, traversing Erie's expanse of warm water from west to east, collected moisture and loft as it came. Compressed against the slope of the continental divide, it rode to the top, vaulted the ridge, and burst out across the Chautauqua County highland. Anyone in the middle of the lake was a sitting duck. Sailing up Chautauqua's south shore one Saturday during a yacht club race, crewing for friend and neighbor Mac Thurston abroad his Thistle, I recall watching as the north corner of the lake was devoured by a squall line that boomed onto the lake and enveloped the main body of the fleet, playing with the boats like a child plays with dominos, lining them up to be knocked down. One after another, sails flopped over and were lost in the dense layer of mist such a squall kicks up off the surface of the lake in the very act of pounding the waves flat.

And here one came, hurtling up behind us smack-dab in the middle of the lake, with a mile of wind scoured water between us and home. It's not clear what we might have done to brace ourselves; and in any event, the storm gave us no time. We were walloped by a blast of air that seemed almost to lift the stern of the boat out of the water, but absolutely almost tore the mast and sail right off the boat. If George had not been there, hanging on to the mast with all the strength he could muster, it would surely have gone overboard. I don't know why it didn't, but it was a good thing. Two things kept the boat from being sucked around broadside to both wind and waves, where one good wave and gust might, in concert, have flipped the boat. One was the sail, pulling like a maniac at the bow as if in frantic dumb effort to stay ahead of the squall. The other was the oar that Hank clung to, dragging out behind and keeping the stern dead on the wind that, with two frenzied miles to lash the water, was piling up waves so large that the dory no longer spanned the distance between them, but crested each in turn, slid down the running trough in front of it, and climbed the back side of the next. Lifting and plunging, we hunched our backs against the stinging rain that seemed to come at us horizontally, and hung on for dear life.

Those necessities attended to, however—and in spite of our qualms about our near total lack of control about the boat's course—I have to confess: that was one thrilling ride. After dragging a moment, as if it felt obliged to put up some show of resistance, the *Empsie* let go with a forward surge that sent spray

Empsie with a Bone in Her Teeth

arching away from its bow as if from a speedboat, while the slender stern trailed a correspondingly narrow wake that continued to inscribe the water six swells behind us. It was the closest thing to a Nantucket sleigh ride that I ever experienced—or expect to. Cries of exhilaration erupted unbidden from our lips as we tore along. No sperm whale, propelled by the pain and terror of a savage harpoon driven deep into its flesh until it lay on the surface of the ocean, exhausted and thrashing, ever towed a boatload of New England whalers faster than that storm drove our dory.

At most, the time required to complete the second mile of our diagonal crossing of the lake took a tenth of that consumed by the first. Alarm intensified, however, as we approached the shore where the waves, lifted by the rising lake bottom, got top-heavy and flopped over. Just short of grinding the hull of Uncle Ed's prized dory on the gravel, we leaped into the breaking waves, guided its nose through the reeds, and hauled it far enough ashore to ensure that the stern wouldn't bounce with every incoming wave.

Now what? We had fetched up just south of "Chedwell," the summer home of millionaire brothers Charles and Edward Welsh, whose Welsh Grape Juice Company straddled Lake Erie's fertile coastal plane ten miles north at Westfield. Looking back across the wind-whipped lake where Chautauqua was just reemerging from the passing squall, it occurred to us that we not only had no ready way home; our parents hadn't a clue as to our whereabouts. There seemed to be nothing to do for it but to find a phone. Checking the dory one more time to be sure it was secure, we plunged into the brush at lake's edge and crossed the narrow right-of-way of The Jamestown, Westfield, and Northwestern Railroad—a diminutive and decaying enterprise boasting 34 miles of track, one four-car train, and a couple of antique trolley cars. (Those early rail lines seemed always to possess names longer than their tracks.)

Clambering uphill through the woods that stretched like a blanket from Dewittville Bay to Midway, we broke into the clear at New York state highway 17 atop the rise and found ourselves only yards from a house. Drenched to the skin and not a little sheepish, we knocked on the door and were relieved to receive both a sympathetic welcome and permission to phone Chautauqua—a long-distance call in those days. Our worst fears were confirmed when Hank's mother answered: the men of the family had jumped into the *Chotsie* when the storm broke with us nowhere in sight. They were still out there, running up and down the lake looking for us. By then, of course, we were no longer on the lake, and they might not see the dory hauled up into the reeds even if they came looking for us that far down lake, which they didn't. Nor had she any way to contact them until they came home. So we hatched a plan: we'd start walking up the highway toward Mayville, five miles north; and when the men got home, Hank's mother would send someone by car to meet us.

Whether the plan would work depended in part on how long they continued to search for us on the lake, their minds agitated by visions of an overturned boat wallowing amid the flotsam and jetsam of shipwreck. Nor could we take the chance of hitching a ride. If we succeeded, we might pass Hank's father coming around a curve or something, with no way to flag him down—and he certainly wouldn't be looking for us in a strange car. We might just find ourselves walking all eight miles back to Chautauqua—and it would take a whole lot longer to walk around the lake than it did to sail across it. Fortunately for us, the men pulled up to the Peters' dock about the time Hank's mother hung up the phone, and we barely walked a mile before his father plucked us off the shoulder of the road.

One more crossing was needed, to retrieve the abandoned dory (amazing how much closer the far shore seemed to be when riding in a speedboat). The *Chotsie's* draft was too deep to approach the shore closer than forty yards, however; so when the rock-strewn bottom became visible in the chop beneath us, we erstwhile and still-damp mariners went over the side one more time, waded to shore, retrieved the Dory from the reeds, and hooked its bowline to the *Chotsie's* stern cleat for the tow home.

I wouldn't want to pretend that we weren't in trouble with our families, although George and I had it easiest. Our folks had been away from home when we came up missing, and knew nothing about it until dinnertime. By then, with us obviously okay, (and with just a bit of editorial license on our parts regarding the imagined level of danger), it wasn't hard to convince them that it was just another invigorating Chautauqua experience. We had, after all, been trained from childhood to survive on the lake—although that training was also supposed to preclude the kind of stupidity we demonstrated that afternoon.

Hank's parents, having experienced the alarm of the thing start to finish, were less inclined to brush it off. Uncle Ed's dory was off limits for weeks, as I recall. And Hank was clearly on notice that, for the foreseeable future, we were confined to the part of the lake that was clearly visible from the Peters front porch—and not more than a hundred yards offshore. Being in no position to argue the point, we agreed to the terms as the fastest way to put the dispute behind us.

To be perfectly honest, though, if I were given a chance to repeat that ride—especially since things ended well and all—I'd jump back into that dory without giving it a second thought.

CHAPTER 15

A Stroll on the Bottom of Chautauqua Lake

Hank and Chaz Suhr sure were ingenious. Or maybe credit should go to their metal shop teacher at the Hill school in Pottstown, Pennsylvania, where they both attended prep school. In any event, when the assignment came to make something, they weren't limited to the sheet-metal flour scoops or cookie cutters that we soldered together in Meadville; and Mercersburg Academy, where I attended (as opposed to studied) my last two high-school years, didn't even have a shop. Hank and Chaz made a diving helmet, and it was a piece of work.

I think it was Hank's seventeenth summer, my sixteenth. He was on our porch minutes after their amazing piece of marine paraphernalia was unloaded from the trunk of his dad's car, inviting me down to the lakefront to see it. He just as well might have invited me to step through a time portal into a Jules Verne novel. "Ingenious" hardly did the thing justice: it was constructed entirely of cast-offs and scraps.

Wielding an acetylene torch, they had cut the bottom quarter off a discarded iron water heater tank, tracing a double curve so that, upended, the thing would rest on the contours of a boy's shoulders while extending down his chest and back, and just tall enough that the end of the tank would not rest on his skull. Cutting a rectangular hole in the front, they welded a two-inch deep box into it and bolted a piece of tempered glass over the opening. Then they welded several heavy pieces of scrap iron to the inside of the tank—sufficient to weigh down a buoyant body and prevent the air-filled helmet from floating off in deep water—an adverse development sure to send an abruptly breathless diver flailing for the surface.

The entire assembly weighed about eighty-five pounds. Lifting it onto someone's shoulders without dropping it on his head posed the real risk, so they welded handles to each side to assist in lifting it on and off. With all that, losing contact with the lake bottom seemed unlikely. Finally, they split several feet of rubber tubing lengthwise, pressed it onto the scalloped edge to protect bare shoulders from the jagged metal, and secured it there by threading thin wire around it and through small holes drilled in the edge of the helmet.

So far, so good. The thing seemed heavy enough; and Hank and Chaz had welded carefully, ensuring it would be leak-proof. Of itself, however, it contained enough air for about 30 seconds of breathing—not enough to support much undersea exploring! No fear: they had the air supply problem solved, too, and it was as inspired as the helmet. Locating two pumps used to inflate footballs and basketballs, they mounted them on a board, their tops facing each other and just far enough apart so that the piston rods touched when one was fully extended, the other fully compressed. Dead center between them, they hinged a two-foot handle onto the board and bolted the piston rods to it. Pushing the handle to one side forced the air out of one pump while the other drew a fresh supply. Pushing it to the other side reversed the process. The result was a steady flow of air. Coupling the tubes from the pumps to one end of a thirty-foot length of hose, they welded a fitting into the back of the helmet to receive the other. All that was lacking was a volunteer diver.

"Why don't you try it?" Hank offered generously.

"Me?" I asked, uncertain that I was eager for the honor. But then, studying the parts of the mechanism laid out on the grass where his family's dock touched shore, I thought, "I can do this. If I get in trouble, I'll just bend over, pop the thing off my head, and swim to the surface."

"Who'll work the pump?" I said aloud, knowing full well that my submarine air supply depended on faithful stewardship of that pump handle.

"I will," Hank grinned cheerfully. He was assuming a lot!

On the other hand, the water wasn't deep enough off the dock to go very far with that thirty-foot hose. To use the thing to full advantage, we'd need to work from a boat.

"So if you're working the pump, who will row the boat?" I queried.

Hank knew he couldn't do both, and I was skeptical of walking the lake bottom with his invention the only thing between me and drowning, pulling the boat after me. Looking at each other, we said as one, "George."

Trotting up the hill, we knocked on George's door. He was always up for an adventure, and today was no different.

Running home, I changed into my bathing suit and "lake shoes." Mother was, as usual, at the Summer Schools office that mid-afternoon, exempting me from inconvenient questions about where I was going. She often chided me about the ear infections I got every few summers that would eventually rob me of a third of my hearing: "Well, it wouldn't have happened if you hadn't spent so much time with your head on the bottom of Chautauqua lake!" But she's the one who insisted that we learn to swim. Besides, she had it in mind that I dove to the bottom too much, looking for interesting rocks or shells or things accidentally dropped from a boat. She didn't envision me putting on a homemade diving contraption and going for a stroll on the bottom of Chautauqua Lake.

Hauling the gear out to the end of the dock, we set the pump in Uncle Ed's skiff and draped the hose over the side. Climbing down the dock's ladder, I stood in chest-deep water while Hank and George lowered the helmet onto my shoulders, careful to keep some bottom edge above the surface until Hank fired up the pump. Everything in readiness, we shoved off, Hank pumping, George rowing, and me (discovering that some leaning and shoving is required to move against that much water) pushing my way down the gradual incline of the lake bottom.

A few lakeward steps brought the water to the rim of the helmet. Disconcertingly, it continued to rise <u>inside</u> the helmet. That wasn't part of the plan. I soon stopped worrying. The reassuring hiss of air entering the back of the helmet quickly equalized the pressure and held the water at bay just below my chin.

Almost immediately, it became apparent that Hank's design failed to account for rising humidity, as my breath steamed the view window to the point of opacity—the same problem I encountered when diving with a face mask. But that problem was easily solved: I needed only to swim to the surface and rinse the inside of the mask with lake water. But this "face mask" consisted of eighty-five pounds of iron. Up was not an option. Nor was there room to reach inside the helmet to rub the window clear. Still, if I could get some water to the glass, it would wash it clear—a step that almost ended my dive before it really began.

Reasoning that bending forward would allow water to run up the front of the helmet and flood the window, and that the flow of air from Hank's faithful labor at the pump would force it out again as soon as I straightened up, I bent forward. The weight of the helmet nearly took me right on over. Envisioning how silly I would look standing on my head in a large iron helmet at the bottom of seven or eight feet of water, I struggled frantically to regain my balance, and did, pleased to find that the trick worked. In the brief sloshing created by my thrashing effort to stay upright, the window was cleared.

Then what a mystical world greeted me. I looked out at the edge of a forest of seaweed, intensely green, anchored to the lake bottom and reaching nearly to the surface. Obedient to the throb of each passing wave, its undulations were a serene choreography in contrast with the darting movements of small fish that sheltered and searched for food among its strands, seemingly unconcerned for the bubbling behemoth that loomed into their tranquil domain. The lake bottom, a sharply defined litter of rocks and shells up close (at least until my feet churned up so much silt that nothing was visible), faded with distance until it melded with the dense medium of the water, gray-green at the surface shading to blue-purple at the bottom. It was startling to enter an environment seemingly devoid of gravity—or possessing a reverse gravity, rather, where air set the balance: given enough of it, things rose to the surface; denied enough, they sank to the bottom.

The temptation to move into deeper water was encouraged by the appearance of an encrusted, half-moon shape jutting out of the muddy lake bottom at my feet, its stark geometry the more evident against the organic softness of its surroundings. It was a mushroom anchor, the kind boat owners set out for permanent moorings. Locating the heavy chain half visible among the bottom litter, I followed it across the lake bottom until it abruptly ascended to the clasp that secured it to the mooring buoy floating above. In the weeks it had hung there, it had been transformed by submarine accretions. Bits of algae drooped like limp icicles from each link, waving back and forth with the same pulsations that set the seaweed to swaying. Small snails moved link to link, at the glacial pace of their species, on what would likely prove to be a month-long slither up a very lumpy highway to exulted altitudes—for a snail. Following the chain, I was shaken by an involuntary shudder as I crossed the edge into a column of black water, as such sunlight as normally penetrated to that depth suddenly was cut off. I glanced up (at least as far up as the helmet permitted without flopping me over onto my back), already expecting what I found: six feet above, its bowline hooked to the mooring, the bulk of the *Chotsie II* loomed directly overhead, its underside trailing its own blanket of algae. (So much for the effectiveness of copper-bronze "anti-fouling" bottom paint.)

I don't know how long I stayed down, but I vividly recall the moment I decided to come up: it was immediately after the moving spots appeared before my eyes. Turning this way and that as I pushed through 12 feet of water, hoping to locate some submarine treasure (like a sunken boat—or at least a lost fishing lure) the view window was suddenly filled with green spots moving past, bare inches from the glass. Startled, I jumped backward (well, okay—fighting several tons of water, I budged backward). Turning in the direction the spots had taken, I found myself looking at the tail-end of a muskellunge moving away with the deliberate ease of a critter that knows it is on the top of the food chain. It was a big fish, easily a keeper according to the thirty-inch rule then prescribed in New York fishing regulations. But under water and up-close, it looked like Jonah's monster.

Insatiably curious (a drive likely urged on by its equally insatiable appetite), it was probably drawn to the silver helmet trailing a stream of bubbles—not something it was likely to have seen before in those waters. To its predatory mind, I must have seemed either a curiosity or a banquet. It had come up behind me, and I was unaware of it until I turned and almost bumped into it. Apparently it found me a mere curiosity—either that, or my cast iron hat convinced it that chewing on me was unlikely to secure much by way of lunch. Moving away, its seeming lack of effort eloquent testimony to how utterly at home it was in its medium, it merged with the translucent glow of the water and vanished.

Eager both to share the news of my close encounter with Hank and George (and perhaps hastened by the sudden awareness that I was the alien in someone else's

Close Encounter

universe) I hauled on the airline to signal my change of direction, and headed toward shallow water—and an unpleasant surprise. As I broke the surface and the sudden release of pressure drained the helmet, a searing pain lanced across my forehead as if something were slicing into the bone. I never experienced anything that intense, before or since. For a moment, I thought I would pass out; but the sting vanished as suddenly as it came—so quickly, in fact, that I didn't even have enough time to shed the helmet to tell Hank I was in trouble. By the time I did get the helmet off, I wasn't. It occurred to me, later, that it might have been a mild case of the bends, if there is such a thing. "The bends" is an excruciating agony that threatens divers who rise too quickly from the depths, as dissolved nitrogen—no longer held in suspension by the pressure of deep water—explodes into bubbles in the bloodstream. Severe cases are fatal. But even non-lethal cases are accompanied by pain described by those who have experienced it as the most acute that a human being can endure. I'll probably never know for sure; but I can assure you that if what I felt was indeed a mild case, I never want to experience a severe one.

PART 6

Sunday

CHAPTER 16

Bordering on Mid-Adolescent Glossolalia

The murmuring swelled as clumps of young teenagers rounded the corner from Wythe Avenue or the brick walk, or topped the Cookman hill—girls in floral print dresses and bobby socks, shining hair secured by bright colored ribbons or barrettes; boys in slacks and sports jackets, regimental stripe ties and polished loafers, faces scrubbed and every hair lacquered into place with Vitalis or Wildroot Cream Oil. In growing numbers, they convened on the sun-dappled and white-pillared porch of the Hall of Missions, volume ascending with the addition of each new peripatetic conversation until it became difficult to sort one from the other, the sum of it bordering on mid-adolescent glossolalia. Congestion—both physiological and auditory—surged as they stepped through the French doors into the large meeting room, Cliff, Frank and I among them that last summer of Cliff's high school years, my first, until it seemed that the arrival of one more body might cause the place to explode.

The setting was plain, and always the same: a small occasional table stood near the west wall, equipped with a pair of candlesticks flanking an unassuming vase of flowers borrowed from the parlor across the hall. A lightweight wooden-post lectern on one side was balanced by an overweight piano on the other. The rest of the room, clear to the west wall, was filled with folding wooden chairs into which the teenagers packed themselves, discretely divided: girls in front, boys in back. No one told us to sit that way. Gender separation just seemed appropriate—not during the rest of the week, you understand, but a seemly gesture toward keeping the Sabbath.

This was the High School Club Bible Class and, frankly, it could have met anywhere as long as the one essential fixture was present. That would be the Rev. Dr. John A. "Doc" Reed, Presbyterian by persuasion and director of the High School Club by summer employment, who now stood at the door welcoming his kids with grins and pats on the shoulders as they entered the room. On any roster of clergy who influenced my young life, eventually drawing me into the ministry, Doc's place is secure. His sway over my generation of teenaged Chautauquans was incalculable. Preaching to adolescents has never been easy. Few adults would hazard standing alone in front of a handful of them, much less a whole roomful, even if handed a ticket of admission to paradise signed by St. Peter himself. And if it was easier back then—perhaps because we grew up during the twin catastrophes of economic depression and global war and were more prepared to listen—convincing a hall of hormone-inflamed adolescents to abandon the trivialities we thrived on for more substantial reflection still required a gift. And Doc had the gift.

The agenda was traditional, and we could hardly wait to get started. The hubbub did not so much subside as its focus shifted when, at 9:00 sharp, Doc stepped to the front of the room. First and always, it was time for song. And that bunch sang. Opening the thin, brown-jacketed and very old songbooks that were on our chairs, we quickly scanned the frayed pages looking for favorites (the order of song was always determined by request)

"Number 17," came from somewhere in the room.

"Number 17," Doc echoed. The pianist (usually one of the girls present) struck a cord, and we were off. For most of half-an-

"Doc" Reed's Bible Class

hour, we sang at the top of our lungs—and in four-part harmony. And we sang the whole Gospel hymn repertoire. We beamed our way through "Brighten the Corner Where You Are" and urged each other to "Follow the Gleam;" crooned "Sweet Hour of Prayer" as if we actually observed it; vowed that we "...would be true, for there are those why trust me;" tapped our toes while marching in place to "Onward, Christian Soldiers;" and felt a special resonance in

"This is My Father's World," because we were at Chautauqua, where

> *...to my listening ears*
> *All nature sings, and round me rings*
> *The music of the spheres.*

It is difficult to judge, across the intervening years, what we sounded like. No one ever made a recording to remind us now of the quality of our singing then. That may be a good thing. Denied objective evidence to rectify memory, I am free to think that, in the ears of both heaven and passersby, our joyful noise was not only eager but sweet. In any event, what we lacked in musicality we more than made up for in zeal, and and never more so than when the call came (as it did every Sunday of my high school summers) to sing "The Old Rugged Cross." If the class had an *alma mater*, that was it. Hardly needing our hymnbooks to sing it, we were claimed by the intensity of feeling reserved for those who love unconditionally and have no better way to express it than by wrapping it in song.

I would later be forced to reassess my feelings about such old favorites. Theological seminary does that. Carrying several decades of religious baggage along with their clothing and personal effects into the residence hall when they enroll, most seminary students discover that their "faith" is holier than Swiss cheese. Then begins the often difficult, always disconcerting, process of letting go of what had seemed certain. The journey is seldom fatal and, entered into open-mindedly, is liberating in ways not easily appreciated by those who never experienced it. At the time, however, it was enough to make me wonder whether I was even in the right place.

But that was in my future. Approaching the end of the 20th Century's fifth decade, my second, I neither knew what was coming nor cared. I was swept along by the emotional intensity of my age group, relishing every minute of it. I sometimes wondered, during the testing and purging experience of seminary, whether that detour into emotionalism had been a waste of time, and why my elders and mentors had not challenged it long before. Then I became director of education and youth activities at an urban church in Syracuse, New York and discovered that emotional intensity both burns religious sensibility into young minds and provides a manageable pathway from childhood innocence to mature spirituality. Had not Doc's high school class, and experiences like it, forged my sense of religious vocation, I probably would not have bothered to continue the trip. And those old hymns were part of the forging fire. So I still feel, somewhere deep in my viscera, the grip of that chorus:

> *So I'll cherish the old rugged cross*
> *'Til my trophies at last I lay down.*
> *I will cling to the old rugged cross*
> *And exchange it some day for a crown.*

Plowed by all that singing, we were fertile ground for Doc to plant the seed of whatever he meant to teach us on any given Sunday. I recall only a few occasions during my early years when singing was not preferable, by several degrees of magnitude, to listening to some preacher talk. (One shortcoming of choosing religion as a profession is that it has subjected me to more bad preaching than I can possibly enumerate.) It was indicative of the uniqueness and the power of those high school classes that we looked forward as eagerly to Doc's lessons as we did to singing. And he never disappointed us.

Looking back, it is clear to me that the model embodied in Doc's preaching style was seminal in shaping my own. Certainly, one of its most important elements was first observed in the Hall of Missions: forget vacuous appetizers—get right to the main course. Sermon introductions too often serve mainly to reduce the number of minutes a preacher feels obligated to fill with something of substance between the scripture reading and the benediction. That, in turn, raises question whether what we are about to hear is worth listening to at all. I especially distrust canned jokes, the sort recommended by public speaking gurus as a way to "warm up the audience." In my experience, audiences generally arrive in the hall pre-warmed. Were they not in a state of expectation, they would not have come. To indulge in stories that do nothing to move the process forward demeans the congregation's readiness to learn.

We came ready to learn, and Doc came ready to teach. And teach he did, from the first word out of his mouth. By the end of the opening sentence, he had tugged our brains out of juvenile self-centeredness and focused our attention on things we'd seldom thought about: moral responsibility and commitment, obedient discipleship, and love so intense that it becomes redemptive. And he never let us down easy. The challenge ran right up to the benediction. Doc's lessons never ran more than twenty minutes. It was all he had left after all that singing, not to mention announcements, prayers, and the offering. But by the time he finished, we were both exhausted and energized, and spewed out of that room with our heads smoking from the passion of it.

I have tangible proof that some of it—in style if not substance—sunk in. This intelligence came as a surprise, actually. While browsing through the stack of scrapbooks that Mother compiled for me, hoping to refresh my memory for writing this book, I was stunned to come across two brief items clipped from the *Chautauquan Daily* for July 14 and August 18, 1951. That would be the summer following my freshman year in college, only one summer after I "graduated" from the High School Club and Doc's classes. The first item simply announced that at Sunday morning's Bible class, "Donald" (I hate that; my name is not now nor ever has been Donald, but newspapers don't seem able to get it) "Skinner, a former member of the High School Club, will deliver the sermon in the absence of the Rev. John A. Reed."

The second item announced that I would fill in for Doc again, and stated my topic as "Beware of Falling Rocks." (At least it's provocative; I could preach on that topic starting right now, without further preparation.) What followed, however, stunned me: "Don has already conducted one class this summer, and was very enthusiastically received...." Even allowing for the *Daily's* long-standing and well-documented penchant for complimentary reporting, it was moving to read that passage. It, and the accompanying information, must have been penned by Doc himself.

But I had forgotten all about it. At the time the two items appeared, I was suffering from self-induced amnesia. A steadily declining academic record and the attendant disapproval of my elders (the end product of undiagnosed dyslexia), had reduced my self esteem to tatters. I was sunk in a pervasive negativity that left me little incentive to absorb praise or approval. Four years and a stint in the U.S. Army would be required finally to come to terms with it all; but much of what had occurred in the intervening years was carefully suppressed and locked away in one of those compartments by which we human beings insulate ourselves from the pain of failure. My discovery of those two clippings left me with my jaw hanging open and astray in a mental vacuum: I could conjure no recollection of having taught those classes. But I must have, and done a passing-fair job as well, else I would not have found yet a third clipping, this from the *Daily* for July 5, 1952 announcing that I would teach the opening class that season, speaking on "New Conceptions."

If I was prepared to do that, Doc gets at least part of the credit. I have difficulty, even now, thinking that I was even remotely qualified to step into his shoes, even though it would not be the last time. Much more would follow. But like I said, on any roster of clergy who influenced my young life....

CHAPTER 17

Awash in a Flood of Protestant Christian Piety

Emerging from the Hall of Missions at the close of Doc Reed's Bible class and turning up the brick walk toward home, we stepped into an intermittent stream of folks exiting Sunday morning denominational house services. The hike comprised a tour of the Protestant Reformation of the 16th and 17th Centuries, by genera: for whatever reason, when Chautauqua's Christians organized themselves into associations and started to acquire building lots, theology determined geography. Churches with a bent toward liturgical orthodoxy clustered at the south end of the brick walk, those with a free church tradition grouped toward the middle, and Reformed theology settled the north. Furthest south was the tiny Good Shepherd Episcopal Chapel—one of only two free-standing chapels that, oddly, bracketed the denominational houses like bookends. Walking north past the nearby Episcopal Cottage, we first mingled with Lutherans, then

Baptists and Disciples of Christ, all of them fresh from early worship. A block on, Presbyterians flanked the south side of the Amphitheater, the Congregationalists the north. (Earliest to organize in response to Bishop Vincent's invitation for all the denominations to do so, the Congregationalists erected their cottage on a lot assigned for that purpose by the bishop himself—who, just as soon as it was completed, asked to use the second-floor conference room for his ecumenical Sunday School Committee meetings!) Overlooking the back of the Amphitheater, centrally positioned as befitted Chautauqua's founding communion, were the Methodists. A block further north, at the corner of the plaza, the Reformed Church House hosted sectarian sisters: the Evangelical and Reformed Church and the Reformed Church in America. Furthest north, half a block west of the Plaza and sandwiched in between two units of the St. Elmo Hotel, the United Presbyterian Chapel served as the second bookend.

While Roman Catholics and Jews, Unitarians and Christian Scientists were present in significant numbers as well, they enjoyed neither quarters nor official recognition. Each would, in time; but that was all in the future. To wander around Chautauqua on any Sunday morning during the late 1940s was to be awash in a flood of Protestant Christian piety—intellectual in character, sober in temperament, moderate in theology—and eager to participate in the most encompassing symbol of Chautauqua's long-standing ecumenical spirit: the 10:45 a.m. "union" service in the Amphitheater. Never to have attended that service was to miss the most abiding evidence of Chautauqua's religious grounding.

It started like scattered showers. Individuals, couples and families, bib-and-tuckered for the occasion, stepped off cottage, rooming house and hotel porches and, in Chautauqua's version of "all roads lead to Rome," began to wend their way toward the center of the grounds. Joined by visitors threading through the gate (Sunday was, after all, a free day), the flow soon became a torrent that filled the streets, bearing down on the Amphitheater. The pace quickened when, turning a corner or rounding a building, worship-goers were met by strains of music from the mighty Aeolian-Skinner pipe organ that, focused by the arched wooden ceiling, flowed out the open sides of the building and rolled up the street to draw them on.

As a fast-moving river churns and eddies when it encounters a dam, the flood that swirled up against the Amphitheater turned turbulent. Milling about, people searched for companions who had said, "We'll meet you there," or stalled in clusters around blue-jacketed and white-panted ushers fixated on trying to place a bulletin into each outstretched hand. When the flow resumed, it was like water swirling into a dozen separate drains, pouring down the steep-pitched ramps arrayed like spokes on the horseshoe-shaped sides of the auditorium. Seated at the four-manual console, George Volkel—Chautauqua's official organist—urged them on with spirited music, as if the Pied Piper suddenly had acquired an entire orchestra and was spiriting off not just Hamlin's children but the whole town. The flow dammed up in spots—here behind an elderly couple pausing to negotiate the turn off the ramp and into one of the rapidly filling benches; there where a young family tried to sort itself out and decide who would sit next to Mom and who next to Dad. Disorderly though it seemed, it was chaos with a purpose. As rapidly as they found seats, people settled back to wait and watch and exchange greetings with friends seated nearby. And with a reliability that bordered on the mystical, the flood crested two minutes before the service began and concluded two minutes into it. It was a spectacle that never failed to amaze me: an Amphitheater half-empty at 10:43 was overflowing at 10:47.

Calm finally prevailed when a diminutive man, head like a snow-clad and sun-drenched mountain peak, rose from his chair and stepped modestly to the ponderous dark-wood podium at stage center. The Rev. Dr. Alfred E. Randell was director of the Chautauqua Religion Department, and may just have been the most beloved figure ever to hold the post. Even with shoes on, he barely reached five feet four inches; but the heart wrapped in that pocket-sized breast was huge, a worthy match for the profound depth of the man's spirit. Presiding at the 10:45 service was his most visible duty, and he accomplished it with matchless dignity.

Well, except during one season, perhaps. Calling for the offering one morning, he informed the congregation of a lamentable discovery: the previous week's collection, divided by the number reported to be in attendance, revealed that the average gift had been ten cents per person. A muted moan, indicative more of embarrassment than peevishness, swept the hall. To lift both the spirits and liberality of the gathering, he quoted the apostle Paul's counsel in his second letter to the church at Corinth: that they should not contribute to the needs of the saints "reluctantly or under compulsion, for God loveth a cheerful giver." Pressing his point home, Dr. Randell explained that the Greek word translated as "cheerful" is *hilarion*. Therefore, he urged, we should give liberally, for "God loveth a hilarious giver!" As expected, that lesson got a rousing laugh—and the average gift rose all the way to a truly stratospheric twenty-five cents.

Unfortunately, Dr. Randell was so impressed by both results that he repeated the story every Sunday for the rest of that season and all of the next, demonstrating that even a man of his distinguished demeanor may become guilty of beating a good thing to death.

Moving promptly through the announcements and the introduction of the chaplain of the week, who occupied the other chair on stage, Dr. Randell yielded to choir director Walter Howe, who signaled the 150-voice choir to rise for the introit. For there to be a choir at all for Sunday worship was an act of faith—especially on the opening Sunday. There were no sign-ups, no auditions, and few rehearsals. It was simply assumed that Chautauqua would draw a lot of singers possessed of some talent; that singers like to perform; and that, given the opportunity, they would show up. And they did, every Sunday of every season, never fewer than seventy-five, some Sundays three times that number.

Our family had a special affinity for the choir. We all sang in it at one time or another, with some unanticipated results. There was, for instance, the summer of Mr. Howe's uncertainty. Fretful that not enough competent singers would appear, he pressed the Chautauqua Opera Company chorus into service as reinforcements. It proved unnecessary, but changed Frank's summer in a hurry—he who, by the time he was sixteen (which he had turned that spring), could hit a low E with compelling authority. Seated next to several opera chorus members, he became aware that they were nudging each other and looking at him after he hit the low note at the end of the anthem. They accosted him at the close of the service.

"How'd you like to try out for the opera chorus?" they asked.

"Me?" said Frank, understandably taken aback.

"You've got the range, and you obviously read music. And we need more basses. If you want, we'll introduce you to the director."

The following day Frank was introduced to Alfredo Valenti, director of the opera program, who would judge whether or not Frank qualified. He qualified. Missing only the opening opera of the season, which was already in production, he sang in the chorus for the remainder of the summer.

None of us, however, could hold a candle to Mother in her loyalty to the choir. She was not only an accomplished pianist and organist, she plain loved to sing, and did so every summer for forty-three years. If ever evidence was required to prove that vocal power doesn't necessarily depend on physical stature, that woman demonstrated it. We own a videotape of a Sunday service recorded in 1988, complete with choral anthems. Taping on a small Canon camcorder and mindful of the prohibition against photographing from inside the hall, I remained on the perimeter. Even though the rule was not enforced during Sunday services, I was loathe (being a clergyman and all) to disrupt a congregation at worship. Besides, I knew what Mother would say if she saw me. I stayed outside! But I treasure those minutes of tape above most others because, when we play it, her voice sings for us again. Invisible among 150 shoulder-to-shoulder singers, 147 of them taller and heavier than she, the concentrated timbre of her voice yet dominated the alto section. She sang one more summer in the choir before standing down for her 90th year, and died that November.

Two things otherwise dominate my memories of those services: congregational singing and preaching.

The singing of hymns was always... well... splendid. How could it be otherwise when so many who both loved music, and felt that God was indeed in that place, opened their mouths together and let fly—and never more so than during the opening hymn. For as long as I could remember, every service began with the same hymn: "Holy, Holy, Holy." I would discern later, when I began regularly to lead public worship, that there are four kinds of hymns: those that combine shabby music with a feeble text (and are uniformly unworthy of inclusion in worship); those that either combine shabby music with a profound text or splendid music with a feeble text (and should be used seldom and only if nothing better is available); and those that wed a profound text to splendid music, and should form the core of public hymnody. "Holy, Holy Holy" is among the finest of the best.

The text is from the 6th chapter of Isaiah. The prophet has entered the temple in Jerusalem and finds himself suddenly and unaccountably face to face with God, seated on a lofty throne and attended by six-winged seraphim calling to each other in voices of thunder: "Holy, holy, holy is the Lord of hosts; whose glory fills the whole earth." Stark terror is the mood of the encounter. In Hebrew theology, no one can look upon the face of God and live—that is, no one can stand in the presence of pure holiness and not be consumed by the experience. In mortal consternation, Isaiah cries out: "Woe is me! I am undone! I am a man of unclean lips and live among a people of unclean lips; and my eyes have seen the King, the Lord of hosts!" But he is not destroyed: taking a pair of tongs, one of the seraphim lifts a burning coal off the altar, flies to him and touches it to his lips. His sin thus cauterized, Isaiah hears God: "Whom shall I send, and who will go for us?" Fired—and freed—by the redemptive encounter, Isaiah answers, "Here I am! Send me." So began one of scriptures most sublime prophetic careers.

And it was the opening hymn during Amphitheater worship since before I could remember. By the time I was ten, I knew the verses of that hymn by heart. So, too, I suspect, did most veteran Chautauquans. At least, standing in the Amphitheater at 10:50 of a Sunday morning, the voice of the 5000 raised in chorus, few eyes were on the worship bulletin, and more than a few turned misty at that convergence of personal faith and long-standing tradition. And if I could have known the elevation above sea level of the Amphitheater ceiling, and measured it during the singing of that hymn, I would not be surprised to find that it had gained two inches in altitude.

But not consistently during the sermon. Even as a youngster, I sensed that while all preachers may have been created equal in the sight of God, their preaching wasn't. My early intuition in this regard was only refined during high school, when I came to the Amphitheater with my ears still tingling from Doc Reed's Bible class. Sundays on which Dr. Randell had chosen especially well were like sitting down at a seafood festival during which broiled lobster followed fast on shrimp cocktail. But even Dr. Randell could not be expected to pick nine winners in a row. And since the preaching of the Word—not liturgy or the sacraments—stood at the heart of Chautauqua's ecumenical covenant, the sermon climaxed the service.

Chaplain-of-the-Week

So it was a gamble, on any given week, whether the final half-hour of a Sabbath morning would be an uphill or downhill ride.

On days of an uphill sermon, I had double cause to be grateful. But even a downhill Sunday wasn't a total loss. Like as not, Doc had already given me more to think about than I could process in the ensuing six days. Besides, the lake lay right there at the bottom of the hill, more than able to compensate for poor preaching if need be, but always to reward Sunday morning virtue with an afternoon baptism of pure play.

CHAPTER 18

Scared Song Service

Returning from Sunday afternoon diversions—sailing or aquaplaning or swimming—we gathered at the dining room table for our favorite meal of the week. I'm not sure just when this Sunday evening custom began; it was part of family ritual long before conscious memory caught up with me. The menu was always the same: everything in the kitchen. Or at least everything in the icebox that did not require cooking or was not on Mother's menu for a left-over supper later in the week. All of it was piled in the center of the table, limited only by its suitability for making sandwiches—leftover meatloaf or ham; cheddar, Swiss and cream cheeses; butter of both the creamery and peanut persuasions; jelly and honey; lettuce, mayonnaise, ketchup, mustard, relish, and pickles—together with loaves of white, whole wheat and rye bread, bottles of milk, a selection of whatever fruit was in season, and at least three kinds of Mother's home-baked cookies.

Serenity, such as it was, prevailed only until the blessing was spoken. Then it was open season on the victuals, and you'd think we hadn't eaten for a week. Let it be said that, during those years when all four of us were teenagers, the amount of food we could pack away was staggering. I can't fathom how mother managed to stretch the family budget that far. I still remember the most amazing feed of them all. The census of Mother's children-at-home had just declined by one, actually. It was in August 1949, and Ruth Ann had been married in Hurlbut Memorial Church, home of Chautauqua's only year-round congregation, the weekend before. By the time we sat down to Sunday supper the next weekend, she and her new husband were already settling into their "starter" house in his hometown of York, Pennsylvania. Measured by the volume of food consumed, however, her absence hardly registered. Her appetite had long since paled in comparison to her younger brothers anyway. However, a more-than-adequate stand-in had been invited to supper that evening, in the person of Jack Clark, Cliff's life-long Chautauqua friend. By the time the four of us got up from the table, we had consumed two loaves of bread with all the stuffings thereunto appertaining (confirming Jesus' admonition that man does not live by bread alone; he requires baloney, cheese...), and drunk two gallons of milk less maybe a quart. I have, in the intervening years, lost the ability to do that; indeed, I have trouble remembering how it was possible both to do it and to stand up afterward. At the time, however, it was just another—if record-breaking—Sunday night supper.

Having thus attended to our stomachs, we often turned our attention again to the Sabbath, ending it as it had begun. Chautauquans, in case the point has not already been made, cherished tradition. So, as evening came on, the streets again bustled with people, fewer in number and quieter now, moving toward the Amphitheater to settle in for what Cliff liked to call the "Scared Song Service." And, like that morning, we drew on Isaiah's vivid imagery to affirm the majesty of a holy God. As the organ sounded the opening bars, the hall filled with the soft accents of Chautauqua's own hymn. The lyric, written at Chautauqua by Mary Lathbury (1841-1913), and set to a hymn tune titled "Chautauqua," by William F. Sherwin (1826-1888), echoed again the cry of the six-winged seraphim, but quietly now, and hauntingly reflective:

> *Day is dying in the west;*
> *Heaven is touching earth with rest.*
> *Wait and worship while the night*
> *Sets her evening lamps alight*
> *Through all the sky.*
> *Holy, holy, holy Lord God of hosts!*
> *Heaven and earth are full of thee!*
> *Heaven and earth are praising thee,*
> *O Lord most high!*

Like the morning's exuberant counterpart, we sang that hymn until it was imprinted on our souls. We had no more need for music or words than we did for a printed text of the Lord's Prayer.

For most an hour, then, sometimes longer, the gathering night filled with sacred song as Chautauquans both expressed their sense of the transcendent, and indulged their bottomless appetite for music—some performed by the choir or on the organ, less frequently by an instrumental ensemble. But always, the congregation itself must have opportunity to contribute, singing one cherished hymn after another. Talk was generally minimal—a few readings and prayers, perhaps a brief homily. To my taste, that was just fine. The less said the better. I was there to let the music do the speaking, whether instrumental or vocal, and found verbal intrusion a distraction. There are mysteries too profound, moments too freighted with meaning, to be encompassed by meager talk. At a minimum they demand poetry, perhaps fine visual art. But on Sunday evening at Chautauqua, they were most surely lifted on wings of song. So we sang our faith and hope and love—but also our joy, our foreboding, our trust, and our garden-variety exuberance. And when it ended and we made our way home through Chautauqua's twice-shadowed streets—first by the night itself, then by the overarching canopy of ancient trees that snatched away whatever light heaven had left to send us—we moved in an enveloping peace that really did persuade us that nothing in life or death could separate us from the love of God. And if that was not why God gifted us with the Sabbath, I couldn't imagine what reason there was.

True to its religious origins, Chautauqua always began and ended its season on Sunday, and the two events were as distinct as were our weekly morning and evening observances. Things officially began with morning worship on the first Sunday of the season—a kind of blow-out celebration that we had survived another winter and were back together and God was in heaven and all was right with the world—at least our most beloved piece of it. Swarming into the Amphitheater, we waited expectantly as Dr. Bestor approached the lectern, tapped on it three times with the antique gavel and, in his sonorous baritone, convened a new Chautauqua assembly.

But the opening Sunday never could generate the depth of feeling that accompanied the closing Sacred Song Service eight weeks and a day later. Sweaters and jackets were more in evidence, and friends and lovers hunkered closer together than on most evenings, warding off the promise of fall that rode in on the late August evening. But there was also a poignancy to it that dogged the steps of the smaller-than-usual crowd as we entered the hall, a recognition that we were at best a spotty sort of multitude. There were rather more empty spaces than congregation.

Our diminished number was not without compensation, however. Also missing was the undertone of commotion that had accompanied every Amphitheater gathering all summer—the murmuring spillover from half-engaged patrons that circled the hall like satellites orbiting a planet, unwilling to come in under the roof to sit down and give the program their undivided attention, yet equally unwilling to shut up. They had mostly packed up and left Saturday morning, when their assigned rentals expired. Exiting the gates, their cars found their way along two-lane state roads and U.S. highways toward homes scattered over half the country. Truth be told, we were relieved to see them go. It was the hard core who gathered that closing Sunday evening, what long-time Chautauquan Peg Simpson has aptly called "the faithful remnant." It was just the right depiction, both expressive of the way those present, if asked, might describe themselves; and a worthy biblical allusion to the place that owned so large a share of our affection. It spoke as well to my wife Patricia. Adopted mid-life into the Chautauqua family, she immediately sensed the unique nature of that closing evening, naming it "The most moving night of the whole summer."

The close of that final service differed in one other regard from the eight that preceded it, and added to the depth of sentiment. By tradition (yes, another Chautauqua tradition) organist George Volkel's postlude at every Sacred Song Service was the "Largo" from Handel's *Xerxes*. However, unlike most church services at which the postlude served mainly to cover the hasty exodus of congregants from the building (including those who hustled out of the Amphitheater Sunday noon in a vain attempt to be first in line at the Glen Park or Starr or Davis Cafeterias), we didn't move when the first strains of the "Largo" floated onto the Sunday evening air. Nor had we to be reminded to stay put. We listened, and never tired of doing so, until the finale faded to its last echo. Only then did calm give way to the bustle of quiet chatter as people ascended the ramps and set off toward all the points of the compass from which they had gathered in the first place.

But not the final Sunday. The playing of the "Largo" concluded the service, as always, but we didn't simply listen: we drank it in, sensible to the fact that everyone else in the hall was doing the same, and was moved by the same depth of emotion that we were feeling. It would be ten months, not necessarily before we heard it again, but until we heard it again from this organ, in this place, among these friends. And when, as the sacred strains faded, Dr. Bestor rose to adjourn the assembly with three more taps of the gavel, and the congregation raised their voices to sing one more time, the feeling was almost too intense to endure. Looking around, we knew that the places of some few among us would be vacant the next time we assembled. Perhaps it was to

"Largo"

them, especially, that we offered the last gift of a Chautauqua summer:

> *Blest be the tie that binds*
> *Our hearts in Christian love;*
> *The fellowship of kindred minds*
> *Is like to that above.*

The night had a different feel to it then. The settling chill was augmented by the cold realization that both summer and season really were over. But it would not hold. Even as we stepped through the door of our unheated cottage and shivered our way to bed, knowing that the residual heat of summer would not likely return that year to warm its rooms, our minds were already settling on spring. And even though we may not actually have spoken the words, the thought was clear: "Just wait 'til next summer!"

PART 7

A Succession of Boats

CHAPTER 19

An Exponential Leap into Uncharted Waters

The adage holds that the happiest day of a man's life is the one on which he buys a boat, and the second happiest the day on which he sells it. For those blessed to grow up on the shore of Chautauqua Lake, that observation was only partly valid. No one I knew, given the privilege of owning a boat, would willfully choose not to. But we were not strangers, either, to the ambivalence that attended the relationship. Like a marriage—even a good one—owning a boat could be hard work.

The Skinner family's first experiment with boat ownership was a mistake, actually. It was 1946, and our family's assets had only marginally improved over what they had been since Dad's death. Indeed, things were tight enough to restrict us not just to the used boat market, but to its swampy bottom. Too, while we children had acquired some feel for boats both at Club and from friends, we knew nothing about owning one. And for her part,

Mother was (how can I say this nicely?) clueless. She loved few things more than getting out on the lake. But her parents were so terrified of the water that she not only was not taught to swim; becoming proficient with watercraft was out of the question. In brief, we were ripe to get taken—and were.

Mother never even drove up to Norton's Boat Yard, just short of Mayville at the north end of the lake. She knew without wasting a trip that she couldn't afford anything that Paul Norton had for sale, and would spare us the pain of getting keyed up over something that was clearly beyond our reach. So we watched the classified ads in the *Chautauquan Daily* until a promising item appeared: "16' rowboat, outboard motor. $15.00." The ad alone should have put us on notice: it was clear evidence that someone wanted to unload an elephant, not make a buck. But we knew the man selling it—or thought we did; how bad could it be? We were about to find out.

Going together to see it, we were directed to an overshadowed and reedy stretch of shore where we found a graceless, battle-ship gray barge half in the lake and awash with rainwater. With the help of a rusty tin can that was sloshing around in the oily bilge, we baled it out, only to discover that it was not appreciably lighter empty than it had been when full, sure evidence that it was waterlogged. It took all four of us children to shove it, bottom grinding on the gravel, into water deep enough to float it. Cliff, being both the oldest boy and the most seaworthy, got first dibs at rowing the thing out onto the lake a few yards where we really could see it. I still remember the uneasy feeling that overcame me on seeing how hard Cliff had to work just to get it to move, much less to maneuver. It was a piece of junk. But like infatuated lovers, we were prepared to overlook not just blemishes but evidence of sclerotic terminality. Maybe, we agreed, we could get some small pleasure from it. At least we could go out on the lake when we wanted to. And we did. Several times. We still own the snapshot Mother took of the four of us with her old Kodak box camera: Ruth Ann and Frank in the role of passengers and me at the oars, while Cliff tinkered with the outboard motor. As I recall, the motor ran at least a couple of times, sending us skimming across the waves at about 0.8 knots for a couple of minutes. Its failure to perform beyond that was a blessing in disguise: had it run for more than twenty minutes, the vibration might have ripped the stern off the old girl and left us treading water while the whole assembly sank beneath us.

As it turned out, only the grace of God prevented that from occurring anyway: late that summer we discovered a large patch of dry rot in the floorboards under the back seat. The more we probed, the more we realized that there was no way to repair it, because most of the frame was too soft to withstand having new wood screwed to it. Once begun, we'd have to replace half the boat. So we burned it, destroying the evidence of our inaugural, and hapless, venture into boat ownership. It was fortunate that we never had named it; anonymity diminished our sense of loss. And the immolation yielded one clear advantage: it cauterized our naiveté about buying an antique boat. We'd never make that mistake again.

Being the most impetuous member of the family, I was first to conclude that we should try again. I knew that buying a new boat was out of the question, but an ad I found in a magazine convinced me that I could build one. First, I'd need to persuade Mother. She did a good job of disguising her skepticism, actually, though she certainly had ample justification not to: I'd never built anything more substantial than a clap-trap tree house and a few woodshop projects at Boys' Club. Building a boat would be an exponential leap into uncharted waters.

But I was determined. For $25.00 I could send away for a kit of pre-cut parts to assemble an eight-foot pram—a tubby little rowboat with curved bottom and sides and a flat prow and stern. It was made of marine plywood, a product developed during World War II when American ingenuity fabricated an astonishing array of new materials and designs. Included among them was the plywood Patrol-Torpedo boat, the best-known incarnation of which was future U.S. President John F. Kennedy's luckless PT-109 that got sliced in half by a Japanese destroyer while on nighttime patrol. For a time after the war, the Higgins Company—which designed the P-T boat—marketed a diminutive version as an inboard runabout. A durability problem brought Higgins up short: the design encouraged the same kind of dry-rot that had finished off our anonymous swamp scow.

But none of that was yet apparent in the fall of 1946, when I was entranced by the prospect of building my own boat using the same technology that produced the storied P-T boats of the Pacific theater. And if my version looked more like a Dutch clog with oars than a tiger-of-the-sea, what did I care? Mother struck a deal with me: if I could save enough to buy it without help from her, I could do it. That way, at least, if the thing sank on contact with water, the loss would be entirely mine. I went to work with a will, squirreling away every cent I could earn until, the following May, I mailed the order form and a check for $25.00, with instructions to ship the kit to 14 McClintock Avenue, Chautauqua, New York. Then I settled back to "allow thirty days for delivery."

I was off my bike almost before it stopped rolling the afternoon I turned down McClintock to see an eight-inch thick, three-by-nine-foot carton leaning against the porch wall. "Your boat came," Mother announced matter-of-factly, as if I might not have noticed. It only took up half the porch. Mother issued a restraining order as I started digging through the kitchen junk drawer and the back porch storage closet looking for tools, as if I meant to have it assembled by dinnertime ("No, you have to eat your supper *first*"). It took almost a month, actually, less because the assembly was difficult—which it was—but because our collection of tools ranked somewhere between World War I and a Salvation Army store. Most of them were fugitives from Dad's furnace room shop in our Meadville home, and some of them were far from new when he fell heir to them. My brow knit as I sat, boat parts strewn from one end of the porch to another, studying the manufacturer's list of "Tools Needed for Assembly." Reminding myself that I was still on my own, I took my meager purse to Colton's Hardware on the main floor of the Colonnade building to see how far the cash would stretch. Not far, it turned out. But by concentrating on tools totally missing from our collection, like a pair of "C" clamps and a set of small drills, I scraped by.

Every spare minute for three weeks found me on the porch, setting up the jig on which the boat was assembled, mastering a marine vocabulary of strange words like cleat and transom, skeg and chine, and uttering a number of expletives the nature of which would have excited Mother's wrath had she been within earshot. My labor was productive nonetheless. As day passed to day, oddly shaped parts left off leaning against the porch wall or railing and took their place on the jig until, almost by surprise, I found myself standing back to admire an honest-to-God boat, and all mine.

Mother made one thing clear from the outset: the boat would not be painted on the porch. She knew which of her sons was most likely to slop paint, and had no intention of having her robins-egg-blue and white porch decorated with random splotches of highly durable marine enamel—especially in the red and black

I had chosen for the boat's color scheme. So Frank and Cliff helped me carry it down to the shore and prop it up on a couple of old saw horses, where I spent two days decorating eight feet of boat and several yards of beach. In a fit of adolescent enthusiasm (and unable to resist the plywood parallel to the Pacific war), I even painted eyes and a toothy shark's mouth on the bow. Finally, late one afternoon, came the supreme moment: across the stern I painstakingly painted the name: *Gleep*.

"Gleep"

It came from a neighborhood joke that Cliff acquired from his friends, one of those absurd bits of silliness that adolescent boys delighted to share, chortling loudly while adults looked at them as if they had taken leave of their senses. Question: "What's a 'gleep?'" Answer: "It's a 'peelg' backwards." I had no idea what it meant, nor did I care. *Gleep* it was, and *Gleep* it remained. At least it was unique.

By that time, the habit of saving for my boat had become ingrained; and by the next spring I had saved enough to buy a splendid little 2.5 horsepower Evinrude outboard motor that purred like a kitten and, throttle wide open, shoved me and my pram along at a breathtaking 5 knots—as long as I was alone. Each additional passenger cut the boat's speed by half, largely because each passenger reduced the boat's freeboard by three inches, and it only had twelve inches to begin with. It took only marginal reflection to conclude that a third body might reduce forward momentum to zero by swamping the boat.

Okay, so it wasn't much. But it was a start. Indeed, it was a bit like the birth of a first child: I would have other boats, and love them just as much; but the uniqueness of that first experience could never be repeated.

For eight summers I ran all over our end of Chautauqua Lake in that little tub. This was not always a wise thing. At eight feet long and over three wide, with flat ends, it wasn't always easy for the pilot of a craft on a converging course to tell whether I was going forward, backward or sideways. Indeed, when the lake was on a snort, piling up whitecaps faster than arpeggios in a Rachmaninov piano sonata, it wasn't always clear to me which way I was going. Keeping the *Gleep* on course in rough water was like trying to drive a jalopy with the front tire blown.

Things only got worse when a cabin cruiser—some family up for the weekend and hosting company for a leisurely cruise—wallowed by close enough for me to grab their stern line and hitch a tow, the passengers waving and grinning inanely and the boat trailing a wake as big as a junk steamer. One incident like that was all it took to persuade me thereafter to compress my 150 pounds as low as *Gleep's* hull would allow and turn her bow into the onrushing waves before I got to them—or they to me. It didn't seem likely that a tub nearly half as beamy as it was long would easily turn turtle; but when the turbulence got serious, profile was less a factor than scale. I especially appreciated it when some friend in a powerful Chris-Craft inboard hoved in to cut concentric circles around me until the water was so agitated the pram almost bounced clear of the surface, the while calling to me about some plan he had for the evening. I wanted to yell back, "I'd love to, if I get off the lake alive!" But I was young and proud of my maritime mastery, and didn't want to have him think that his churning of half the lake directly under my keel was cause for apprehension. I sure was relieved when his boat pulled away and raced up the lake as if it was inspired, while my aquatic bathtub and I wallowed homeward as fast as 2.5 horsepower could push us.

Fortunately, few excursions were that traumatic, and some were the stuff of January daydreams. Among the best occurred when a summer day had exhausted its ration of wind and evening caressed the lake, soothing its nervousness until the last ripple vanished. I loved, then, to row out into the middle of the lake, drop the oars, and let the boat drift while the sun played artist on a canvas of sky that ranged from azure to cobalt, painting the clouds pink or frosty blue or gold, or yet a rainbow, as its mood dictated. In 1950, the year I acquired a 35-millimeter Kodak Pony camera, I often took it with me, wanting to cage the evening and take it home with me. I failed, of course—except when I succeeded. Even in the hands of a master, a camera never traps what is by nature mystical and ephemeral. But the image of it, spread across a screen on the light of a projector bulb, was sometimes the key that unlocked some inner door of mind, restoring summer experience to mid-winter memory.

Looking back now at the several dozen slides that resulted (the several dozen that I kept), I am struck by how varied those evenings truly were, with moods ranging across as broad a spectrum as ever my late adolescent temperament could have conjured.

I never lingered beyond sunset. As should be obvious, craft the size of the *Gleep* didn't come equipped with running lights, and trying to affix them would make my small boat sillier-looking than it already was. So Mother made it clear that she did not want me to overstay the light. Having my plywood vessel split in two by a fast moving speedboat, like Jack Kennedy's P-T boat, was not her idea of how she wanted her youngest remembered in the annals of Chautauqua Lake.

Eight summers of wallowing around the lake took their toll of both boat and motor until—as if to honor their lifelong bond—they collapsed in concert. The motor quit and the boat ruptured a seam. When it became evident that the motor would cost more to repair than I paid for it in the first place, I sold it for a few bucks to a man who operated a filling station and garage a quarter-mile up the road toward Mayville from the Chautauqua gate, where state road 394 intersected sharply with the Panama road. (21st Century Chautauquans know his building—though seriously altered—as Andriaccio's Restaurant.) He repaired outboard motors on the side, and could pirate it for parts

Too, investigation of the ruptured seam made clear that it could never be repaired in a way that would hold; and going out on Chautauqua Lake in an eight-foot pram about to pop a three-foot leak was ill-advised. Late that season, on the cusp of September, when the neighborhood patriarchal council—Dick Jones, Don Patton, and Campbell Brandon—issued the call for firewood donations for the annual Labor Day picnic, I consigned *Gleep* to the same fiery end that had claimed its un-christened predecessor. I watched with a heavy heart as her paint bubbled and her thin plywood began to fragment and separate, evaporating in a hell of flame. It was hard to let go of a boat that I had assembled by my own labor and ridden over the breast of the water for half my teen years.

At least we got some great corn out of the sacrifice.

Fortunately, she wasn't my last rowboat—though that's a larger story, and must take into account a much larger boat.

CHAPTER 20

Boiling Mahogany over a Driftwood Fire

"It's only a thousand dollars," I said to Mother, trying to sound off-handed and convincing while the voice in my brain erupted: "What are you <u>talking</u> about? A thousand bucks!? For an old boat?" Her almost casual response stunned me.

"Well, we could go look at it."

She had been talking about buying a boat that entire spring, but had wanted one for far longer. Not a dinghy or an outboard, but a seaworthy beast that could carry her securely across the lake free of any foreboding about not being able to swim. She had just celebrated her fifty-fourth birthday and was financially more secure than she had been since Dad's death fourteen years before. The dream had been postponed long enough.

My mind was still processing the improbabilities as we passed among Miller Park's columnar maples and beeches as if striding the aisle of a temple. We were on a bee line for the *Gadfly III*—at seventy feet, one of the largest boats on Chautauqua Lake. It floated quietly between six pilings the size of telephone poles, driven three on each side into the lake-bottom mud south of the College Club pier. More than a mere boat, *Gadfly* was the home of Bill and Kay Marsh, who made their summer living taking people on regularly scheduled cruises. Invited abroad, we crossed the passenger deck to the port rail and looked down at the object of our visit: a smaller boat lashed to the outboard pilings, where it rose and fell at the bidding of the waves. At thirty feet long and nine in the beam, *Shadow II* was not a petite craft; it only looked modest against the ponderous bulk of its big sister. Too, viewed from the loft of *Gadfly's* deck, it possessed little grace and no luxury.

Six feet of her knife-like prow stretched forward of a squat windshield wrapped around the first of two boxy-spare passenger compartments, providing spurious protection from wind and spray. Directly behind lay another open cockpit, dominated front-and-center by a motor cowling flanked to port by the steering assembly and a chrome gear lever. Bringing up the stern was a third passenger compartment that reminded me of the open cockpit on a World War I seaplane. Of proper seats there were none. Ten folding lawn chairs, divided four, four and two, stood in the passenger compartments. The only other amenity was a pile of life preservers stacked under the bow deck against an emergency.

Looking it over intently, Mother furrowed her brow, less in censure than uncertainty. Her grasp of things nautical had not notably improved since the day we bought that waterlogged, no-name gray barge, and this big a leap justly gave her pause.

"Do you know how to run this thing?" she asked, looking at me.

"Oh, sure," I replied carelessly, directing a look at Bill Marsh that pleaded, "Hey, back me up here."

I might as well have been talking to a fish. I got to know Bill—a socially reticent animal to begin with—through my casual friendship with his son Tom, so knew that he did not suffer fools gladly. And while he was never overtly unkind to me (indeed, I would shortly earn his friendship and the marine education that came with it) I knew not to presume on his kindness. He was not about to climb out on any limb with Mother about how well I could handle the *Shadow*. I tried to ease him into it by asking several intelligent-sounding questions, but quickly abandoned that effort, too. Bill's manner of selling a boat was terse to the point of brusqueness, and I didn't care to push his brusque button.

"I've told you its history, what it can and can't do, and the price," he'd pointedly remind a fussy customer. Then he'd walk away, saying over his shoulder: "If you want it, buy it. If you don't want it, don't buy it." He didn't say it unkindly; he just refused to take responsibility for a buyer's decision one way or the other. What did irritate him was having someone try to get him to reduce what he already knew to be a scrupulously fair price, and he'd wait until hell froze over before he'd betray anxiety over the outcome. It wasn't some kind of sales ploy; Bill honestly didn't care.

Walking back through Miller Park, Mother continued to quiz me and I kept trying to lay her concerns to rest. Where would we moor it? What would we do with it over the winter? Could I put seats in it? How much would it cost to run it? How many people would it hold? She was at once the child desperately excited over a new toy and the child's mother trying to be sensible about the whole thing. One by one, her concerns were satisfied—or she just couldn't resist any longer. She went to her desk and wrote out a check for $1,000.

"You realize that I don't know anything about boats," she said, handing me the check (as if I needed reminding). "I'm going to have to trust you."

"Don't worry, Mom," I replied brightly, looking at the check like it had fallen from heaven. "You won't be sorry. I can handle this." She never was, and I did—mostly.

Sprinting back across the park, I stopped to catch my breath before stepping out on the *Gadfly's* dock. It would not do to conclude an exchange with Bill Marsh in a panting rush. He and Kay were below getting supper when, the very soul of detachment, I stepped to the rail and called down the gangway.

"We'll take it," I greeted Bill quietly as he came on deck. I held out Mother's check.

Without even looking at the amount, Bill folded it carefully and placed it in his wallet.

"When do you want to take it away?" he asked.

"Well, I need to buy a mooring. Can you wait until I get that put out?"

"That'll be fine. I'll take the lawn chairs out of it tomorrow. Unless you come around by boat, you won't be able to get on board when we're out on a cruise. But you're welcome to come by when we're in dock to work on it if you'd like."

Looking full into my face with the most guileless eyes I have ever known—akin in color to a Caribbean lagoon and seemingly able to see clear to Toronto—he extended a hand that felt like finely tanned leather, shook mine, and smiled so reservedly that, had I glanced away just at that instant, I might have missed his change of expression altogether.

"Thanks," I said with a slight nod, trying to repay one spare smile with another, and started home. With that man, words were superfluous anyway.

By the time Bill Marsh acquired it, *Shadow II* had a history half as long as Chautauqua Lake—and *Shadow* was a singularly appropriate name; it was something of a leftover. We called it a launch, but when built early in the 20th Century it was one of the fastest recreational speedboats ever produced. I know, because of Bill's penchant for learning everything he could about every boat he ever bumped up against. Combing through a stack of boating magazines from the 'teens and 'twenties, he had found its pedigree. When we bought the boat, he gave me one of the magazines. I couldn't even imagine what it must have been like to settle onto the leather-upholstered bench seats that once filled the now chair-less cockpits. And when the straight-eight, 270 horsepower engine that crouched like a tiger beneath the hatch doors of its engine compartment roared to life, the thing must have seemed a creature possessed. Full throttled—the magazine reports attested—it had a top cruising speed of 50 miles per hour. Landlubbers accustomed to 65- to 80-mph speed limits on today's interstate highways are not likely to be impressed by that. But experienced boaters knew that 50 mph on water was like flying a plane while straddling the fuselage. Any boat capable of that kind of speed was on the verge of going airborne. The only boats I ever saw running that fast were flat, no-draft racing craft; and I never knew anyone who took the family out in one for a spin around the lake.

Shadow's hydrodynamic design was fine for its intended use. The prow—sharp, deep-keeled and concave—lent stability forward at high speeds, while a flat-bottomed stern provided the platform for it to get up out of the water and plane. A double-planked bottom ensured that it would withstand the pounding of high-speed running in rough seas without leaking. But the framing was too light to hold together forever against the stress created by that overweight engine. Sooner or later, the strain would take the boat apart, and did.

To Bill, that simply posed the kind of challenge he loved. Propping the worn hull up on blocks, he pulled the motor and stripped the boat of everything that was nonessential or worn out. Then, starting with a new keel, he gave it a skeleton suited to its length and profile. Made of white oak three inches thick, the keel spanned the middle two-thirds of the boat's length, cut ruler-straight on the bottom edge, concave on top to accommodate the gentle curve of the hull. Inside, set on edge and bolted to the keel, he added half a dozen white oak "ribs" an inch thick and eight deep. Finally, he screwed twin 2" x 4" white oak "stringers" onto the new ribs, precisely spaced to receive the mounting flanges of a new, 120 horsepower Palmer marine engine. By the time he finished it off with parts scrounged from the crammed storage barn he owned on one of Mayville's back streets—an oval instrument panel, upright steering wheel, gear shift linkage, and a hand-powered brass bilge pump, everyone of them a genuine antique—it was an odd but charming craft, sound and seaworthy.

Bill intended to use it in his lake tour business. Putting out in the *Gadfly* with fewer than ten passengers cost him more than he earned, and Bill was not in the business to be charitable. He and Kay lived on a shoestring as it was. They needed it to be a dependable shoestring. At the same time, he disliked losing nine fares for the lack of a tenth. And he realized that many customers might not be at Chautauqua long enough to have more than a single chance; if he missed his first opportunity to take them, he'd not likely get a second. So he meant to take undersized groups out in the *Shadow*. It didn't work. Clients expecting to board a spacious yacht lost enthusiasm when told to clamber down into a low-slung launch—especially the frailer among them who had long since given up clambering anywhere at all. So *Shadow* spent most of a season tied up at the pilings, going nowhere, and Bill didn't even make enough to cover insurance and Coast Guard inspection fees. Deciding he'd been better off canceling trips after all, he put it up for sale; and for a dozen years, the Skinners were privileged to own one of Chautauqua's most unique boats.

There wasn't time left that season to do much with it. Mother did get to take several long rides around the north end of the lake, poised on a folding lawn chair like it was an angel's throne. And at that moment, it might just as well have been: she thought she was in heaven. Beyond that, we had mostly to content ourselves with the simple joy of looking out at breakfast each morning to see its long, low profile riding at anchor. Never did a summer end so quickly. The hundred-pound mushroom anchor had barely settled into the lake bottom mud before I had to haul it out for the winter—and it takes a lot more effort to pull a mushroom anchor out than it does to drop it in.

Only an overwhelming desire to graduate in 1956—reinforced by Mother's order that I stay put in Meadville until winter vacation!—kept me from compromising my senior year at Allegheny College by driving home every few weekends just to admire that boat, cradled like a beached whale against the back wall of the boat yard's cavernous storage building at Mayville. So it was probably good that I remained ignorant of how seriously it had been damaged when taken out of the lake that September. That discovery would come in the spring. For the moment, I had to be satisfied with plotting the work I would begin in June.

And I did—the day after commencement. The work went well at first. Free to devote full time to it, I drove into the boat yard as it opened each morning, almost like I had a job there, lunch box on the front seat beside me and the car's trunk full of tools. I even became something of an honorary member of the yard crew who—exercising egalitarianism at its basest level, were soon throwing the same obscene remarks at me as they did at each other. I repainted all thirty feet of *Shadow's* hull in a striking black, white and aquamarine blue design, fabricated seats and back rests for passengers from slats of oak, cleaned and gapped the spark plugs, changed the oil, and polished every scrap of brass.

By the third week in June, *Shadow II* was sparkling and ready for launch. Jumping aboard as it slipped free of the lift slings, I revved up the motor, eased her down-creek between lines of boats moored by both banks, cleared the channel at the creek's mouth, and turned south, steering on Miller Bell Tower and home. Everything seemed fine until I sensed that the boat had begun to wallow sluggishly. I pulled up a floor panel and stared uncomprehendingly at almost a foot of water sloshing around in the bilge. I'd only made half-a-mile. Where had it come from? Bill had warned me to expect some leakage each spring, but cautioned me not to caulk the double-layered bottom boards.

"They'll separate as they dry out over the winter," he had said, "and leak for a while in the spring. But if you caulk the cracks, the boards won't be able to swell, and their edges will be crushed. Next year, the cracks will be even larger. The boat was designed to seal itself. Give it a chance."

I took him at his word, but couldn't imagine I'd have to sink the boat to accomplish it! Indeed, I couldn't imagine how that much water could get through the cracks between the bottom boards, no matter how dried out they were: I'd checked the entire length of the hull, lying on my back under the cradle applying a fresh coat of copper-bronze bottom paint.

Scrambling fore and aft checking the hull, I saw nothing to concern me until I lifted the small hatch door astern of the rear cockpit. Enough water was gushing in at both back corners to supply a fire hose. *Shadow* was in serious trouble and—given my location—so was I.

Knowing that getting the stern up out of the water would slow the leaking, I throttled the engine up as much as I dared. (There was just a possibility that the added strain of several tons of water sloshing around in the bilge might blow the stern completely off.) Then, like a man with the devil at his back, I worked the old brass bilge pump until my arm muscles burned from the strain. The torrent shooting out the side of the boat was impressive, but I wasn't fooling myself: my best effort couldn't turn the tide. All I could hope for was that the raised stern and pulsing pump might together buy me enough time to make Chautauqua before the boat foundered completely.

Bellowing past home, one hand steering and the other pumping furiously, I was grateful that Mother was at work and wouldn't have to witness another emergency with another boat—at least not until the immediate crisis was past. I didn't even slow down, just went right on around Miller Bell Tower point, curled in past the *Gadfly*, ran *Shadow's* bow five feet up onto the sand of the Children's Beach, cut the engine, and sagged down on the motor cowling to catch my breath.

Glancing over at the *Gadfly*, I was not surprised—but surely was chagrined—to see Bill and Kay standing at the rail watching me. They'd heard me come in. Large motor boats did not usually snort past their portholes and up onto the beach; and if one did, they knew something had to have gone wrong. Seldom was I more grateful for their unflappable temperaments. They just stood there, waiting, knowing that I'd explain when I got ready.

"Something's wrong in the stern," I panted at last. "Water is pouring in at the back corners."

Bill said not a word, just stepped off the *Gadfly*, came around to *Shadow's* bow and climbed aboard. Working our way to the back, we stood squinting down the stern hatch.

"The transom is sprung," Bill said as calmly as if he were announcing a trip to the grocery for bread and milk. "You'll have to take it out of the water and rebuild it."

That fast, what must have happened dawned on me. Bill didn't trust the people who ran the boat yard, and had counseled against taking *Shadow* there for winter storage. But I had nowhere else to take it.

"Well," he had said, "if you take it there, be sure that they position the slings under the keel, about a foot from the front and a foot from the back, when they take it out of the water. If they lift it by the bottom boards in front and behind the keel, they'll wreck the boat."

He knew better than anyone what he was talking about. Having rebuilt it, he knew that its structural integrity out-of-water depended on resting all its weight on the new keel. Lifting the keel lifted everything. But lifting the hull by its bottom boards before and after it would hang Bill's meticulously designed reinforcing structure—keel, ribs, stringers and engine—like dead weight in the unsupported center. The middle would go down and the ends up, stressing the frame. Looking into the stern, Bill didn't have to explain what was only too clear: whoever took the boat out of the water the previous fall had ignored my explicit instructions. I knew it hadn't happened that morning when we launched it, because I was there to position the slings myself. But I'd left for school before the boat came out the previous September. Improperly supported, the boat sagged in the middle, wrenched the stern, and tore the transom corners.

My heart sank. The Chautauqua season would open in ten days, and I had neither the place nor the equipment to haul several tons of boat out of the water. Nor was I sure I'd know how to fix it if I did. If I'd taken it back to the boat yard, Bill might never have spoken to me again. "They know how to paint and varnish and tune motors," he snorted, "but they know nothing about building and repairing boats."

For just a moment, I was immobilized, knowing only one thing for certain: Chautauqua Institution was not about to allow thirty feet of launch to sit on the Children's Beach during the season.

Regaining my composure—such as it was—I was just resolving to take the boat back around the point and run it up on Jones Beach where I could at least work on it, when Bill spoke again. But his customary crustiness was gone. Sensing my helplessness, he spoke matter-of-factly, almost gently. Never did the man's generosity come through more clearly than at that moment.

"I won't be taking any groups out for a few more days. We'll pull it out tomorrow, up at my yard, and I'll help you repair it."

That was it. No negotiation, no mention of a price, not even a suggestion that there would be one. Just a friend's help, generously offered and oh-so-gratefully received.

Looking over his shoulder as he walked away, Bill said, "Shove some oakum into those cracks. It'll slow the leaks down until we get it out of the water."

Next morning's sun had barely cleared the low hills across the lake when I arrived at the Children's Beach. Bailing as much water as I could out of the boat (and thirty feet of boat holds a whole lot of water), I caulked the sprung stern seams with oakum, cranked the motor, and gunned *Shadow* backwards off the beach. Kay was at the *Gadfly's* rail as I hauled around and headed for deep water, her smile and wave a gesture that said "Good luck" in a way no words could convey. It would be hard to say how much that smile lifted my spirit; and it lifted further when a glance at the stern confirmed that the oakum indeed had slowed the leaks. Between it and the brass pump, I was able to keep the water under control.

Bill's boatyard was just a single lot a half mile south of Mayville between state road 394 and the lake, sandwiched in by cottages on both sides. He had laid ties and railroad track down the slope and out into the lake to a depth of about five feet, on which he fabricated a steel I-beam truck ponderous enough to cradle the *Gadfly* when he pulled it ashore for winter storage. The front end of an old pickup, welded to the top end of the tracks, provided power. Driving a winch fitted with steel cable and geared down so far that the truck moved only inches a minute, Bill had enough power harnessed there to haul the old *City of Jamestown* into dry dock.

Lying off to one side in the weeds was a smaller pair of trucks that he had fabricated to store the *Shadow*—until we bought it. By the time I nosed in to the shore, he had levered them onto the rails, attached the tow cable, and run them out into shallow water. Waving me in, he guided the bow until the keel grounded reassuringly on it, and I cut the engine. While I lashed *Shadow* into place, Bill cranked the old pickup's engine and engaged the winch. An inch at a time, the hull lifted clear of the water, resting—as it ought to have all along—on the unifying keel. Crawling underneath to wedge blocks under the hull to hold it upright, I watched bilge water drain from the broken stern. It was worse than I had realized. Bill was right about having to rebuild it.

For four days, we worked to undo the damage. It was like watching a man court the woman of his dreams. Bill spoke lovingly of marine design, of the merits of various kinds of woods, why one pattern of setting screws was better than another. He was patient, methodical. Every movement had a purpose. No energy was wasted. When we pulled two of the three transom boards, it was clear that they would have to be replaced. They were made of 5/8" mahogany—a fine marine wood, but soft. The edges were stressed, the screw holes frayed. They might not withstand being drilled and screwed a second time; and as fast as they failed, the boat would have to come out of the water again. So, too, the "shapers," or corner pieces, that connected the sides and back of the boat. The stress of lifting the boat incorrectly had split them. They would have to be replaced, too.

That last gave *Shadow* a component unique to Chautauqua Lake. Digging through the clutter of lumber in his Mayville barn, Bill flashed a grin as he liberated two 1" x 4" boards about four feet long. He handed me one.

"Know what this is?" he asked. (He so loved being the teacher.)

"No," I said honestly, turning it in my hands. Lighter than oak or maple, it was smooth, finely grained, and seemed extraordinarily dense.

"That's the most rot-resistant wood in the world," Bill said with satisfaction. "It's Cypress."

"Cypress?" I asked in surprise (like he hadn't already told me). "The stuff that grows down south, standing in water?"

"That," he replied, "is why it's so durable. It grew in water. Being wet all the time doesn't hurt it."

That evening, using the split shapers as templates, he laid the boards on his band-saw table and returned to the yard next morning with brand new Cypress shapers that slid into place as if they had grown there. Setting me to work screwing the side planking home, Bill laid a driftwood fire on the beach: not the usual compact pile, but strung out a foot wide and five feet in length. From somewhere in the weeds, he hauled out half of an old iron water heater tank cut length-wise, like a sausage sliced up the middle, and laid it on the wood, open side up.

"There," he ordered, striking a match, "fill that with lake water. To the top."

Grabbing a bucket, I dutifully waded into the lake a dozen times, returning until the long, slender pot was brim-full. Finally, I got up enough nerve to ask.

"What are we going to cook?" It occurred to me that the thing was about the right size to cook me, that maybe I was Isaac helping to prepare the altar for my own sacrifice—fitting retribution for letting *Shadow* get busted in the first place.

"Mahogany," Bill said simply.

I stood, looking quizzically at him, knowing that more explanation had to be coming.

"If you boil wood, it bends more easily. And if you bend it hot and wet, and clamp it in place, it retains its new shape when it dries."

He glanced at me, blue eyes probing to see if I was keeping up with him.

"Look here. The transom of your boat is curved. We can bend the new stern boards into place, but they'll always be under pressure, trying to pop their screws. If we screw the boards on hot and wet, they'll mold themselves to the curve of the stern."

I never realized that boiling

New Stern for *Shadow*

mahogany over a driftwood fire could be so useful. Or that working with a piece when it came fresh from the tank would be that painful. Chuckling at my discomfort, Bill drilled and screwed, leaving me to figure out how to hold the steaming wood in place without parboiling my fingers.

By the fourth afternoon, when *Shadow II* rolled down the ways with her stern freshly painted, no one could tell how close we had come to losing our launch before we even got to enjoy it. Hoisting myself up over the topside as it floated free of the trucks, I cranked the motor and threw it into reverse. Bill stood at water's edge as I backed away, his weathered face creased by that hint of a smile, nothing more; but by then I recognized the look as one of satisfaction. He barely acknowledged my wave as I hauled around south and, again, made for Miller Bell Tower. This time I stopped at home. Tying up to our mooring, I screwed up my courage, took a deep breath, lifted one of the floor panels, and looked into the bilge. Dry as a bone.

Walking in off the dock to tell Mother about the *Shadow's* reprieve, I heaved what may well have been the biggest sigh of relief in my entire life.

CHAPTER 21

God Saved the *Shadow*

If Bill Marsh saved *Shadow* the first time around, God got the credit two years later. It was the conclusion of a three-year trial-and-error search for some way to store it through the winters without having to take it back to the boat yard at Mayville.

The fall after Bill took me under his wing to repair its sprung stern, he offered to store it behind the *Gadfly* at his lakefront lot. There would be no charge—except that he'd appreciate my help in taking *Gadfly* out of the water in September, before I left for school. *Shadow* would be brought up astern of it. It seemed a more-than-fair offer.

Except that I did not yet realize how interesting pulling 70 feet of yacht out of the lake could be. *Gadfly* displaced 15 tons, and its topsides rose six to eight feet above the waterline—a configuration bound to catch any breeze that happened along. To hold it in place, much less to stop it once it started to move, all while standing chest deep in water, was not a lightweight assignment. But that's what Bill had in mind for me. He and Kay had done it for several years until, her protestations to the contrary notwithstanding, he worried that it was too much for her. So he elected me.

The difficult thing to control was not the boat, however, but the weather, over which we had no control whatever. The lake must be dead calm—everywhere. A glassy surface in the lee of Miller Bell Tower, where *Gadfly* was moored, was of no value if gusts were playing along the shoreline up near Mayville. Chautauqua Lake was that calm maybe one day a week, and then only at the crack of dawn. So we waited.

For five days, I climbed out of bed before sunrise to look out across the lake. If any breeze at all was evident, I went back to bed. On one iffy morning, I dressed and walked quickly across Miller Park, silent and deserted that tenth day after the season ended. Bill was at the stern rail surveying the lake as I stepped aboard.

"Not this morning," he muttered without a hint of annoyance. Bill and Kay Marsh were imbued with one of Mother Nature's elemental traits: they would not be rushed, yet never grew impatient. I turned around and walked home.

The sixth morning, I woke and looked out on a liquid mirror. Had I paused right then to take a picture of two sailboats still moored off the end of our community dock and mounted the print upside down, most people wouldn't have known the difference. There wasn't so much as a ripple out there. Something told me that this was the day. I bolted breakfast and ran across the park.

"We go today," asserted Bill, that inscrutable hint of a smile on his mouth. "How soon can you leave?"

"I'm ready," I replied (terribly pleased with my prescience). "I can leave right now."

"Good," he said. "I ran the truck out into the lake last week. Go check the tracks from water's edge clear to the back wheel. There can't be so much as a pebble on them, understand?"

"Got it," I said. A single pebble caught under one of those steel wheels while it was bearing that much weight could create a huge amount of resistance, stressing both the tow cable and the winch.

"I'll leave in a few minutes. Kay will drive our car up. When I get there, be in the water beside the truck. I'll tell you what to do."

"Okay."

Barely ten minutes had elapsed by the time I pulled onto the berm next to Bill's old tractor. I had no problem locating the truck, even though it was submerged under several feet of water: its steel-pipe struts, slotted into the ends of both I-beams, angled up out of the water marking a precise square for Bill to slide into. By the time I reached it, *Gadfly* was already well up the lake, the clean cut of its hull barely marring the mirror-flat surface of the water. That boat created less wake than any comparable-sized craft I ever saw. I stood for a moment, admiring it. A perfect replication of it floated upside down beneath the bow wave, reflected by the dead-calm water. Then I started awake to the realization that I hadn't checked the track yet. A week of calm weather had been my ally: only a scattering of small gravel, easily brushed off, had washed onto the tracks at water's edge. But I still had to check the entire length of both tracks, and that required diving under water.

When I surfaced, satisfied that all was well, I looked up to see *Gadfly's* prow, swung in toward shore, ghosting right at me and only yards away. Something else caught my eye as well: a dark riffle spread across the water fifty yards north, evidence that an offshore breeze was building. We weren't going to be as lucky as we'd hoped. Bill saw it too. Letting go the wheel, he stepped out from behind the windscreen.

"We have to move quickly," he called through cupped hands. "Climb up on the front end of the truck to port and hold me in place until I can get lines on the struts."

I swallowed hard, but hauled myself up on the I-beam, gripping the strut for balance while fifteen tons of boat whispered past, inches from my fingers. It was hard not to think what it would feel like if the wind took it in mind right then to let go a sudden gust and grind the boat on the strut with my fingers trapped in between. It almost happened anyway: arriving where he wanted to be, Bill threw the twin engines into reverse, checking the boat's forward motion... and drawing the bow to port. Instinctively, I brought my shoulder around against the looming topside and shoved hard, surprised—and relieved—that it worked.

Being in the lee of *Gadfly's* bulk, I couldn't feel the breeze, but I knew it was building: water had begun to eddy around the bow and stern, and *Gadfly's* desire to side-slide down-lake grew more insistent by the minute. Bill's voice came again, out of sight now, and overhead. Being under the curve of the bow, I could no longer see him; but I heard the uncustomary tinge of urgency in his voice.

"Get inside the strut and try to keep the boat centered!"

I moved around the strut, turned to face it, and put my back against *Gadfly's* massive hull. It felt like pushing an elephant that had lost interest in the game. The soft calm of dawn had given way to a stiffening breeze and falling temperature. Every time I pushed, *Gadfly* pushed back. About the time I wondered how much longer I could control it, the pushing stopped, and Bill's voice again came from overhead.

"Okay, I've got it."

Relieved, I dropped off into the chest-deep water. It was like stepping into a warm bath. Preoccupied with winning the test of wills with *Gadfly*—or at least not losing it—I hadn't realized how chilled I had gotten.

I also had failed to notice Kay's arrival, pulling their black Cadillac sedan in behind my Chevy. (Bill would own no other make of car; never bought one new; never exceeded 35 miles-per-hour—anywhere; and changed the oil every two thousand miles. It was the same kind of fastidiousness with which he maintained his boats. That's why he drove every model he owned until the odometer turned over 150,000 miles.) Kay's appearance was announced by a guttural snort from the old pickup. I looked up to see her vanish in a cloud of exhaust; but when it blew off, she waved and smiled with the kind of warmth that I had come to expect.

On signal from Bill, she engaged the clutch. Slowly enough that if you weren't watching, you'd miss it, the slack was drawn out of the tow cable and it lifted off the ground. Momentarily, it became so taut that it sounded a musical note like the C string on a double bass. For a brief moment, nothing happened. Then, as the strain on the cable exceeded the dead-weight of its burden, the truck shuddered and inched forward. Soon the pace was set: to the steady grinding of the engine and the curl of the geared-down winch, *Gadfly* inched toward the beach. The while, Bill moved about the deck, fine-tuning the strut ropes to align *Gadfly* with the center of the truck. After a few minutes, almost imperceptibly, the prow began to lift from the water, evidence that the forward I-beam had caught the boat's massive keel.

"Hold it there," Bill called to Kay. The winch stopped and the truck rested.

For a moment, as I stood soaking wet and shivering in the now stiff breeze, nothing happened. Then Bill reappeared at the rail and lowered a bucket over the side on a rope.

"Here," he said, his face lit by something brighter than his normally spare smile. "This will warm you up."

I looked into the bucket. It held a bottle of whiskey and a glass. I looked up at him, the warning flags of my abstemious upbringing flapping as if lofted onto the chill September breeze. Bill, as was his wont, just looked at me, and Kay's smile assumed a teasing edge. They knew what was going on in my head. They did not share it, but they would not dishonor it, either. It was up to me, and I was freezing. Reaching into the bucket, I lifted out the bottle and poured out a half-inch of the pale golden liquid. Returning the bottle to the bucket, I lifted the glass and sipped gingerly. I can't say that it warmed me up, but it sure took my attention off the chill in a hurry. The acerbic vapor exploded up into my head and down my throat. I'm not sure how much the smarting altered my expression, but when I looked at Bill and Kay again, both sported full-toothed grins.

Hanging a ship's ladder over the side, Bill climbed down, pulled a large chine block out of the overgrown weeds, set it on the I-beam and firmed it into place with a few well-placed smacks of a maul. Having set its mate on the starboard side, he called to Kay, the tractor engine re-engaged, and *Gadfly* resumed its snail-paced ascent into winter storage.

Now that I had earned *Shadow's* keep, we repeated the process the next morning, reversing rolls. I rowed out soon after dawn, clambered aboard, and laboriously hauled the mooring assembly—buoy, chain and encrusted mushroom anchor—out of the lake and into the engine compartment. Returning it and *Gleep* to the dock, I turned up-lake and retraced Gadfly's course from the day before—leaving a far larger wake. Within an hour, *Shadow* was blocked up on the smaller trucks. By lunchtime, her bow was pulled up under *Gadfly's* stern. That afternoon, after we drained the cooling system and poured a tablespoon of motor oil into each cylinder, Bill drew on his seemingly bottomless accumulation of scrap lumber and guided me in fabricating a frame to fit over the deck. Its ridge was raised, like a shallow-pitched house roof, and open fore and aft for ventilation. Next morning I lashed and nailed a pair of ten-by-sixteen-foot canvas tarpaulins over it for cover, and *Shadow* was ready to withstand whatever winter threw at it.

And it did. But things got complicated in the spring. Bill put *Gadfly* back in the water before I got home from school. I arrived to find the track empty and *Shadow* resting on a makeshift framework ten feet off to one side from where we'd left it, already hedged in by early summer weeds. Bill also made it clear that, this time, he was not in a position to help me. I'd have to get *Shadow* back on the trucks and down to the lake on my own.

"But how am I going to do it?" I asked, my anxiety more evident than I wanted it to be whenever he was involved.

"Oh, that's no problem," he replied, ignoring my disconcertion. "Just bring the trucks along side, rig some ties across the opening, and move the boat across on the rollers that I stored under it."

I drove up to the yard, studied the thing further, concluded there was no way I could tackle it alone, and recruited two friends. It took a day of figuring and two hours of white-knuckled labor, and we only almost flipped it over once (I sure was glad that neither Bill nor Mother was there to see that one!). We also had to ease the trucks down the ways by hand. Dependent as he was on his winch, Bill understandably wanted no one but himself or Kay to operate it. So we rigged a drag line, wrapped it around a post three times, and let friction be our brake. Shoving the trucks back up the track and levering them off into the weeds, I looked at *Shadow* riding proudly a few yards off the beach waiting to go home, and determined that I would never do that again.

That September, however, I hatched a new scheme that was not a notable improvement: I determined to store the boat on Jones Beach in front of our house. I always was a slow learner.

Trying to appear the soul of confidence (at least when Mother was nearby), I assembled a cradle rather like a giant sled, with doubled two-by-twelve runners and three stout crossbars positioned to support the all-important keel. Recruiting a bunch of neighborhood boys who were always looking for some challenge to add zing to their weekends, we lashed the cradle under *Shadow's* midriff and dragged it into shallow water until it touched bottom. Then I got daring. Haltering one pulley of a fifty-foot block-and-tackle to a beach-side maple, I hooked the other to the cradle and tied the free line to my car. Working in tandem, boys laid round posts under the runners to serve as rollers, retrieved them as the cradle slid beyond them, and moved them forward again. By dint of Chevy-power, we towed *Shadow* so far up that its prow nearly touched the tree, jacked up the cradle against the possibility of high water, and set large blocks under it. Finally, I winterized the engine, reassembled the frame Bill and I made the previous fall, and lashed on the canvas tarps. *Shadow* was bedded down for the winter, right there where Mother could keep an eye on it.

As it turned out, I hadn't jacked it up any too far. The lake rose so high that year that it reached clear in under *Shadow's* elevated stern—the highest the water came during Mother's 40 years in our North Lake home. She was so impressed that she took pictures from several angles—you know, just to get the full effect—and mailed them to me at school. I didn't mind the foot of snow resting on the canvas roof, but that ice nipping at the heels of the stern blocks didn't do much for my concentration that term.

Asleep for the Winter

The expected spring drain-down of the lake was both good news and bad. By the time I got home and went to pull *Shadow* off the beach, we had plenty of beach to work on again, but the lake level had dropped to below normal. That's when it dawned on me that, to pull Shadow back into the water, I'd have somehow to reverse my ingenious device for pulling it out in the first place. Driving my Chevy out into the lake didn't appear to be a good idea. Fortunately, it was the Memorial Day weekend, and all those neighborhood boys were still looking to be distracted. Recruiting roller-attendants, we mauled a stout post into the lake bottom as far off-shore as my block-and-tackle would reach, and haltered one end to it and the other to the back end of the cradle. Then I tied the free end to my faithful Chevy again, and pressed on the gas. It worked like a charm. In fifteen minutes we moved *Shadow* twenty-five yards offshore. Which is where the block-and-tackle ran out of rope, twenty yards short of water deep enough to float the boat. Only the propeller and rudder even got wet. Never ones to give up without a fight, a dozen young boys pushed and hauled and grunted and pried for an hour. It was labor to no purpose. *Shadow* didn't go anywhere—but they did. Memorial Day expired and their parents took them home to await the opening of the season a month hence. I was back to one-man ingenuity.

For several days, *Shadow* sat like a beached whale. Under the circumstances, Mother was remarkably calm. She knew I was stuck. She also knew that, as desperately as she wanted to see her boat afloat, she had nothing to add by way of a solution. But God did. On Tuesday the sky became overcast. On Wednesday it began to drizzle, then to rain, then to pour. That wasn't unusual in early June, when nature could get downright nasty over that lake, and did. Had such a storm broken then, it might have gone hard for *Shadow*. It was designed to take a terrible beating when afloat; but half in and half out of the water like that, it was a sitting duck. God apparently thought so, too: the wind seemed to be corralled by providential restraint. But not the rain. It came on like Noah's flood. And if it fell for four days and nights instead of forty, the result was comparable: by the time Saturday dawned to clearing skies and warming air, the lake had risen a foot. *Shadow* was by no means afloat, but its entire stern-half was awash.

Although it was the weekend, Mother was already at work, readying her office for the rush that inevitably attended the opening of a new season. I didn't even hesitate. It seemed better to seize the moment and explain to Mother later—especially since the odds of success were at best about even. I grabbed the ignition key off its hook in the cellarway, waded out to *Shadow*, started the engine, put it in reverse, and gunned it. Even though it didn't move, the churn of muddy water that roiled shoreward was impressive. That's when it hit me. Shifting into forward, I revved the engine and watched with satisfaction as a turbid trail surged lakeward. Shifting once more into reverse, I gunned it again. That's when I felt it: a sudden jolt as the stern dropped several inches. *Shadow* was dredging itself a hole to float in. Thrice more I shifted the gear and revved the engine. Shifting into reverse one last time, I pulled the throttle all the way out and let the engine go full bore. With a shudder, the boat pulled backward and shot free. Relieved of its burden, the cradle floated to the surface. But by then, I was already fifty feet on out into the lake.

That was the last time I tried that, too. Later that summer, I connected with a man who had just opened a new boat yard up Prendergast Creek. When I explained the fine points of lifting and storing *Shadow* to him, he promised to honor them, and did. For the rest of its life, *Shadow* spent its winters up that creek.

CHAPTER 22

Supper in the Lee of Long Point

"Everyone grab something," Mother ordered giddily. "No one goes out on the dock without carrying something! Here, Bob, you can take this thermos. Hazel, can you carry this tray of fried chicken? And Ruth, you bring that canvas bag with the tablecloth and paper plates and napkins, and I'll bring the potato salad," and so on until every hand held something. "Do we have everything?"

Coasting in from its mooring to the end of the dock, I shifted the *Shadow* into reverse and lay over on the wheel to draw the stern up against the old tire bumpers that Dick Jones had hung over the uprights of the metal horses. By the time I jumped out and half-hitched the bow and stern lines to the pilings, the parade already stretched from the front porch, across the lawn and onto the beach. With uncertain gait, people unaccustomed to having a jiggling dock underfoot made their way out the 120-foot length of ours, burdened by their share of the commissary. One by one, I received the ingredients of a picnic supper, lined them up around the engine cowling, and helped Mother's landlubber friends—none of whom possessed anything remotely resembling sea legs—to climb down into the boat.

"All set?" I asked Mother as she came last on board.

"I think so," she replied.

"Then let us away."

Releasing bow and stern lines, I planted one foot on the boat and shoved against the dock with the other. When the space between boat and dock approximated the stretch of my legs, I dropped into the engine compartment, engaged the gears, and *Shadow* slipped through the mooring area into open water. I steered an expansive curve around the Bell Tower Point and lined up the bow pennant to split the difference between Prendergast and Long Points.

Excitement rippled among the passengers. Since we acquired *Shadow*, boat picnics had become Mother's absolutely favorite Chautauqua activity—the kind of thing she had wanted to do all her life but could not, for lack of means. Now she not only had the means, but had them in sufficiently generous dimensions that she could invite any seven friends along. Finding volunteers was never a problem, as evidenced by the seven plus herself now comfortably settled, four and four, on the slat benches in the two forward passenger compartments. But today was unusual. This collection of friends did not have regular access to the lake, and they were ready for just about anything. So Mother decided that the time had come to make the five-mile run to Bemus Bay, and anchor for supper in the lee of Long Point.

It would be a relaxed trip. *Shadow's* top speed was about twenty-two miles per hour, but we seldom cruised above ten. It was restraint that I had learned from Bill Marsh.

"Running a boat wide open all the time is like driving a car wide open in second gear," he said. "You can get away with it for a while; but before long you'll have torn the engine apart. They're not designed to take that kind of strain." Then he'd launch into a grouse about people who bought expensive boats, raced them all over the lake as fast as they could go, and then complained a year or two later that they wouldn't go as fast as they used to. The moral had the clarity of a bat striking a ball; treat your boat's engine well and it will reward you with years of dependable service.

Boat Picnic

So we cruised to Bemus Point gently, and had forty-five minutes to enjoy the passing scene and each other's company, and did. It promised to be just lovely—and for the first hour and a half, it was all of that.

As we passed each landmark—Prendergast, Midway and Maple Springs, Whitney's Bay, Sylvan Park, Long Point—our guests one by one got farther downlake than they had ever been, and the trip turned into a guided tour of the north half of Chautauqua Lake. Interest peaked when we rounded Stow Point and Bemus came into view. The Bemus-Stow ferry, which most of them had ridden but none had seen from a boat, was midway on its yo-yo course across the narrow stretch of water that—according to tradition—was the feature that prompted the Seneca Indians to name the lake "Chautauqua." They said it resembled a grain sack with a rope cinched around the center, so named it "Bag-tied-in-the-middle." According to tradition (but as a matter of fact, no one truly knows).

For full effect, I ran on south through the cinch-point, crossed the ferry's trail, and dropped several hundred yards below Bemus Point before coming around. Aiming for the ferry landing on the Bemus side, I slowed *Shadow* to an idle and glided close inshore so the guests could enjoy the bustle that stretched from the point building past the Hotel Lenhart (a remnant of the heyday of wooden hotels that once surrounded the lake), and admire the yachts lined up the length of the waterfront, noses to the shore.

Once beyond the village, I turned out into the middle of the bay, cut the engine, and threw out the anchor. Mother half-climbed and half-crawled over the divide between the passenger cockpit and the engine compartment so she could take charge, and we got down to the serious business of eating. I never knew that crowd to be off its feed, and that day was no exception. From the cheese and cracker platter to the chocolate chip torte, their appetites didn't flag.

But the weather did. As we ate, a dark band of clouds peeked up over the trees that blanketed Long Point, and continued to grow in altitude and breadth every passing minute. There had been no indications to predict that it was coming, one of those squalls that can surge in from the west almost any summer day, uninvited and unannounced, to pounce on Chautauqua Lake. "Mother," I cautioned, "we're going to have some nasty weather. We'd better get things cleaned up."

"Oh, my," Mother said, looking at the sky while concern darkened the faces of our guests. "Can we make it home in time?"

I surveyed the underside of the storm that by then was coming overhead. It was among the nastiest I have ever seen, on or off that lake. As if from an inverted caldron suspended above us, huge bubbles of cloud boiled down from the storm's underbelly, barely five hundred feet off the water, while lightning scorched their edges. It would not have surprised me one bit to see a funnel cloud bore right through the middle of the mass to reach menacingly for the ground. But it would have scared me a lot worse than I already was. I candidly confess that I was more frightened that moment than I ever had been, or would be again, on Chautauqua Lake. It was one of the few times that I thought we might be in serious trouble and hadn't a clue what I could any longer do to forestall it.

"Not a chance," I replied. "We're not even going to make it around Long Point."

Shadow had no cabin, nor even a tarpaulin to pull up over our heads for whatever shelter it might provide. I was also worried about hail, against which we had no protection at all. As rain drops the size of mothballs began to splatter the surface of the lake, their intensity mounting by the second, I told everyone to button up and to cover their heads with whatever they had, gunned the engine, and bolted in against Long Point—and I use "against" advisedly. The lake bottom west of Long Point sloped gently up out of deep water until it simply pushed above the surface to become the visible part of the point. On the Bemus side, however, it rolled over and plunged so precipitously that a single stride off the point landed average-sized persons in water up to their chins. It was a serious drop-off. Squinting into rain that lashed the lake to a frenzy that was blinding, I ran *Shadow's* bow so far onto the point that brush scraped its sides and lay on the foredeck. And there we sat through the deluge.

Apprehension eased as the sky began to lighten even before the downpour moderated, and it became apparent that the storm would be a flash-in-the-pan—one of those about which Mother was fond of predicting that it wouldn't last long because it couldn't keep raining that hard. (She wasn't always right; but on that occasion I happily ceded her the benefit of the doubt.) The rain quit almost as abruptly as it had begun. Even before we felt the last of it, the sun stuck its face out from beneath the departing clouds and plastered the landscape with warm wet brilliance. The whole thing hadn't lasted fifteen minutes.

Warning the landlubbers abroad that, soaked to the skin as they were, the ride home would be a chilly one, I backed *Shadow* out of the underbrush and retraced our course around Long Point. As often occurred following one of those here-and-gone squalls, this one gathered up the wind and took it along, leaving only an echo of turbulence behind. Rounding the Bell Tower, I pulled up to the dock, lashed *Shadow* to the pilings, and helped the guests climb out. Most of them had by then advanced from saturated to half-dried, but I wasn't sure how they might be feeling about the whole adventure. I needn't have worried. As one took an empty casserole dish from Mother and joined the caravan off the dock and up to the kitchen, she beamed brightly and spoke for the whole crowd:

"Oh, Ruth, when can we do this again!?"

PART 8

Around the Grounds

CHAPTER 23

Riding the Lightning

Residing, as it did, near the eastern edge of the Great Plains—two-million weather-making square miles that stretch from central Canada to Mexico; and located south and east of the world's largest impoundment of fresh water called, appropriately enough, the Great Lakes, Chautauqua was heir to a whole lot of precipitation. During late spring and early fall, it was actually known to drizzle there. But that was the exception. During summer, rain was more likely to come by the bucketful, accompanied by a good deal of very impressive lightning and thunder. Every Chautauquan could tell you at least one personal story of something that happened during such a storm. It was part of the ambiance of the place. I could only imagine what life was like when such a torrent rolled over one of those early assemblies in the late 19th Century, threatening to wash the entire congregation into the lake, tents and all, bringing the whole Chautauqua experiment to a sodden end before it had opportunity to take wing.

Chautauquans never capitulated willingly to the vagaries of the weather. Perhaps it was inbred by tradition. If the pioneers at Fair Point could ride out such gales by hiking up the hems of their skirts and tying down their tent flies, why couldn't we? Or maybe it was the seriousness with which Chautauquans took their cultural opportunities. The only difference between navigating the brick walk on a radiant day and one on which the "waters above the firmament" seemed to have sundered it was the number of umbrellas I had to dodge to keep from getting my eye poked out. If a gaggle of Chautauquans had happened by the ark just as Noah and his boys were trying to herd a pair of each according to its kind up the gangway, they would have swept right on by, brushing aside his warning with some come-back like, "Not until after the lecture." I have seen well-dressed and dignified women and men stop in the middle of the street, stoop down, untie and kick off their shoes, tie the laces together, and go their barefoot way as if nothing was out of the ordinary.

Nor did they become particularly annoyed when an event was disrupted by a display of exhibitionistic meteorological petulance. To have done so would deny them what they had come to attain. Early in its history, Chautauqua's program played out under the open sky. When steps finally were taken to hold inclemency at bay so that programs could proceed with minimal disruption, it appears that the founders wanted to put no more between them and nature than was necessary to keep the seats dry. Among my first and abiding childhood impressions of the place was its open-airedness, and forget the weather. How many times have those on the windward side of the Amphitheater or Hall of Philosophy responded to a sudden squall by getting up, mid-sentence or mid-movement, to move further in under the roof? And while they found new seats, or simply moved in against the dry side of a pillar or tree to lean against, lecturers and symphony orchestras continued their ministrations as if nothing were happening.

My attitude toward thunderstorms was adopted from Mother. As the first flash pierced the gathering gloom and the initial gust tore at the trees, she headed for the front porch. Dinner was on hold until the deluge was reduced to droplets splattering the ground from overhanging branches and the first ray of the late-afternoon sun emerged from behind the departing storm to splash rainbows across every street corner. She was not alone. I never took a poll, but have long suspected that if I did, I'd find that the most heavily subscribed seats for witnessing one of Chautauqua's noisome downpours were lined up on the town's numerous porches. Every one seemed occupied by a group that lined up in rockers pulled back from roof edges, or leaned against clapboard cottage walls, eyes a-sparkle. The more expressive among them applauded each bolt and cheered each thunderclap, or burst out with approving cries of "Author! Author!"

It would be hard for a youngster not to conclude from it all that thunder squalls were fun, an opportunity for the kind of play not typical of an average summer day. Observing the opening peal of an approaching tempest, Cliff, Frank and I did not run for cover; we ran for our bathing suits and lake shoes. Stripped of all else, we started for the door just as the first plop of the first drop sounded from McClintock's asphalt pavement.

"Where are you going?" It was Mother's voice, and it stopped us in our tracks.

"We're just going to ride in the rain." It was Cliff who answered, although all three of us shared the fervent hope that she would not put a lid on our excitement.

"Well, be careful," she rejoined. "I don't want you hurt, and I don't want you to hurt anyone else."

"Okay, Mom," we cried in unison, and shot out the door before she had opportunity to reconsider. Of course she wouldn't; she knew perfectly well what we were feeling. Indeed, had her parents not denied her permission to learn to ride a bike as a child, she just might have jumped into her own bathing suit and joined us!

Indian file by age, we were off like beings possessed, pedaling up and down the streets as fast as churning legs could pump us. Passing the end of a nearby street edged with a deep, brick-lined gutter intended to channel the runoff of just such a flood to the lake two blocks away, and all of it downhill, we circled around. It was running brim-full with racing water. Pausing only long enough to realign our column, we steered into the top end and raced the length of it, bellowing like the three horsemen of the apocalypse, our balloon tired bikes spraying water halfway across the street in a wake that did justice to a speedboat. Reaching the bottom, we turned and pumped back up the hill, so wound up that exuberance, more than labor, carried us to the top. Then we did it all over again.

By the time the storm subsided, we had completed a high-speed exploration of half the gutters on the grounds, and rode home feeling wetter than we had in our entire lives—though I never could figure out why bike-riding in a pelting rainstorm felt wetter than going swimming. And, of course, for the rest of our teenage lives, we repeated the ritual practically every time Chautauqua was gifted by a summer downpour.

It was during one such escapade that I engaged in a business so risky that, looking back now, I wonder how I ever survived it. Mother, of course, could have told you stories about a lot of other occasions when enthusiasm and stupidity conspired to put my survival in jeopardy; but there's no need to get fixated on them here. The event in question was sufficient by itself to make the point, and was rooted in an accident of history.

As mandated for communities across the country during World War II, the people of Meadville, Pennsylvania formed a Civil Defense Corps to organize air raid drills and blackouts, so that we would know what to do in the event of an enemy aerial attack. During such drills, Corps representatives in each neighborhood took to the streets as air raid wardens, felt their way through the night looking for homes or business where someone seemed not to have gotten the drift of what a blackout required of them, and instructed them accordingly. Their only armament was a World War I infantry helmet, rather like an old-fashioned shaving basin, painted white with a civil defense logo pasted on the front. From someplace, I know not where, a helmet came into our possession. I kept it for years, adjusting the webbing to fit my growing head. And one time, as we scrambled to mount our bikes to ride the rain-glutted gutters of Chautauqua, I grabbed it and shoved it onto my head.

It's not clear to me why I thought it a good idea to run around outdoors, naked except for bathing trunks, sneakers and several pounds of metal strapped to my head while riding my bicycle through large accumulations of running water as lightning forked the sky or—now and then—stabbed at one or another of Chautauqua's majestic trees. Nor do I understand why Mother or one of my more-astute-than-me siblings failed to challenge the stupidity of it. I do recall that it proved very effective at keeping the rain out of my eyes, which was not in itself a bad thing. Failing to discern the details of where we were riding, like large rocks or sharp drop-offs where gutters met at street corners, could lead

"Yeee-haw!"

to sudden and very painful trips over the handlebars. Beyond that (and looking at it retrospectively) it doesn't seem like it was a very good idea. But it sure was exciting at the time—though that probably goes without saying. I suppose I should consider it a gift of grace that my brain was not fried; and with that helmet resting atop the highest point of my anatomy to act as a form-fit conductor, it wouldn't have taken much.

I doubt that anyone knows how many times lightning has struck Chautauqua. I recall two incidents the memory of which retain enough current to make my brain twitch. Oddly, both occurred in the 1960s. The first happened around dinner time, and caused quite a community stir. The second occurred in the middle of the night; and while a lot of people must have heard it, its impact was pretty much confined to Mother's front yard.

Most thunderstorms arrive at Chautauqua mid-afternoon, when the day's build-up of heat to the north and west has hoisted sufficient moisture aloft to generate the cumulonimbus clouds that are the engines of midsummer storms. Chautauqua had just emerged from the backside of such a one—a run-of-the-mill affair that generated only modest wind, a respectable shower, and intermittent lightning and thunder. Nothing to draw any particular notice. So word spread like wildfire when the siren raised its doleful howl: one of those barely noticed bolts had landed squarely on the point of a conical tower roof built into the corner of the Hazlett-Jacobs home on McClintock, across the street and up one from the cottage we had owned a few years earlier. President Sam had died by the time the lightning came to dinner, but his sister Mrs. Jacobs, and her family, still owned the house, and understandably found the experience distressing.

By the time the news reached down to Mother's lakefront home, and we ran up to gawk like tourists at our friends' misfortune, everything was under control. Several of Chautauqua's volunteer firemen were just coming out of the house after checking every corner for evidence of fire and finding none. Standing in the middle of the street, I spoke briefly with Mrs. Jacobs, who was still shaking from her close encounter with several million volts of rampaging electricity. I extended what comfort and reassurance I could, which wasn't much. (I would someday conclude that helpful techniques can be taught; but true pastoral skill is the product of years of bumbling through crises and tragedies. Seminaries can't teach it; it must be learned in the field, and I hadn't been in the field long enough yet.) As often happens, the one in distress gave the greater gift. Standing there assessing the wretched scar that twisted down the surface of her tower roof, she thanked me less for my help than for my effort. But the tremble that hampered her speech betrayed the shock she still felt. It was a valuable object lesson: some experiences beget trauma that only time heals. We can be there for our friends, but we cannot always calm the strife that claws at their psyches.

I would shortly learn that for myself.

It came one August night, an hour after the last of Mother's household had settled into bed. And it came with no more warning, nor was it any more welcome, than the bolt that slammed the Hazlett-Jacobs house. The bulb in the reading lamp over the head of the bed had barely cooled when a gust of wind punched the house, shaking the windows and putting us on notice that we were about to be blessed by a night-flying storm.

Climbing back out of the bed, I stepped up the hall and opened the door to our children's room. It was a bowling alley sort of space, directly above and equal in dimensions to the open front porch that it overhung. When Mother bought the place in 1952 and had it refurbished and winterized, that had been my room. It was too narrow for more than a single bed; so when our son and daughter were born, I built a cantilevered bunk bed against the back wall, and they shared the room whenever we came to visit.

It was a light and airy room with four sash windows directly facing the lake and awning windows in each end, providing all the ventilation that anyone could possibly want. Which was precisely what concerned me: when the full fury of the storm came angling off the lake to wallop the house, things would get messy in there real quick. The children, six and four at the time, barely stirred as I shut the windows one by one, snugged the covers up under their chins, and kissed them before going back to bed.

I got no further than planting my right knee on the mattress. My left foot was still on the floor when a cosmic-sized flashbulb exploded, lighting the room ten magnitudes beyond daylight, accompanied by an ear-splitting crack so excruciatingly loud that it lifted my wife right off the bed and left me deaf for several seconds. Knowing what it was, but not where it had struck, I made it back to the children's room almost before the echo died. Both were sitting bolt upright, disoriented and terrified. Oddly, there were neither tears nor wailings.

"Daddy, what was *that*?" they quavered in such unison that they might have rehearsed it.

Relieved that the bolt had not struck their room, I felt the knot in my ribcage unlace and mustered such off-handedness I could.

"It was just lightning, kids. It struck close to the house. That's why the flash and the crack came at the same instant."

I tried to peer out the front window. It was futile. There was no street lamp anywhere along that stretch of North Lake Avenue, and the wind-buffeted rain lashed the windows with such force that I might as well have tried to peer through a bucket of black paint.

"Go back to sleep, kids. The storm will be over in a minute."

Tucking them in and kissing them for the third time in less than two hours, I dawdled for a minute, trying to reassure them by stroking their hair and cheeks, and in an amazingly short time they were dozing off again, as if nothing had happened.

In the house, nothing had. But out on the front lawn we had lost an old friend without ever a chance to say goodbye.

I went outside at first light, trying to figure out where the bolt had struck. Nothing seemed out of place until I noticed a fifteen-foot circle of chewed-up bark littering the lawn at the foot of a stately shagbark hickory tree thirty feet from the house and five from North Lake Drive. A shagbark is a wonderful, and unusual, tree. Its bark grows in long, narrow strips that separate, top and bottom, from the trunk of the tree as it matures, sometimes sticking out a foot or more in ragged slivers twelve or fifteen inches long and six wide. We loved that tree. Shagbarks grow tall and plumb, and ours was straight enough to serve as the mainmast on a clipper ship. More unusual, the tree had stood through so many seasons that the lowest branch was fully forty feet off the ground. God didn't make them better.

A sense of foreboding filled me as I stepped close in against the massive trunk and looked up among the branches. There it was, as if chiseled by a carpenter: a gouge as big as my arm that started near the crown and descended the trunk, curling almost twice around it en route. Oddly, it disappeared halfway to the ground.

"It cut inside the tree at that point," my Maine-bred stepfather explained, "and came down through the core wood." Hutch had seen a lot of trees in his almost ninety years, and I had no reason to gainsay his judgment.

"The tree will live through the rest of this summer," he predicted, "but it'll die over the winter. It'll never leaf out again."

And so it was. Summer drew to a close with no discernible change, and the shagbark's leaves fell as they had every fall since before that multitude of pilgrims gathered to welcome the very first Chautauqua assembly in the grove on the south side of our double row of houses. But the following spring, when tree buds burst up and down the lakefront, the old shagbark stood stark and stripped, locked in a sleep from which it would never awaken. The following summer, when we drove down the lakefront and pulled up on the edge of the lawn to unpack the car for our annual visit to Grandma and 'Uncle' Hutch, only a stump remained, and that cut close to the ground. Knowing it would quickly deteriorate into a hazard for anyone walking near, Mother and Hutch had it taken down.

To this day, I never pass by where Mother's house once stood without thinking of that tree. Maybe if I'd loaned it my helmet....

CHAPTER 24

Incidental Witnesses

It was during the summer of 1942 that our small band of boys crossed the Plaza, minds and mouths occupied with the usual vacuous business of 10- and 11-year-olds. The banter stopped, however, as we approached Ames Avenue. Something was up. A hubbub flowed back and forth under the portico of the Colonnade and poured off the steps to engulf anyone who happened by—like us. A friend from Club, fresh from the commotion and seeing us coming, ran across the street to meet us. His expression was one of bemusement, as if he had just heard what must be good news, but didn't know what to make of it.

"What happened?" we asked.

"They just split the atom!" He said.

Vacuous business evaporating, we stopped and looked at each other under knit brows,

"How do you know?" someone asked.

"It just came over the teletype!"

"But what's it mean?" said another—as if any of us had any idea—that day or for a long time thereafter.

We were incidental witnesses to an event of unparalleled consequence for the future of the world, but were utterly without understanding of what it might mean. Nor were our parents much better informed than we. I recall the traditional explanations, like: "If we can crack the atom, we'll get enough fuel from a cup of water to drive the Queen Elizabeth clear across the Atlantic." That was dramatic enough. It was also misleading. No one talked about enriched uranium or chain reactions or the frightful hazards of radioactivity. Few initially grasped the immense difficulty that would attend our country's efforts to develop machines actually capable of getting any useful work out of the stuff without having it turn to destroy us. And fewer yet appreciated the Faustian bargain we were about to make in hopes of harnessing nuclear energy. The devil, as they say, is in the details—never more truly so than here.

It was another jarred awakening to things going on outside the Chautauqua fence. They had been happening for months; but having no understanding about what it was that had just awakened us, we were left in more than ordinary confusion.

To spend a summer at Chautauqua (or a month or a week) was to escape all that, in more ways than one. Our purpose was not just to abandon hometown routine—jobs and schools and community activities. We meant to lose touch with the world. It was one of those periods in technological history best described as "not yet." Television, in an early stage of development by an infant electronics industry, had not yet impacted everyday life. Cottage owners had not yet equipped them with radios—nor had plans to. To be that much in touch with the world defeated the whole purpose of getting away to Chautauqua. Not yet, thank you.

And traditional rooming houses? Where few doors even had locks? And guests propped them open for ventilation anyway, content to pull a curtain across the doorway for privacy? Where a bathroom at the end of the hall was shared by everyone on the floor? Forget it. A radio would be as much a nuisance as the cellist who practiced all summer in his room one floor above Aunt Helen and Betty Jane McCafferty's rented quarters at the Eau Clair, which is to say intolerable (the Institution erected those practice shacks up by the highway for a reason!). Being forced to listen to a neighbor's radio would be akin to being dragged back into hometown turmoil before your gate ticket expired.

My family didn't even own a telephone until 1952 when Mother moved into her new home on North Lake. And forget the internet, email, cell phones, Palm Pilots, and the rest of the electronic litter by which 21st Century Americans frenetically intrude on each other's solitude, mostly to convey inanities.

Even newspapers were in short supply. Only a few editions—and those printed by publishers located within two hours by truck from Chautauqua—made it into the Bookstore. We learned of developments in the outside world largely from acquaintances lately arrived for their own vacations, or visiting platform speakers whose lectures included mention of recent developments on the national or world scene. But there was not even much of that. Lectures at the time tended toward the inspirational or abstractly educational, less often analysis of current events. It seemed a sensible thing. Most news during the decade of the Great Depression was just that: depressing. People would as soon not learn any more about it than they had to. They already knew enough, and yearned to restore their faith that life is good and the future hopeful. It was a time of willful isolationism.

Things changed in a hurry after December 1941. The Japanese attack on Pearl Harbor and subsequent declaration of war with Germany gave willful isolationism a sharp knock on the head. There still were few newspapers or telephones on the grounds, little radio and no television. But when the 1942 season opened, the quiet of the Colonnade lobby erupted with the rattle of an Associated Press teletype machine that spit out news about global events in a steady stream. Few things so quickly changed traditional Chautauqua behavior: we were privy to more news in an hour than we had been accustomed to receiving in a season. As lines of black ink trailed across the newsprint, the paper jumping from the machine so fast that it sometimes piled up on the floor, segments were torn off and hung on the wall (a new summer job for an enterprising Chautauqua teenager, perhaps?).

All through the day, a stream of folk wandered in to check for hopeful signs that the world was regaining its sanity—or at least

AP Report

that we were winning. What were the latest U-Boat losses in the North Atlantic? What the plight of captive Europe or North Africa? Had the demoralizing retreat of American forces in the Pacific theater been arrested? We children, made newly aware by war that the world we thought to inherit was a lot more dangerous than we had been given to believe, were among them. The Colonnade Lobby became the brain from which news penetrated the grounds like neural impulses through a living organism, as those most recently at the machine returned to the streets and spread the latest to anyone willing to listen.

A new program wrinkle was soon added too, to strong popular approval: Friday's 10:45 a.m. Amphitheater lecture began with a fifteen-minute news report and analysis prepared by a knowledgeable member of the Institution staff or, if qualified, the lecturer-of-the-week. Then the customary buoyancy of veteran lecture-goers turned deadly serious. People listened intently to news possessed of a life-and-death intimacy, no longer to be engaged as an abstract exercise in good citizenship. Those Fridays were among a finite number of occasions on which several thousand loquacious Chautauquans grew so quiet that the sound of a pin dropped on the Amphitheater platform was audible on the front porch of the Methodist House.

Of the thousands of stories spit out by the teletype during the war years, two remain vivid in memory sixty years later. The first was about the splitting of the atom. Then there was the other.

It clacked out on August 14, 1945—cleaner, simpler, and infinitely more welcome: Japan had surrendered. World War II was over and we had won. We had been confident since spring that it was only a matter of time. German resistance collapsed in the immolation of Berlin in April, and the Allied powers had been reassigning forces since, preparing to focus their combined fury on Japan. But we expected the end to be Armageddon. The Japanese home islands, our leaders warned, would be defended with religious fanaticism. The price of final victory would surely be measured in the deaths of thousands of Americans and millions of Japanese.

It was at that moment that the implications of the 1942 teletype story first became clear: the war would end when it did and as it did—with Japan's sudden and meek capitulation before any actual invasion got mounted—because U.S. B-29 bombers had dropped atomic bombs on the Japanese cities of Hiroshima and Nagasaki a week earlier. In two blinks of an eye, two major cities were erased off the face of the earth, thousands of Japanese citizens simply evaporated, and hundreds of thousands who survived the immediate blasts faced agonizing deaths from burns and radiation sickness, or lives of enduring misery. Japan had either to embrace the unthinkable dishonor of defeat or accept utter extermination.

But we barely noticed. The relief of having it finally over, the knowledge that there would now be an end to the killing and maiming—especially of America's sons and daughters—sent people running through the streets of Chautauqua, as through every American community, shouting the thank-God news that it was over. Even staid and proper Chautauqua dowagers hugged total strangers and shook hands and congratulated each other.

The teletype machine disappeared soon after the end of the war, and news briefings no longer preceded Friday lectures. As a nation, we were as weary of the war as we had been of the Great Depression, and yearned for a return to "normalcy"—especially at Chautauqua. It was too late. We had been so distracted by the national outpouring of energy required to win a world war that we failed to notice that other things, some having little to do with the war, were changing. There would be no turning back. The blue-gray flicker of television tubes began eerily to glow from cottage windows, radios were more often heard playing in kitchens or on porches, and national newspapers became increasingly available in the Bookstore. We were still a long way from the wireless internet bubble that now envelopes Smith Memorial Library at the south end of the Plaza. But the process had begun, and Chautauqua would never be the same. If we lost something of the tranquility that attracted us in the first place (and, by some definition, still does), we also became personally and institutionally more attuned to the world beyond the fence.

Perhaps the old teletype stole our innocence. Then again, maybe it just woke us up. The whole experience started the Chautauqua program—and us—back up the road toward the kind of passionate and engaged citizenship that, it seems to me, Vincent and Miller intended for us in the first place, and we are the richer for it—even if only a handful of us understand nuclear energy any better now than we did in 1942.

CHAPTER 25

A Handsome Stranger Named Dominic

Sprung from genetic lines among whom no one, for three consecutive generations, demonstrated any facility for art, I was either a mutation or a throw-back—and if the latter, no one could say to what. But I drew three-dimensional figures by the time I was five, and was painting pictures by third grade. It was a mixed blessing. I soon found myself ordered to "draw something" for Grandma or Aunt Maude or whoever else we happened to be visiting, or who was visiting us, or had a birthday coming. I also discovered that I could, with minimal deception, draw my way through an entire school year. It was either that or study, and I was not much motivated to study—the consequence of that undiagnosed dyslexia that haunted my entire educational pilgrimage. Observing it all, Phil Benjamin—the Allegheny College librarian who rented an apartment of rooms in our Meadville home for nine years following Dad's death—said to Mother one day, "Don is cursed with versatility." Along with music and gym class, or projects where effort, not accomplishment, earned a teacher's approval, my talent for art generated good grades clear up through college. I even earned part of my seminary tuition painting pictures (not a few of them piously and garishly sentimental) for Yale classmates. My peers, I concluded, were better theologians than art critics—probably a good thing in light of their vocational predilections.

So it came as no surprise when Mother encouraged me to register for a painting class the summer after I had "graduated" from Club. It seemed a logical step. I had taken private lessons for several years from Rebecca Lord, a popular Meadville artist, so I already owned the essentials—easel, palette, palette knives and brushes, gummy containers of linseed oil and turpentine and dammar varnish, and a box of half-squished tubes of oil pigment. All I lacked was canvas, and that was readily available at the small art school shop.

Before dawn burned the mist off the first Monday of a new Chautauqua season, I gathered with several dozen would-be Picassos in the large painting studio of the Arts and Crafts Quadrangle at the north end of the grounds. It had only three sides, actually (the quadrangle, not the painting studio); the missing side opened onto a broad lawn that fell away to the lake two hundred yards down-slope. The studio itself would have made a pretty good barn. Its unpainted board walls supported truss-work that was open clear to the roof ridge, and the bare wood floor had never been painted, at least not intentionally. It was, in fact, ornamented in a style that might be termed "Early Random Splotch," the result of forty years' worth of pigment dribbled by amateur artists who then walked around in it as they strove to become less amateur.

I can't speak for the others in the class, but I anticipated a summer of breathtaking creativity under instructor Revington Arthur, director of the Silvermine School of Art in Connecticut and, at the time, head of Chautauqua's art school. "Rev" (as he was known to acquaintances) presented a figure that could fairly be called rumpled. A mop of graying hair that appeared not to have felt comb or brush in weeks, as if he simply ran his hand through it each morning, hung down over the forehead of a ruddy, almost flaccid face. A cigarette seemed always to hang from the corner of his mouth, dropping ashes down his paint-stained and terminally wrinkled shirt. I came to imagine that the ashes of at least a carton of cigarettes were brushed into the surface of every painting he ever completed. Maybe that's why they looked the way they did. His work—at least one large canvas of which, "in progress," always stood in the middle of the studio—was crowded with foreboding. His choice of colors was heavy and convoluted, so uniformly dark (or so it seemed to me) that it was impossible to discern any variation except in direct sunlight, as if every color turned to burnt umber on contact with the canvas.

I would like to think that he helped other students to progress, but cannot claim it for myself. Affable in temperament, he wandered around the studio (scattering ashes on his students' work) talking a kind of painter's jargon that I never understood. I wished I had been registered for the landscape class. I could have wandered the grounds, chosen subjects from among scenes I had loved all my life, and avoided Rev's ashen critiques until I returned to the studio at the end of the day. But I had been signed up for the portrait section, so spent endless mornings in the studio trying to capture the image of a model in whom I had no interest. As the fifth week of the eight-week season approached, I grew increasingly unhappy. The stuff I was producing was dreadful. So I hatched a plan of escape: I volunteered to be the model for a week. Now there was a learning experience. Sitting for half-an-hour at a stretch without so much as twitching proved to be far was more demanding than being the portraitist—especially for a hyperactive teenager!

Allowed a short break each half-hour, I wandered around the quadrangle's cloistered walk one morning, looking in other studio windows to see what other students were doing. Peering in one, I was so arrested by what I saw that I was almost late for my next twitchless half hour. Next break, I returned to stand in the doorway, entranced both by the work and by the obvious pleasure of the students. During my final break, I spoke with the instructor, an older woman with a gentle intensity about her. Even as she answered my questions, she moved quietly around the room, encouraging, teaching, reminding. I was charmed. On my way home that day, I resolved to make my escape permanent: I stopped at the summer schools office in Kellogg Hall and changed my registration from painting to weaving.

For the final two weeks of the summer, I learned about loom and shuttle, warp and woof, the several qualities of threads and yarns and their advantages, and patterns like tabby and herringbone. My instructor understood that success bred enthusiasm, so bypassed the essential but tedious business of warping a loom in favor of actually making something. Sitting me down at a loom, she demonstrated how the pedals dictated what thread pattern would emerge, while choice of shuttles would determine color design, and taught me how to devise a formula to put them to work. Mesmerized, I sat for entire mornings watching beautiful fabric emerge, slowly and incrementally, but dependably—as long as I remained mindful of my hands and feet! More than once, my mind wandered until a flaw in the pattern set off an alarm. That brought another lesson: that it was harder to undo a piece of weaving than to fashion it—and a lot less fun.

About the middle of the final week, lightning struck: Mother discovered that I had resigned from Rev's portrait class without telling her. She was less distressed by my deception than by her assumption that I was doing nothing at all; and since the unrefunded tuition came from her purse (which was not that well-endowed to begin with) she felt entitled to be informed. But I didn't want to tell her because I planned to give her the incriminating evidence for Christmas. Standing silently while she vented her exasperation was one of the hardest things I ever did; and my waffling about what I <u>had</u> been doing with my time only amplified her irritation. But it was that or ruin any chance to surprise her in December. Swallowing hard, I acted sheepish and bit my tongue—and hid the proof of my connivance in the back of my closet.

It was arguably the most inspired deception of my life. Christmas morning, before the family gathered in the living room to exchange gifts, I snuck in and shoved Mother's present back behind the other brightly-wrapped packages under the tree. It worked. When the next-to-last gift had been given, I retrieved the small parcel, crossed the room, laid it on Mother's lap, and retreated to my chair without a word. For a second, as she recited the obligatory "What ever could this be?" the emotional confusion in my breast became almost intolerable. Even if she had forgotten that bruising August confrontation, I hadn't. And my delight at having so thoroughly fooled my Mother, not by lying but by silently enduring her censure, was delicious. But what if she didn't like my present? Might it re-stoke her August anger? What would I do then? Can Christmas, once tarnished, be made innocent again?

I didn't have long to fret. Untying the ribbon, she lifted first one piece, then another, a third, finally the last, out of its wrapping, held each up and studied it in turn, mystified. The four were about the same size, suitable to scarf a dresser or small chest, but dissimilar in color and weave. I said nothing, just waited, as did my siblings, who had no inkling of the history behind the gift. Finally, Mother looked at me.

"They're lovely," she said softly. "Where did you get them?"

"I made them," I replied with as much relief as pride. "Remember last summer when I dropped out of Rev Arthur's painting class? I signed up for a weaving class instead. I made them for you."

The expression on her face made her August anger worth enduring ten times over. She did not easily yield to emotion; indeed, her tough-as-nails response to life's most difficult moments was legendary. But as she sat there, the pieces spread on her lap, smoothing each in turn with her hand, her eyes welled up with tears, and I knew that everything was better than fine again.

Forty-five years later, when we undertook the sad work of breaking up Mother's lakefront home following her death, the four pieces still lay atop chests or dressers (wherever she had placed them after that feeling-full Christmas) as bright as the day they were cut from the warp. As her executor, the task fell to me to fulfill her directive—and Mother's directives were never less than emphatic!—to give to any member of her extended family such of her possessions as each might desire, without regard to value. In the end, no one had asked for the early American secretary that stood in Dad's medical office in our Meadville home until his death, thereafter to serve as Mother's living room desk for the rest of her life. So Patricia and I took it home—together with the blue-and-white scarf that had adorned its top since that

Christmas day. It is still there, reminding me of the joy—and risk—of changing art classes mid-season.

My personal nominee to receive the excellence in teaching trophy was Richard Duhme, professor of art at Washington University in St. Louis and for many years sculpture instructor at Chautauqua. Dick was not simply a fine teacher and artist; he was a gentleman in every sense of the word—kind without artifice, patient without patronizing. He never talked down to a student, even a complete novice. His eyes reflected a different light, an awareness of beauty that the rest of us had not yet discovered, and he could not help but be in love with it. Perhaps that was why his countenance was so serene. I was instantly drawn to him, and the feeling never left. I learned from him not because he demanded it of me, but because his manner made me demand it of myself.

My first subject remains my favorite—an affectionate kid with white hair, slightly-crossed eyes, aquiline nose, expressive mouth, and ears that flapped when scratched. He was maybe eighteen inches tall and twenty-four long. Oh... did I mention he was a goat?

Dick borrowed him from a nearby farm and kept him in a wire-fenced enclosure in the yard behind the sculpture studio. Almost before I knew it, I was sharing the pen with the goat, armed with a work stand, a large lump of clay, and a handful of tools—but not the Capricorn equivalent to Benjamin Spock's *Baby and Child Care*.

"Put the goat on this," Dick said matter-of-factly, lifting a chair over the fence with a teasing twinkle in his eye.

"How am I going to keep him up on it?" I asked, puzzled by how any baby animal could be kept from bolting off to explore everything in sight. But Dick was already walking away. I picked the little guy up and set him on the chair. He never moved, just stood there looking at me as if to say, "Well, when are we going to get to work?" Taking him at his word, I attacked the lump of clay, gouging, slicing, patching, and molding, trying to capture his delicate baby-animal form.

Everything went well until I knelt down on one knee to work on the belly and legs of the model rapidly taking shape on the work stand. Without so much as a by-your-leave, the kid stepped off the chair and onto my thigh. There I knelt, clay-smeared hands reaching around the little beast, trying to mold his image while his tiny hooves poked into my leg muscle, his head rubbed the bottom of my chin, and his ears batted my nose. Apparently concluding that this perch was more comfortable than the abandoned

Who's in charge here?

chair, the kid shifted his hooves slightly as if to say, "There, that's better," and froze. I don't know how long he might have stayed there. But he hadn't budged—save for his flapping ears—by the time I concluded that it was not possible to sculpt a goat that was standing on my lap. Returning him to the chair, I moved around the work stand out of reach. He bleated his disapproval, but remained the perfect model for another twenty minutes. He sat still better than I did.

I always regretted that I was not able to keep that model, not for its artistic merit (though Dick pronounced it a pretty good piece—for a beginner) but as a memento of guileless friendship. I have raised a lot of animals in my life, and have befriended many more both domestic and wild. But none was so serendipitous, or won my heart with such ease. He stamped his image into my affection in a fraction of the time it took me to form his in clay.

The following week, Dick upped the ante. We arrived Monday to find a handsome stranger named Dominic waiting in the studio—a swarthy young man from Jamestown with finely chiseled features, black eyes, and dense, lightly curled hair and beard. He was, Dick announced, our model, and the assignment was human portraiture—the hardest skill of all to master. It was like being back in Rev Arthur's painting class, with one exception that I quickly embraced: Sculpting is a 360 degree enterprise. Before long, the half-dozen students in the class were circumambulating Dominic like dancers around a Maypole, weaving in and out and dragging our work stands after us. Impressions that didn't work from one angle could be amended from another. It was an exhilarating discovery—and just plain fun.

Dominic's sharply-drawn features were a real help to our neophyte class—but not enough to deliver us from a pitfall universal among greenhorn sculptors. By the second day, as globs of clay became recognizable as models of a human head, we studied each others' work and made a startling discovery: there were not six likenesses of Dominic taking shape in the room; there were likenesses of six students—so pronounced that, had we scrambled our work stands, an impartial judge could have matched art to artist without apparent difficulty. Having let us first discern this for ourselves, Dick moved quickly to confirm it:

"Beginning sculptors, working from a live model, inevitably sculpt themselves rather than the subject. Part of the task of learning to be a sculptor is to see the model before you rather than your features reflected in the model."

That quickly, we also learned that amending a clay likeness, once formed, is a lot harder than shaping it in the first place. And that led to a second, more difficult lesson. A piece of art—even a bad one—takes on a life of its own and resists change; but unchanged, it fails as portraiture. It was one of the few points at which Dick pushed us, hard. Sometimes, we discovered, it was necessary just to throw something away and start over. But doing that required us to leap over the other hurdle that hampers amateur artists: an unwillingness to let go of our precious creations. Having fashioned them, our natural impulse was to preserve them, to resist letting go. We had not yet learned that first efforts should be treated like pencil sketches: an experiment to be learned from and discarded. If Dick allowed us to cling to faulty work, we never would move on to something better.

I didn't have to let go of Dominic, as it turned out. I was prepared to, assumed I should, was about to, when Dick arrested me with a compliment.

"Your head has a lot of you in it," he admitted, assessing it through narrow eyes, "but it also has many features that are faithful to the model. It's worth keeping."

"Keep it? Is that possible?" I asked. "Won't the clay dry and become brittle?"

"Oh, you won't keep the clay head. It will be lost in the process of reproducing it in plaster-of-Paris."

For the rest of the week, he painstakingly talked me through a seven-step process to do just that, detailing a dozen do's and don'ts along the way, lest I reach the step where the clay model had to be sacrificed, never to be recaptured, in order to secure the plaster image. I could only imagine how frustrating it would be, having come so far, to fail at just that moment of transition. I may never in my life have remained so focused on a teacher's instructions.

Through the weekend, my plaster head—faithful in every detail to the one I had created from clay—stood curing in the dark and empty studio, bone-white and sterile. I didn't think it very pretty, to be perfectly honest, and told Dick so. He reassured me that there was more to be done, and that I would find the result more than satisfying.

Come Monday, he proved it.

"The next step is to create a base for your head to stand on. It needs to be stable enough to prevent it from toppling over. But it also should be artistically pleasing, something that will complement the work without detracting from it."

For once, I had the answer.

"Uncle Edgar," I said.

"Come again?" Dick asked.

"My uncle lives in Blockville, about ten miles away. He has all kinds of hardwood. I know he'll give me something that will work."

And he did. Uncle Edgar, our father's only brother, owned a woodlot—a northern hardwood forest in miniature, actually. Next day I was back at the studio with a lovely piece of maple. Again pressing me to the work, Dick guided me in shaping and staining a block the color of dark honey, with a strong post angling up into the hollowed-out center of the plaster image. Then came the best (and to me the most surprising) part of all: dressing the barren white plaster with a five-layer veil of shellac, three colors of artist's oil paint, and graphite. In the end, you'd swear that Dominic was cast in bronze.

Finally, Dick paid me the best compliment of all:

"The Plaza art show is next week. I think you should register your head in the portrait division."

The annual Plaza art show, sponsored by the Chautauqua Art Association, was an all-day exhibit, demonstration, and general celebration of creative effort at which all Chautauquans were welcome to display the products of their artistic labor, and sophistication was not a consideration. Who was I to argue?

Early on the assigned morning, I labored toward the Plaza lugging a large cardboard box in which Dominic lay, nestled in wadded-up newspaper. My arms ached long before I found a place to put him down. Twenty pounds of plaster-of-Paris came as close to defining "dead-weight" as anything I could imagine—or wanted to. All day long, "my head" stood atop a large folding table among other sculpture entries, gazing up the Vincent walk as if looking for a friend to arrive at the Main Gate. And all day long, interested Chautauquans streamed by, weaving their ways in and out among two-dozen rows of art and craft work created by a thousand pair of hands. As was always so, the work reflected a range of both talent and training, from neophyte to expert; but in aggregate it illustrated the uniquely Chautauquan ingredient of excitement at learning to do something new, or of learning to do it better. So I was stunned when I retuned as the late afternoon sun lit Dominic full in his westward-gazing face, to find a bright blue ribbon laid across the corner of the maple base bearing the golden words, "First Prize." It was doubly gratifying, because I knew that my teacher was not the judge.

I think often of Dick Duhme—and not only because, for years after, he greeted me warmly every time we ran into each other on the grounds, his kind eyes still aflame with wonder at the beauty of created things. I recall him to mind because his thoughtful instruction ensured that I would always own a tangible illustration of good teaching. Half a century later, as I sit at work on this book, Dominic—all unyielding twenty pounds of him—looks across my study from the top shelf of a bookcase, indifferent to having been packed up and moved several dozen times—two of them coast-to-coast. More than once his surface got chipped or damaged. But so thorough was Dick's instruction that I have been able to repair him, making him look as fresh as on the day he stood in the middle of the Plaza gazing into the setting sun, oblivious to the blue ribbon laying across his base. But there's more; I can still detail for you every step of his construction, from slapping the first lump of clay onto the work stand to applying the last graphite highlight to the bridge of his nose.

That is one tough piece of art.

CHAPTER 26

The Valued Possession of the Many

It was earlier than we were accustomed to being up and about. By family tradition, our leap from bed was triggered by the first clangor of the Bell Tower chimes that filtered through the trees of Miller Park and ascended the hill, putting Chautauqua on notice that a new day had begun. In Chautauqua's own version of nepotism, the chimes were played by Arthur Bestor, Jr., son of Chautauqua's 6th—and arguably one of its finest—presidents. For as long as I could remember, each dawn recital began with the same descending scale, every day of every week of every season. (Chautauqua cannot be accused of slighting that tradition, either!)

Mother's capacity for near-military coordination conditioned us to the point that we were nearly able to make our beds in the act of climbing out of them. In rapid succession, then—and served by a single bathroom—four of us managed to wash our faces, comb our hair and get dressed; prepare and eat breakfast; wash, dry, and put away the dishes; brush our teeth; retrieve our swim suits and towels off the back porch clothesline; and mount our bikes for the ride down the lakefront in time for the 9:00 assembly that launched each day at Club.

But today was different. Mother summoned us from bed an hour early, threatening the morning routine with a measure of chaos. So it was, when we rode up McClintock and south along Pratt Avenue that Norton and Normal Halls, Hurlbut Church and Kellogg Hall were still dark and bolted, and would remain so for another half-hour before most Chautauquans were roused by the morning chimes. The grass was dew-strewn and cool as we rode through the Plaza, its giant sugar maples still holding back the bolt by which dawn intended to fire the pillars of the Colonnade. And such light as penetrated to ground between the Amphitheater and the Methodist House vanished when we passed beneath the massive trees that shadowed the junction where Pratt merged into Clark Avenue (though no one I knew called it Clark; it was simply "the brick walk"). By habit, we strung out single-file to thread our way between the twin, ball-topped iron posts that spiked Clark's intersection with each cross street, making clear to motorists that they were not welcome on the walk. Those posts carried so many coats of white paint that they resembled bleached elephant hide. The paint may well have outweighed the iron cores within; and when one got seriously chipped, the cavity looked to be a half-inch deep.

Few people, and less noise, disturbed the early stillness. Habit placed a restraining lid on voices obedient to years of official pronouncements calling for quiet between 11:00 p.m. and 8:00 a.m. Only the hum of our bike tires rippling across the bricks was audible, a rolling figured-bass line upon which the birds composed a soprano obbligato.

The minute we saw the dozens of bikes already littering the grass in front of Alumni Hall's angular Victorian bulk, we knew we'd arrived not a moment too soon. Dozens of children ranging across half as many years of age milled about on the walk and clustered on the porch, awaiting their assignments.

The CLSC (shorthand for Chautauqua Literary and Scientific Circle) was founded in 1878 by John Heyl Vincent—only one of several hundred novel ideas generated by a mind whose originality seemed as inexhaustible as it was visionary. "Education," he argued, "once the privilege of the few, must, in our earthly estate, become the valued possession of the many." That vision undergirded his establishment of the CLSC, the world's first and most enduring book club, at a time when only a miniscule fraction of Americans received a formal higher education. Most could not afford to absent themselves from the essential business of eking out a living to attend college, even if blessed with the financial resources to pay for it—which few were. But the hunger was real enough, and it bordered on starvation: Vincent announced the organization of the CLSC on August 10 of that year, expecting at most that a few dozen would participate. Before the week was out, registrations were in the hundreds; and they surpassed 8,400 by the close of the first year.

At a time when a "typewriter" was still a human being, not a machine, the clerical demands alone must have been staggering. But that didn't stop Vincent and his colleagues. In the next few years, they set thousands to work at home, reading four serious books a year and writing reports on what they had learned, and how it might make a difference in their lives and that of the world.

From the start, Vincent and his colleagues realized that the experience would be enhanced if readers worked in groups, sharing their insights and debating the issues. Overnight, reading circles sprang up like cone-flowers in a prairie summer, and not just in America. Folk in other countries, better informed than we tend to give them credit, clamored to join. Soon they, too, were reading, their reports flowing in from halfway around the world.

As typically happened when people of diverse languages and cultures began to explore and share ideas, global friendships began to sprout. Through the offices of CLSC's leadership, reading circles abroad were put into contact with classmates in the U.S., while Americans were encouraged to write to readers half a world away. It would have been fascinating to be part of those friendly exchanges, slow-paced precursors of our computerized chat rooms, a global intercourse in culture and opinion. Many of their exchanges were lost, because they remained both personal and scattered. But many were captured, too, and remain the heritage of the CLSC to this day.

My favorite, learned not at Chautauqua but from a source the reference for which, I regret to say, got lost during one of Patricia's and my serial, cross-country migrations, involved an American churchman who had never heard of Chautauqua. A rare Cold War visitor to the Soviet Union, he attended the Sunday gathering at Moscow's Baptist Church—the only Protestant congregation permitted the privilege of public worship during the Communist captivity of the Russian people.

During the service, he later reported, a curious ritual was observed: on signal from the minister, the worshipers lifted white handkerchiefs over their heads, held by one corner so that the cloth hung down limply. Slowly, ceremoniously, in silent unison, they lowered their hands. Fascinated, the visitor later asked his hosts what the ceremony meant. It was, they replied, to honor their dead, and was a custom received decades earlier, before the

Bolshevik Revolution in 1918, when members of the congregation formed a reading circle under the sponsorship of an organization in the United States called the Chautauqua Literary and Scientific Circle. A pen-pal correspondence sprang up with CLSC members in America, who responded to pleas from the Russians for stories about Chautauqua, its character and history and customs. Among them, the visitor was told, was the description of an annual tribute to deceased Chautauquans, called "the drooping of the lilies," observed every summer on Old First Night, Chautauqua's official birthday celebration. So moved were the Muscovites that they adopted the custom and wove it into their Sunday liturgy during the portion of prayer called the Communion of Saints, where it had been observed since. Bursting with curiosity, the American visitor returned home intent upon learning more, and visited Chautauqua for the first time.

After completing their four-year course of study and fulfilling the expectations of the program, CLSC members "graduated." Commencement occurred on Recognition Day in August of each summer. Economic constraints or sheer geographic distance prevented many graduates from participating. Indeed, many enrollees—especially those from foreign lands—never got to Chautauqua in their lifetimes. For those who did, however, the exercises were a solemn but high-spirited business. Convening at the foot of the shady, two-square-block grove where Merrill and Fletcher Avenues intersect, the graduating class passed through the Golden Gate (a privilege strictly reserved for them) and ascended the rising path and broad steps that led into the Hall of Philosophy, Chautauqua's version of the Parthenon Temple in Athens and the CLSC's historic meeting hall..

Clothed in white, the graduates seemed a procession of angels into heaven, their path blanketed by a mid-summer blizzard of flower petals thrown down before them by pre-schoolers enrolled in the Children's School who, dressed in their frilly Sunday best and bearing floral baskets, had processed all the way from the opposite end of the grounds to pay tribute to grown-ups they did not know for achievements they did not understand—but loving every minute of it. Around the children gathered a large and light-hearted aggregation of CLSC alumni, come to welcome these latest inductees into their ranks.

It was that procession that we set off to join on our quiet morning ride. We had signed up to carry class banners—multi-hued and mottoed paraments representing successive CLSC graduating classes. Emblematic of the years that had passed since the founding of the CLSC, each banner was designed by someone among the alumni who marched behind it. Ornate or simple, they shared two features in common: their graduation year and a class motto. Some mottos were adopted from some person of letters whose writing symbolized a class's collective literary journey; others an idealistic phrase reflecting a consensus among its members about the events of the day. The latter were more likely to be chosen during periods of global turbulence, like a world war, and were inevitably more political in temper.

We children didn't care what motto a class had picked. On the other hand, it didn't much matter, because we were given no choice as to our assignments. Banners were handed to each of us according to our height, the smallest pennants to the littlest bearers. It made perfectly good sense to the parade organizers to do it that way. But we children saw it differently. We eschewed 19th Century banners, tried even to avoid the pre world War I years. Because we yearned to carry the banners of classes that graduated in the 1920s and 30s, at the appearance of which eager hands thrust forward and children began to vibrate with enthusiasm, like school kids flailing their arms in the air and muttering "Me, me!" in hopes the teacher would call on them to respond to the one question for which they thought they had the correct answer. Our motive was entirely pecuniary. By the mid-1940s, infirmity and mortality had seriously thinned the ranks of the early classes. And the point of carrying a banner wasn't to collect the .25¢ stipend budgeted by the CLSC; it was to collect the often generous tips pressed into our palms at the end of the procession by members of the classes whose banners we carried. An ill-suppressed groan could be heard escaping the throat of some youngster handed the emblem of the class of 1894 or something equally ancient. And ill-disguised envy was directed at the lucky kid who was handed the banner of alumni still short of their tenth reunion.

Finally, when the last banner had emerged from the cavernous and allergenic rooms of Alumni Hall for its one-day-a-year in the sun and fresh air, and chronological order had been established among the bearers, the whole entourage unwound like a gigantic, polychrome centipede walking in reverse. Herded by volunteer adults and paced by the bass drum boom of a small marching band, its music reverberating brassily off the close-set cottages lining Clark Avenue, we banner-bearing and tip-hopeful children followed it all the way to the Plaza, where generations of alumni waited. The procession halted when the youngest banner (that of the previous year's graduating class) reached the junction of the brick walk with Ames Avenue, across from the Colonnade. There we executed a grand about-face and, the band again in the lead, started south again. First in line, in the place of honor, went the hand-painted and gold-fringed banner of the Chautauqua Literary and Scientific Circle, picturing the original, white-wood Hall of Philosophy, followed by the tots of the Children's School toting their baskets of petals. Finally came the increasingly populous stream of alumni, now in ascending order by class, who poured off the Plaza curbs and fell in behind their class emblems.

The trip back down the brick walk required more care than the earlier one up it. On our way to the Plaza, I had an open field, so to speak, with little to hamper my progress except an occasional tree branch that hung down far enough, if I grew careless, to entangle the top of my banner pole. Walking south, however, I was caught up in the helter-skelter enthusiasm of alumni, some of whom (especially the more elderly among them) tended not to march with a lot of precision. Thus pressed before and behind by walkers only scantily focused on the task, and blinded by the banner hanging six inches in front of my nose—especially if I happened to have been given one that was almost as big as me—I was in constant danger of whacking some hapless alumnus of the preceding year's class on the noggin. While the alumni were generally tolerant of such awkwardness, it was still embarrassing, especially when one of my troop rushed forward to assist—usually making matters worse. A banner with four or five hands grasping for the pole was a banner out of control. I always had the edgy feeling that the tips I hoped to receive at the end of the procession would be reduced by some fraction per whack.

By the time the most recent classes joined the procession, the head of the creature was long gone from sight, well beyond the Amphitheater, and was only minutes from its terminus at the Hall of Philosophy. There it applauded and cheered that year's graduates, newcomers to the ranks of world-class readers, ensuring that, decades into the future, Chautauqua children not yet born would have the opportunity to carry *their* banner—and receive their coveted tips.

Lined out along the ten blocks between the Plaza and the Hall of Philosophy, Chautauquans of all ages waited to cheer the alumni on, calling greetings to those they recognized and exchanging light-hearted banter—with one exception. Something like a hush invariably came over the spectators as the first class banner passed, as though a bubble of reverence was floating along at the head of the column. Even the sporadic clapping and calling out of greetings that erupted along the line of march, as parade watchers spied friends in the procession, became sustained and respectful, as befits the veneration in which sensible communities hold their true elders. These were the Pioneers, members of the very first CLSC class in 1882. When they graduated, they were 1,518 strong and hailed from thirty-five states, the District of Columbia and five foreign countries. Inevitably, their numbers ebbed with each passing year of my youth until only two—a woman and a man— remained to march. But they proved to be astonishingly durable. Their names were Jessie Duncan Grassie and John M. Edwards. At the time they graduated, she was from Massachusetts, he from Pennsylvania. Years after I lifted my last banner, there they came, side by side, silent, erect and dignified. Among the hundreds of color slides I took over the years of Chautauqua in action, none is more prized

The Last of the Pioneers

than the 1956 image of the two of them, both in their nineties, leading progressive CLSC generations in solemn procession.

Something tangible was lost the year they first failed to appear, some touchstone of human flesh by which we Chautauquans compassed our community history and were still able, by pressing their hands and hearing their voices, to know that we were exchanging greetings with someone who had heard the voices and touched the hands of John Vincent and Lewis Miller. Involuntarily, I find myself still looking for them each summer that we are at Chautauqua on Recognition Day, and feel a void when their station passes, silent and vacant, along the brick walk.

Yet there is something soothing even about their absence. There are those who think that the CLSC is a quaint anachronism, an irrelevant remnant of a bygone era. Perhaps it is. Yet Chautauquans—even those who graduated from college, some who went on to earn doctoral degrees—continue to join, to read, to graduate, and to process in undiminished numbers. Some suggest that this is because Chautauqua is an ivory tower unstitched to the world of real human events. I prefer to think that it is because we know our history. Indeed, as a group, Chautauquans are not only as aware of their history as the majority of citizens in any community in the country; they are far better-informed about world events as well. It is not because Chautauqua makes them that way; it is because they make Chautauqua that way. And the procession that winds its way down the brick walk every summer is a conduit to our past. Somewhere up ahead, out of sight around the curve of time but still leading the way, walk the shadows of generations who not only claimed to value learning but were willing—in their own times and to the limit of their own resources—to pursue it until they earned the right to pass through their own Golden Gate. And that, Vincent would smile, is what it's all about.

PART 9

On the Lakefront

CHAPTER 27

Learning the Hard Way What They didn't Know

C lub had just dismissed at the close of a not-very-fun day. Agitated by a chill wind that had come huffing out of the northwest, shoving a dark tangle of low-flying clouds, the lake had grown restless. It was not the kind of weather that made young children eager to do much of anything outdoors, least of all strip off their clothes to go swimming. But at Club, twice-a-day swimming was so ritualized that little short of a lightning strike cleared the waterfront. Cliff and Frank were getting ready to head home when their attention was drawn to something floating about four-hundred yards offshore. The simple fact that it was visible was enough to get their attention. Anything that could be seen floating that far away had to be pretty big; and anything that big floating in the middle of the lake was a curiosity.

"What do you suppose that is?" they asked each other.

"Dunno," they answered each other.

It appeared as an elongated hump, hugging the surface. Concern began to rise, however, when several smaller shapes bobbed up, seeming to accompany the hump but not to be part of it. By silent consensus, the realization dawned on them that those were human heads, and the bodies they were attached to were in the water.

With hardly a pause for breath, they ran to the boat ramp, grabbed an extra pair of oars, and shoved off in one of the Club's large rowboats. With twin pairs of oarlocks and double oars in the hands of experienced rowers, those boats got up and moved, and my brothers were soon sprinting toward whoever it was that was out there. Their fears were confirmed as they closed in on a capsized boat with four fully-clothed men hanging onto the belly-up hull. And they were in serious trouble. Two could barely talk, and one showed no sign of even realizing they were there.

"What happened?" they asked the man who seemed most alert.

"We tipped over...a mile or two up the lake...we've been in the water for an hour."

At least the men had known enough to hang on to their boat. It was their only salvation: they had ventured out without life preservers. But they didn't know enough to right their boat and climb back into it. Even swamped, it would have floated under them, and they could have paddled toward shore with nothing but their hands. That effort alone would have helped them stay warmer. But they just drifted while the wind carried them down the middle of the lake, no closer to shore than when their boat capsized. Given their state by the time Frank and Cliff got to them, there was every likelihood that, dazed by hypothermia, their judgment and resolve gone, they would weaken one by one, lose their grip, and slip away long before their boat—perhaps only their boat—fetched up on Prendergast Point.

Brothers to the Rescue

Rescuing such a dismally unqualified quartet was touchy business, and my brothers knew it. Hauling four half-comatose men into a rowboat with little cooperation on their part was prickly work. Seldom did the rigorous training that Club provided—and which Cliff and Frank by then were teaching to younger children—pay off so handsomely. Pulling in so close that they almost ramped their boat up on the bottom of the overturned craft, they helped three of the men work their way to the bow and stern of the Club boat. The fourth man—the one who failed even to register their arrival—didn't move. So desperately were his fingers clamped to the upended keel that they might as well have been frozen there. He seemed not to comprehend that it was time to let go. Finally, Cliff reached out, grabbed the man's wrists one at a time, wrenched his hands loose, and replanted them on the Club boat between his companions.

Once the four victims were secure, Frank and Cliff turned their attention to their overturned boat. Gripping whatever came to hand, they rolled it upright to break the suction that held it fast down in the water and lifted the bow, balancing it on the gunnels of their own boat. When most of the water had sluiced out the back (and while the men in the water looked on as if watching a miracle unfold—which for them it was), they rolled it onto its topside again and dragged it aboard, where it lay athwart their boat as if they had just landed a huge fish. Satisfied, they flipped it back over onto its keel, launched it back into the lake, and secured its bowline to the Club boat's stern cleat.

Then came the hardest part: painstakingly, they hauled the half-drowned castaways one by one into the Club boat, making sure that each man already aboard shifted his weight as necessary to stabilize the boat as the next body came up and over the side. Finally, everyone secured, they laid to on the twin oars and headed for shore. Given the added burden of four sodden men and the just-resurrected boat trailing astern, the row home understandably took longer than the trip out.

It was two wearied brothers who nosed the Club boat in to the waterfront dock to be greeted by a considerable welcoming committee. Word of what was unfolding on the lake had spread rapidly among the professional staff, half of whom—Tom Moore, Andy Landis, Sheridan Hardenburg, Paul Arnold—were on the dock to help the waterlogged foursome, cold, miserable, and grateful, out of the boat. By the time Cliff and Frank, the rescued tub still hitchhiking at their stern, rowed around to the ramp and hauled both craft out of the water, the victims had disappeared, hustled upstairs where several wives of senior staff had gathered blankets and boiled up pots of coffee. By the time someone arrived to retrieve them, they were only half-dry, but a lot warmer, and more than ready to go home.

I suspect they were also wiser than when they set out that morning.

It was inevitable, living at the edge of water, that we would be witness to more than a few events where someone needed rescuing because they went about learning the hard way what they didn't know. I don't recall a summer of my youth when

Chautauqua Lake did not claim at least one life. Biking the lakefront drive four times a day to Club and back, it was hard to miss the grim business that followed each loss—a flotilla of boats summoned by the county sheriff's office in Mayville, crisscrossing like a caucus of troll-fishermen, but following the lines of an imaginary grid laid out on the surface. They weren't out for muskellunge or northern pike, either; they were "dragging the lake," as the sad expression had it, trailing grappling hooks in hopes of snagging the body of someone who drowned in deep water and sank to the bottom.

Lakes, rivers and seas are, after all, insensate. We love to speak of their "personalities" or "moods" or "behavior." But our tendency to anthropomorphize does not change the hard truth of the matter: they will neither to help nor to harm the human beings who are drawn to them, because they will nothing at all. Yet they, and all who venture onto or into them, are alike subject to natural law—mindless, immutable and unforgiving. Chautauqua Lake was an exquisite playground for those prepared to learn the rules and abide by them; but lacking sensibility—moral or otherwise—it had no mercy on those intent on writing their own rules.

There was the man who took his family to a July 4th picnic at his fraternal lodge's campground, across the lake below Midway. He decided to take them out in a rowboat, but he was drunk, and for that alone his friends should have chained the boat to the dock and bodily pulled him out of it. But they didn't, and it soon became apparent that he was ignorant as well. He couldn't swim, and knew next to nothing about rowboats. More by random thrashing than anything, he got the boat fifty yards from shore where, with a particularly inept motion, he dislodged one of the oar-pins from its lock and lost his grip on the oar. Having no experience, and failing to realize that the oar he still possessed could serve as a paddle, he leaned out in a vain effort to reach the oar, already twice as far away as he could stretch, lost his balance, and fell out of the boat. He never surfaced. Frantic cries from the family brought help, but it was far too late. Plunged into the cold water head down, disoriented by weightlessness, his judgment clouded by alcohol, the man probably struggled deeper and deeper, searching frantically for the surface that was somewhere above his feet.

Not all tragedies involved alcohol abuse, however, or occurred during the summer. Arriving home on Thanksgiving break from Allegheny College, I looked out toward Mayville to see the too familiar and macabre sight of drag boats once again tracing the invisible grid. It was a cold day on the cusp of winter. Weighted with the promise of snow, clouds that seemed too heavy to rise higher than a thousand feet were driven before a bitter west wind that stirred the uniformly battleship-gray lake into a ragged chop. Unless they were extraordinarily well-prepared, the people in those boats had to be miserable. None would choose to be out there on such a day but for the hopeless mercy that moved them. They knew that the best they could do was find the lifeless but still precious body and return it to its family, so they had something tangible to grieve over.

I found Mother peering soberly out the picture window in the dining room.

"What happened?" I asked.

"It's a Mayville boy," she replied. "Today was his fifteenth birthday, and his parents apparently gave him an outboard motor boat. He couldn't wait to try it out."

"On a day like this?" I asked, incredulously.

"Apparently so," she said. "They found the boat circling in the middle of the lake, empty."

She turned away. Living year-round on the lakefront, she had seen enough. It was never easy for her to look anyway; but she was doubly troubled because she had so many times swallowed her anxiety as her own children headed out onto the lake, convinced—in spite of our years of training—that God's mercy, not our skill, brought us home to supper. Her heart ached for the boy's parents. Imagine giving your child the one present he probably had coveted most of his life, but failing to make him wait for a better day. It promised to be an anniversary forever haunted by grief and self-accusation.

I was pretty sure I knew what had happened. Ecstatic at his luck, but lacking enough judgment not to push it, the boy headed out onto the water. It would not do just to cruise about for a while, giving the motor a chance to get "broken in," as all motors then required. He must see what it would do, and opened it up. That far, the damage might have been confined to the motor, but its life expectancy was still greater than that of its young master. Boys have a congenital need <u>not</u> to use the seats in small outboard motor boats; they must perch on the gunnels athwart the motor where they can feel the full thrill of the ride. Nor had the boy sense enough to wear a life preserver—the more needful because he was out there alone.

Given the chop, safely operating a 14-foot outboard would require care. At high speed, it would dance around like a Mexican jumping bean, leaping and bucking in response to the erratic waves. And the bounding could only have been accentuated by the boy's decision to ride the stern gunnels. His weight, combined with that of the motor, would pull the boast's center of gravity to the rear. At every surge, the underweight bow would leap into the air where it was subject to the careening wind. Keeping to a straight course under those conditions would be next to impossible, and the boy compensated by jerking the motor back and forth. It was only a matter of time until the boat, wrenched by the conflicting forces of wave, wind and motor, threatened to capsize. Already on the low side of that fling because his weight tilted the boat to his side, and failing to have an iron grip on something, the boy was thrown backward out of the boat and into the frigid water. I can only imagine how shock turned to terror as he righted himself to see his boat bounding away at top speed, leaving him a mile from land in any direction while his clothing, suitably heavy for a November day, filled with frigid water. Even simple strokes needed to keep his head above the waves demanded a supreme effort, while cold sapped his strength and his saturated garments dragged him under.

Standing in the dining room, I watched the depressing, snail-paced waltz of the drag-boats that sought to return all that was left of their son to his family before he was lost altogether. And I reflected again on how swiftly our beloved lake could penalize heedlessness with enduring consequences.

Fortunately, not all crises ended so badly. And no description of Chautauqua Lake rescues would be complete without recalling the most dramatic one of all. (I suppose that's a bit hyperbolic. The rescue efforts that attended the burning of one or more of the old lake steamers must have been pretty dicey. But having occurred before my time, they are beyond the reach of my memory.)

It began in Virginia, actually, at the Norfolk Naval Air Station, when a pair of single-engine tactical bombers took off on a training mission. Their objective was Buffalo International Airport, which they were to attack by stealth. Their counterparts in Buffalo, unaware of their approach, were being tested at least as much as the flyboys. Their flight plan directed them to Jamestown, where they dropped below the line of hills bordering Chautauqua Lake, off Buffalo's radar. Flying up the center of the lake to

Mayville, they were to hedge-hop over the continental divide, drop in against the bluffs along Lake Erie's south shore, and skim the surface all the way to its eastern end. If all went as planned, they would roar into the Buffalo airport at roof-top altitude before anyone saw them coming.

They never made it—but not because Buffalo saw them coming. They were way too low for that. So low, in fact, that one of the pilots, glancing down at his instrument panel somewhere between Miller Bell Tower and Point Chautauqua, failed to notice how close to the water he truly was. In the kind of second-splitting that transformed A-OK into Mayday before he could even utter the words, his propeller blades struck the surface and immediately bent back over the engine cowling. Stunned by the cracking jar, the pilot instinctively jerked back on the stick. In a sickening arc, the plane lifted a few hundred feet off the water, stalled at apogee, and plunged into the lake. Even before the colossal splash of its impact subsided, the plane plunged below the surface, and did not stop until it came to rest on the bottom in thirty-eight feet of water. The hapless pilot's wingman pulled up and banked into a gut-crushing turn only to see the point of impact vanish. Nothing smothers evidence more quickly, or more efficiently, than deep water.

On the bottom of the lake, the sunken pilot worked frantically to extricate himself, knowing his cockpit would flood the instant the seal was broken; and the pressure of thirty-eight feet of water is crushing. Human lungs lack the strength to draw breath against the pressure of more than a few feet of water—a realization that dawned on me the first time I strapped on a snorkel and diving mask. He would have one chance, no more. Popping the canopy, he kicked desperately to get loose from the cockpit and pulled the ripcord on his mae west.

On the surface, meanwhile, high comedy threatened to submerge anguish. Every boat within eyeshot rushed to the scene and milled about, creating so much turbulence that no one any longer could tell just where the plane had gone down, much less where the pilot might come up—if at all. Confusion was further compounded by the dramatic arrival of an overzealous sheriff's deputy so distracted by the unexpected call to function in a genuine crisis that he lost track of himself. Rushing this way and that in his speedboat, he bellowed, "Cut your engines! There's a gasoline slick on the water! Cut your engines!" The millers-about could be excused for their amusement at the contrast between his words and the cigarette hanging from the corner of his mouth, trailing sparks and ashes into the wind that he himself was creating.

The agony of uncertainty evaporated as the pilot suddenly broke the surface with an explosive gasp. (I still don't understand why he didn't crack his head on the bottom of one or another of the boats that, by then, constituted an aquatic parking lot.) He later confessed that he didn't think he'd make it, that his lungs felt like they were on fire by the time he burst into delicious air. He also said that he was more terrified than he had ever been in his entire life. Who can blame him? It was a touching admission from a man who flew war planes for a living.

Don't go looking for the plane, however. It isn't there. It was crammed with sensitive equipment and cost the taxpayers a cool million and a half. The Navy wanted it back. A salvage team arrived a few days later. Divers ran a mile-long cable to the plane from a winch set up on Point Chautauqua, and harnessed giant air bags to the fuselage. Inflating the bags just enough to free the plane from the bottom muck, they signaled the winch. The cable went taut, and the plane flew slowly toward shore at negative-35 feet altitude. Each time it ran aground, they repeated the process. Finally into shallow water, they manually lowered the landing gear. A short time later the plane rolled up on shore, where it stood for several days before the wings were removed and it was hoisted aboard a flatbed truck.

Several of us drove over to see it before it got away. It was remarkable. Except for the contorted propeller blades, the craft exhibited no signs of damage. And the divers, climbing out of the lake and stowing their gear, shook their heads in wonder and reported that, in all of their dives, they had never seen so many fish.

CHAPTER 28

A Pretty Good Definition of Successful Fishing

*C*hautauqua Lake attracted many serious fishermen, but none more serious that Fred Heinz, the father of five whose coming of age at Chautauqua pretty much synchronized with our own—Babs, Sally, Peggy, Skippy, and Ginger—and if I never meet a handsomer quintet, I won't have missed much. (The Heinz home and dock on South Lake Drive were magnets for young people—especially admiring young men.) Skip and I traveled through Club together.

Mr. Heinz owned an unassuming Chris-Craft cabin cruiser named *Whitecap*, and no boat at Chautauqua—perhaps even on the entirety of Chautauqua Lake—spent more hours of more days of more seasons plying its waters. Commuting from Pittsburgh every weekend, Mr. Heinz took no longer to park his car, change his clothes, and cast off in *Whitecap* than most people did carrying a suitcase upstairs to their room.

Hour after hour, he trolled up and down the lake, one fishing pole bracketed to starboard, another to port, both trailing several hundred feet of line at the end of which wriggled a large, sparkling lure. And Mr. Heinz wasn't after small fry. His prey was the mighty Chautauqua Lake muskellunge, a member of the pike family. Full-grown—and lucky enough to have avoided the hooks of the likes of Mr. Heinz—a "musky" could reach forty inches and tip the scale at twenty pounds, dominated by a head-full of vicious, dagger-like teeth that confirmed its standing atop the food chain.

When John Vincent and Lewis Miller first arrived to assess the Fair Point campground as the site for their Chautauqua Assembly, fish of that caliber could be had in half-an-hour of intelligent fishing. It was not by happenstance that muskellunge was featured on the breakfast menu served President "Teddy" Roosevelt when he visited Chautauqua in 1905. And there was more: northern pike nearly as impressive, large- and small-mouth bass weighty enough that a single fish sufficed to make dinner for a family of five, and pan fish too numerous to imagine—perch, bluegills, sunfish, and rock bass. But years of increased fishing pressure inevitably took their toll. Only a few real monsters were left by the time I became conscious of how addicted a man might become to musky fishing, and fewer busting-with-pride fishermen came home with the kind of trophy that sent ripples of excitement up and down the waterfront, drawing people from blocks away just to see it. But the musky was still king, and Mr. Heinz was out for royalty.

Whether he caught many or few, I never learned. You'd think that any man who devoted that much time and fuel to it must have caught a good many. Or, if he didn't, it must have been because he didn't want to. Maybe he wasn't after musky at all, just wanted to be out there, free for a while from the demands and frustrations of life, to relish the serenity of being on the lake alone. Now that I think of it, Mr. Heinz was almost always alone.

But, few or many, I did learn about one fish that he didn't catch. It must have been around the summer of 1950. Chautauqua County's commissioners decided that a law enforcement presence was needed on the lake. I never understood why they thought it appropriate. Chautauqua Lake was not notably overrun by scofflaws needing apprehension. Whatever their reasoning, it was sufficiently compelling that they voted to extract enough tax dollars from county residents to purchase a pair of speedboats and employ deputies to operate them—like the one who so agitatedly appeared at the spot where of the Navy tactical bomber took its ill-fated plunge. And they made them obvious: painted white with large blue letters on both sides, as tall as the boats' freeboard would allow: SHERIFF.

Let it not be assumed, however, that vigilance overpowered common sense. Living around a lake like that, more than one officer—including the sheriff himself—had the foresight to throw his fishing pole and tackle box into his patrol boat, just in case there wasn't much to do on the water that day—which there usually wasn't. So it came to pass that Mr. Heinz, trolling slowly down lake one morning, passed the sheriff moving smartly northbound, presumably completing his appointed (pre-fishing) rounds. Mr. Heinz was no stranger to anyone who spent much time on the lake. As their boats converged, the two men acknowledged each other with a wave, and the sheriff called, "Morning, Mr. Heinz."

An hour later, still without a nibble and coming in against Prendergast Point, Mr. Heinz executed a languorous half-mile wide turn and started back north. Long before he came in sight of home, he again encountered the sheriff, coming south. The sheriff didn't cruise on by this time, however; he came around easy, parallel to *Whitecap* and close as he dared go without tangling with the trolling line that stretched, taut and quivering, from his side of the boat.

"You should stay home, Mr. Heinz," the sheriff teased. "I just caught a 32-inch muskellunge off the end of your dock." Indeed he had, lifting almost a yard of fish off the floor and holding it up for the startled Mr. Heinz to see. Grinning in supreme satisfaction, the sheriff lay the fish down, saluted smartly, peeled off, and sped down the lake.

I never learned what, if anything, Mr. Heinz said when he got home. But the story spread around the grounds with the speed of gossip which, as everyone knew, was only one microsecond slower than the speed of sound.

While many around Chautauqua took their fishing seriously, not many matched Mr. Heinz's single-minded passion for it. And there were a few—among whom I count myself—who went fishing less to indulge the pastime than to indulge an appetite for fish.

It took a while for me to get the hang of it. As a child, I fished off half the docks along Chautauqua's north shore, learning pretty much by trial and error until, finally, I hit on as surefire a system as I either wanted or needed.

Years later, while chaplain of Northland College on Wisconsin's Lake Superior shore, I met a charming older gentleman and consummate trout fisherman. Having devoted half his life to it, he penned a manuscript the title of which ("Coming Up to Trout Level Thinking") reflected his singular blend of wisdom, humility, and panache. I moved away before he was able to get it published; but if he succeeded in doing so, even experienced trout fisherman could learn something of value. The idea first came to him, he said, on the day he told his wife he was going fishing and she responded, "Oh, good. I'll call the Connors and invite them over for dinner. They love trout." In his wife's view, there was no longer any difference between him saying, "I'm going fishing" and "I'll bring home trout for dinner." He was that good at it.

I was delighted by his story because, in a more modest way, my trial-and-error education earned me the same success as a Chautauqua teenager. Except the quarry was rock bass, and the meal was breakfast.

Early on, Chautauqua Lake docks were most often suspended between posts driven into the lake bottom. And the broad "tees" at the ends of most docks, particularly those where large boats tied up, were hung from posts slotted into permanent cribs— heavy wood boxes filled with large rocks. Over time, as docks increasingly were set on portable horses so they could be easily removed from the lake for winter storage, the cribs were abandoned. As their wood rotted, the stones settled into loose piles on the lake bottom. They were seldom disturbed further—unless they happened to lie in someone's navigation lane. Having your speedboat propeller chewed to scraps or shearing the pin on your outboard motor justified the labor needed to move the offending boulders. Left alone, however, collapsed cribs provided important habitat, attracting small fish in need of places to hide from all those toothy members of the pike family.

Just such a crib lay abandoned on the lake bottom a few yards off the end of the dock belonging to the Reid Babcox family at 7 North Lake Drive. It was fifty feet south of our community dock and, because it stood in deeper water, was twenty-five feet shorter. Soon after we formed the north shore association that owned and maintained our community dock, I discovered the Babcox crib by accident. It was late on a splendid summer evening. The sable air was motionless, the lake smooth as glass, as I stood quietly on the end of our new dock casting a jitterbug in a fan-shaped pattern, starting north and working around south, just to see what might turn up.

My jitterbug was a squat little plug, rather like a roma tomato with a triple hook dangling from its belly, and hollow so it floated. Affixed to its snout was a concave oval made of bright metal, nearly as wide as the plug was long. Dragged slowly across the surface, it bobbled back and forth, sounding like a small animal thrashing its way to safety after falling in the lake.

It drove bass nuts.

Standing on the dock that night, hardly expecting any response, getting none, and not caring (one of those few occasions when just

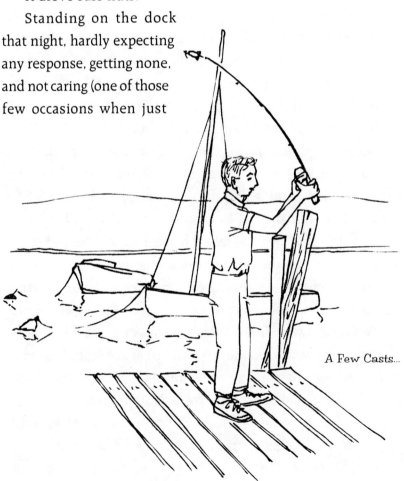

A Few Casts...

fishing was good enough, catching anything was secondary) the angle of my casts came around until I finally dropped the plug a few yards from the end of the Babcox's dock. That's when I first suspected that the old crib was there (a discovery confirmed a few days later when I put on my diving mask and flippers, and swam over to check it out). The jitterbug had bobbled its way across the water for all of ten feet when the peace of the night was startled by a wet sucking sound and my pole was almost jerked from my hand. For most of a minute, I worked to reel in the light monofilament that throbbed with resistance. Whatever was out there, it wasn't coming willingly. The only light at the end of our dock consisted of whatever was left over from street lamps and porch lights, the closest of them fifty feet beyond the beach. So it wasn't even clear what I had caught when I caught it, until I was able to pull it out of the water and hold it up toward shore. Only then did I recognize the silhouette of a rock bass easily ten inches long—the biggest I had ever seen.

Not expecting to catch anything, I had neither bucket nor hold-line to secure it, so walked in off the dock and dropped it on the beach to await cleaning. But not yet. My appetite was whetted, not just in anticipation of how good it would taste, but by the thrill of that pole jumping in my hand. Back on the end of our dock, I abandoned the fan pattern and again sent my jitterbug arching straight toward the Babcox's dock, heard another strike disturb the night, and brought in a second bass as big as the first.

Two casts, two fish. That was my kind of fishing.

Twisting my arm around to catch a shard of light, I squinted at my watch: 11:10 p.m. The bewitching hour, I thought, and quit. I knew that I would be enjoying my fish alone next morning. No one else then at home would likely join me—even less would any of them volunteer to kneel on the beach with me at 11:15 at night, cleaning bass by flashlight.

Next morning, I dropped the two fish into a small bag in which I had combined several tablespoons of flour with a dash of salt and pepper, shook them, and gently laid them in a skillet bubbling with melted butter. It was the first time I had cooked fish myself, and I was caught off guard by how quickly they got done. I had barely poured a big glass of orange juice and made a couple of pieces of toast when it was time to lift the steaming bass from the skillet and carry it all out onto the front porch. I had eaten a good many meals on that porch already—and would eat many more out there in the years ahead. But none equaled, in flavor or satisfaction, that breakfast of orange juice, toast, and piping-hot, butter-soaked rock bass fresh from Chautauqua Lake.

That single event set my fishing style for fifteen years. Every summer that professional duties allowed me to get to Chautauqua, I waited for the first dead-still evening, walked out on our dock at 11:00 p.m., and cast my jitterbug across that rock crib. And every one of those summers, I sat down the next morning to relish the blessing of two or three rock bass fried in butter.

It was enough. I never fished at any other time or place, or needed to. I knew just where to go, and when. Best of all, I knew that when I did, I'd bring home what I went for. And that's a pretty good definition of successful fishing.

Oh... I never told the Babcoxes. They were fine neighbors. But some secrets, like a surefire place to catch bass, were too valuable to share with anyone—even if it was right off the end of their dock.

CHAPTER 29

The Long Swim

I would not want to claim that I never did anything really stupid in my lifetime. Some of the stupider among them are covered in these stories. But one of the dumbest was the time I followed Cliff on the long swim.

It may well be among the dumber things that <u>he</u> ever did, too, although I am reluctant so to demean my eldest brother. I never allow myself to forget that it was he who struggled to be an example to Frank and me after Dad's death. That's a heavy burden for any ten-year-old to pick up and carry for a decade.

Besides, Cliff was not, for the most part, given to doing dumb things. I make bold to defame him concerning the swimming incident because he already authorized me to tell the story about the sailing incident. That would be the time when the lake was on a howl and he took it into his head to go sailing in his *Lightning*. Alone.

Several things need to be clear at the outset.

First, Cliff had sailed his *Lightning* solo many times. He loved the sport like few other things in his whole life.

Second, he was good at it. Twice—first while crewing for Miriam "Mim" Sample in her Lightning, then with John Bierley, with whom he jointly bought a boat—he helped to retire the Lightning trophy. That means that they won the pennant three years in a row—more wins in six years than many people get to experience in a lifetime. (Still, in my opinion, they were better at sailing a boat than they were at naming one. Johnny was going into law and Cliff into medicine. A friend—clearly an inspired individual—suggested they call their Lightning *Scheister-Quacker*. Exhibiting a total lack of panache, Cliff and Johnny instead painted the thing black and named it *Raven*. I never forgave them. But I digress.)

Third, while remarkably seaworthy, a Lightning normally carried a crew of three including the skipper. When the weather got really rough, some skippers opted to add a fourth hand, not to throw the original two overboard.

None of which fazed Cliff. So what if the lake was behaving like a wart hog that had stumbled into a bee's nest? He would go sailing anyway. Nor was it that cautionary counsel was lacking. Mary Ann and Sally Evans, good friends and seasoned sailors themselves, were there, and spoke up.

"Gee, Cliff, is this a good idea? Shouldn't you maybe reconsider?"

"Nah," Cliff snorted. He would not be dissuaded.

By his own accounting, he had barely reached deep water when the boat convinced him that there was a lot more to do on that rough a day than one pair of hands could manage, and tipped over. Now, a Lightning has few drawbacks; but one of them is that, when it capsizes, it quickly fills with water; and if care is not exercised, it turns turtle. That means that the centerboard points at the sky and the masthead at the lake bottom. Under any circumstances, righting it is a tough job.

That seemed dumb even by my standards. But not necessarily dumber than the next maneuver.

It was hot on the day in question. A brilliant sun pounded the water and the breeze was barely enough to wrinkle the surface and scatter the light as sparkles. Such hot days were rare on the Chautauqua lakefront, especially along our stretch of it where an onshore breeze reliably pushed the coolness of the lake up the lawn and through our kitchen door. That day was an exception. A short swim was just what was needed to take the edge off the heat that had been building since sun-up. I was halfway out the dock before I realized that Cliff was standing on the end. He looked like his mind was focused on something very far away. It was. Without a backward glance, he dove in and swam out into the lake, angling south at a languorous crawl.

"Cliff," I shouted from the end of the dock, "where are you going?"

"To Sample's boathouse," he called over his shoulder, hardly breaking rhythm.

I stood a moment, considering the matter. The Sample's imposing home stood atop a steep slope above the ball diamond, alongside Hawthorne. A Roman numeral V had been cut through each left-hand shutter, and an X through the right, symbolic of Paul Sample's position as chairman of the board of the G.C. Murphy Corporation, operator of thousands of five and dime stores across America. But it was a long way from the lakefront, so Paul arranged to build a handsome sandstone boat house at water's edge, fronted by a substantial dock. The boathouse was a favorite gathering place not just for the family but for half the young people of Chautauqua. Paul and his wife Helen Heinz Sample, niece of the founder of the H. J. Heinz Co. in Pittsburgh, had four daughters: Miriam, Dorothy, and twins Rebecca and Matilda. That gender profile was significant: it imparted a decidedly male cast to the company who called at the boat house. And Cliff's interest in Miriam was more than casual.

Beyond that, Helen Sample and her two sisters, known affectionately as Auntie Helen, Auntie "Iz" (Elizabeth) McCreedie, and Auntie "Beck" (Rebecca) Lytle were, as that appellation suggests, surrogate aunts to every kid in Chautauqua. With them, we felt free to share our dreams and fears, and to confess things we'd never admit to our parents. They listened patiently, reproved without condemnation, and counseled with wisdom—the quintessence of the trio of good fairies in Walt Disney's movie version of "Sleeping Beauty."

But let's get real. Samples' boathouse was at the south end of the grounds, beyond the Boys' and Girls' Club and easily a half-mile bicycle ride. And it was some further when the route was a hundred feet off the Bell Tower point and the length of the south shore mooring area that stretched from the Institution boat dock to the south bathing beach. None of which appeared to faze Cliff any more than had the weather the day he climbed abroad his Lightning and sailed off into disaster. A stroke at a time, his arms rose and fell and a fountain of water erupted in the wake of his powerful flutter kick.

Watching him go, anxiety welled up in my gut. He was out there alone—as clear a violation as I could imagine of the rules drilled into us about safe swimming. But I was even more concerned because he was headed out where a lot of boats, some of them power boats driven by people paying only marginal attention to what they were doing, came and went around the Bell Tower Point at high speed.

To this day, I cannot explain why, but I dropped my towel on the dock, dove in, and set off after him and discovered three things in rapid succession. First, the distance separating our dock from Miller Bell Tower doubled in the fraction of time that it took me to dive into the water. I felt like Alice in the land beyond the looking glass, where things instantaneously change to suit their own pleasure.

Second, while it was easy to see Cliff from the dock, it was anything but easy once I was nine-tenths submerged myself. Looking across the water between strokes, I periodically saw his arm flash in the sun, or his head lift as he checked his bearings. At other times, I wasn't sure he was there at all—which did nothing to ease my apprehension about us being out there, or how either of us would explain to Mother if the other of us got run over by some inboard jockey. And who would be able to explain to her at all if, borrowing from the language of probate, we were "taken in a common disaster"?

On which—third—boats looked a whole lot bigger, and more dangerous, when I was thirty yards off the Institution boat dock with nothing but my head above water and no assurance whatever that the people running them saw me nearly as well as I saw them.

I suppose that I might also have considered whether either of us was in condition to make that kind of swim in the first place. But to be perfectly honest, I wasn't thinking about conditioning right then; I was mainly concerned to reach the boathouse without getting my backside lacerated by a propeller. That we were in any kind of condition at all was a credit to the training we received at Club, and to the fact that most of us who grew up summers at Chautauqua spent several hours in the lake almost every day of the week.

Still, what conditioning we had was none too much, and the lack was evident by the time I passed the Athenaeum. I could have quit at any time, of course—just turned in toward shore and climbed out at the nearest dock. But there was the pride thing. I had started out after my big brother; and even though real weariness began to set in about the time I realized that neither of us would likely get run over by a boat, my craving for his approval wouldn't let go. So even if, poking past the bathing beach, the distance left to Samples' dock seemed about equal to what we had already covered (though it was at most a tenth of it), I couldn't bring myself to give up. Looking ahead the last forty yards (the gap between us had not materially changed since we swam away from home) I thought that Cliff climbed up the ladder onto Sample's dock much more slowly than usual. Until I got there myself and wasn't sure I'd be able to climb up it at all.

As it turned out, the trip hadn't been worth it. No one was there, and we still had to walk all the way home—barefoot and

Almost There

wearing nothing but our bathing suits in an era when Chautauqua regulations specified robes over bathing suites for anyone going to or from the beach. The south shore waterfront was never that long before, and I intended to make sure that it never was again. Cliff could swim off alone next time he insisted on going. I'd stifle my brotherly concern.

He never did. And from the way my body ached the next two days, I'm pretty sure I know why.

CHAPTER 30

"What's the Course?"

The door was open when I stepped up on the Hukill's porch at 38 South Lake Drive. It was about 10:15 on a Saturday morning. I tapped on the screen door, opened it, and stepped into the living room.

"Hello," I called

"Hi!" Nancy Hukill's smiling face appeared in the kitchen door. "Coffee?"

"Love some."

I pulled out a chair at the dining room table and sat down. Sally emerged from the kichen, two mugs in one hand, a steaming pot in the other, and eyes smarting because smoke from the cigarette hanging out the corner of her mouth had gotten into them. After a couple of years, our Saturday morning kaffeeklatsch was something of a ritual. Sally was my crew of one during the summers that I was vice-commodore of the Chautauqua Yacht Club and responsible to run races every Saturday and Sunday afternoon from late June to Labor Day. Given that we averaged six to eight hours together every weekend of the summer, anchored somewhere or other aboard *Shadow*, it's good that we got along so well.

And we did it in every kind of weather imaginable. Except for a hurricane, nothing I knew of ever persuaded Yacht Club aficionados to stay off the lake. They would race, and that was the end of it. Was the day sultry hot without a breath stirring, the whole fleet bunched together on the starting line like cows waiting for the barn gate to be opened at milking time? Sally and I sat and baked with them. Were gale-force winds shoving boats around the lake as if the devil was breathing fire behind them, while *Shadow* rolled and heaved and strained at its anchor line? You could count on us. If we didn't look like summer apples by day's end, we looked like drowned rats. Having lived through ten to twelve weekends a summer like that, we developed a camaraderie that made even the worst of it seem like part of the fun. So I'd stop for coffee every Saturday morning and we'd clear signals for the weekend.

Sally sat down at one end of the table and slid an ashtray over beside her saucer. Drinking our coffee, we engaged in the obligatory round of gossip by which friends keep up with the stuff of each other's lives and families and communities. After a few minutes, Sally brought the conversation back to business.

"Is the course set?"

"All set," I responded. "Point Chautauqua, Lighthouse Point, home. We'll set up off the Bell Tower."

One eyebrow lifted mischievously. "Are you sure of the wind?"

"Sure as I can be," I replied, refusing to be baited. It was the guessing game that I played every weekend, and the part of the job I enjoyed most: predicting at nine in the morning what the wind would be doing at two in the afternoon, and laying out the course accordingly. I was only badly wrong once that I recall, but that was enough. I had to postpone the race half-an-hour while I crossed the lake to reset one of the buoys. It was more trouble than it was worth, and I didn't care to repeat it. Sailors do not like postponements. Drinking the last of my coffee, I stood to go.

"Another cup?" she asked, lifting the pot.

"No thanks, Sally. I need to buy gas for the *Shadow* and grab some lunch. I'll pick you up at the end of your dock at one."

"Good enough," she smiled. "I'll be ready."

Standing on the beach that morning, swamped by the reverberations of the eight-o-clock chimes, I studied the lake. The far shore was completely obscured by a dense wall of fog that lay up the middle. Unusual that early in the summer. Still, the sky overhead was mostly clear, and the breeze was light out of the south. I couldn't feel it from where I stood, in the lee of the point. But it was there, betrayed by a flurry of ripples that moved up the lake out beyond the Bell Tower. Still, to be sure, I walked around the corner and across Miller Park until I could see the flag pole atop the Athenaeum Hotel's truncated tower. It was the highest thing on the waterfront, and a more accurate indicator of air movement than anything at lake level. As it did on every summer morning when the wind was likely to come on fine for afternoon sailing, the flag floated gently on a south-easterly drift of air. Returning to the beach, I studied the sky again. Such high-altitude wisps as were evident were moving smartly from the northwest.

"Good," I thought. "The wind will shift around to the northwest early this afternoon. It should be a perfect day for a three-point race."

My mind settled, I walked out on the dock and untied *Spook*, the rowboat we acquired when *Gleep* had run its course and was sacrificed to the gods of the Labor Day corn roast. It was a step up, as rowboats went. A round-bottomed fourteen-footer, oak ribbed and clad in cedar, it handled well in rough weather yet was light and maneuverable, perfect for getting to and from *Shadow's* mooring, thirty yards off the end of our community dock, no matter the weather. I tied *Spook* to *Shadow's* stern cleat, mounted the yacht club's lightning bolt pennant in the bow socket and the Union Jack at the stern, and checked the bilge (it was dry) and the fuel tank (it was dryer than I liked). With a final glance at the fogbank (it hadn't shifted), I cranked the engine, pulled *Spook* around to the bow, and traded cleats on the buoy, setting *Shadow* free. (I had seen others learn the hard way that it is unwise to cast a motorboat loose before starting the engine. On some days, boat engines don't start, and one can drift into a lot of trouble discovering which days they are.)

I brought *Shadow's* bow around due north, where Point Chautauqua was supposed to be, out there beyond the fog bank. Finding it might not be easy. Driving a boat blind on a dead-calm day too easily led in a circle, or at least well off course. I had nothing to go by except *Shadow's* own trail. Once into the fog, I looked ahead only often enough to be sure that some fisherman hadn't materialized twenty yards dead ahead, but otherwise steered by looking backward, nudging the wheel this way or that just enough to keep the wake arrow-straight. It worked. After what seemed like more time than the trip should take, I glanced forward to see the Point Chautauqua pier dead ahead and a few hundred yards distant. There was less haze there than out in the middle. I was reassured. It meant that the fog was confined to the lake—cool air lying on warm water—not a blanket that covered half the county and might keep coming all day.

I reversed *Shadow* to a stop, lifted one of the marker buoys out of the stern cockpit and threw its anchor overboard.

Watching the anchor line unravel, and sure it was not tangled, I tossed the buoy out after it, brought *Shadow* around to the west, and headed back into the fog, watching astern as long as I could, to keep my union jack aligned with the Point Chautauqua pier. I didn't have to run blind for very far that time. While yet a half-mile from Lighthouse Point I broke out into sunshine. Another good sign: the fog had started to lift. Terribly pleased with my meteorological prowess, I ran in a hundred yards from shore, dropped the second mark, and steered home on Miller Bell Tower.

Feeding myself lunch and *Shadow* twenty-five gallons of fuel, I checked the lake one last time before starting out. A fresh northwest breeze had blown the fog to memory and was churning the expanse of water that stretched from Miller Bell Tower to Hartfield Bay into white caps. It was going to be a splendid sailing day.

Sidling in against the Hukill's dock, I grabbed a piling long enough for Sally to clamber aboard and shoved off again. Five minutes later we threw the third marker buoy a hundred-fifty yards off the Bell Tower point, moved fifty yards closer inshore, and turned *Shadow's* nose into the wind. As we drifted to a stop, I heaved the sharp-tined stockless anchor over the bow, waited for the line to snap taut indicating that the anchor had snagged the bottom, and cut the engine. While Sally assembled the clipboards and laid out the flags, I raised the flag staff, mounted the signal cannon on the bow, set out a box of blank 12-gauge shotgun shells, and loaded one into the breach. We were in business. We might have looked like a river-raider from a low-budget movie, but we were arguably the most distinctive committee boat in the history of the Chautauqua Yacht Club.

"What's your watch say?" I asked Sally, checking my own.

"About One twenty-eight."

"Good." At 1:30 I pulled the cannon's lanyard and punched the knob on the stopwatch hung around my neck. Before the watch needle twitched, an ear-splitting thud flamed from the muzzle of the cannon, and acrid smoke enveloped *Shadow's* bow. Simultaneously, Sally ran a pennant up the flag staff and ten echoes bounced back at us from the shore. With that, the entire fleet was put on notice that the first race would begin in precisely half an hour.

Up and down the lakefront, brilliant patches of white bloomed alongside two-dozen docks as the fleet made sail. One by one, they cast off and converged on *Shadow*.

"What's the course?" someone hailed as each boat got in range. Lifting a large megaphone, I pointed my mouth at them.

"POINT CHAUTAUQUA, LIGHTHOUSE POINT, CHAUTAUQUA."

They veered off, having learned all they needed to know. Such a triangle was both the most common, and the most popular, kind of course. The first "leg" was straight upwind, called a "tack" or "beat-to-windward." The second leg was across the wind, and was called a "reach." If the course was well-designed, the wind would be exactly perpendicular to a boat's long axis as it sailed between the first and second marks. The final leg was called a "run," and was directly downwind toward home. It was on such a third leg that a boat equipped to carry one, mostly among the Lightning class, flew a spinnaker—a giant "pillowcase" (as Lightning sailors often called them) that rode high and forward and spotted the lake with galloping splotches of color that never failed to thrill lakeside visitors or to set camera lenses snapping.

Soon we were hedged about by huge spreads of sail as fifteen C-Scows—shallow, flat-bottomed boats like streamlined barges with a single giant "mainsail," the fastest boats in the fleet—jockeyed for position downwind of the starting line. Each boat's start was official when its mast crossed that invisible line that ran between the *Shadow's* flag staff and the third buoy marker. The best skippers positioned their boats not just toward the windward end of the line—where they could "blanket" other boats by blocking the breeze—but in a position to move across the line at the instant the starting flag ran up the staff. Timing was everything. A boat that arrived too early and had to fall back lost its advantage. One that came on time but hit the line too fast had to stall, "luff" its sails to dump wind, then scramble to get under way again at the flag. It was tricky business; any boat that hit the line under full sail at just that instant tore right on past them.

A few boats in each class were at a disadvantage, however: their crews didn't own stopwatches, and had to try to track the time between the half-hour warning gun and the start of the race on a wrist watch. Being off by only a few seconds made the difference between crossing with the lead boats and being caught in their backwind. To even things up a bit, I called the final countdown through the megaphone for the benefit of the stopwatchless:

"FIVE... FOUR... THREE... TWO... ONE...." The cannon boomed, the flag snapped up, and fifteen milling C-Scows suddenly formed up and moved as one, as if the fleet was on review. With the breeze up and huffing, fifteen boats crossed the starting line as close-hauled as they dared in such tight quarters, sails so taut they hummed and masts heeled over thirty to forty-five degrees. Fifteen skippers, one hand grasping the tiller and the other tugging on the sheet (the rope that controlled the position of a sail), rode with their derrieres hanging out of their boats; and fifteen crew members, clear outside the boats, planted their feet on the leeboards and leaned back as far as possible to hold their boats down and hustling.

Clean Start

It was a clean start, with no one to challenge. It wasn't always so. If a boat's mast crossed the line before the signal, it was disqualified and must be challenged.

"C-43, YOU ARE OVER THE LINE!"

Sailors got really irritated when I called them on a faulty start. To get back into the race, they must haul about, drop below the line, and start over—a process sure to be accompanied by a lot of very loud and colorful language. To turn a sailboat around so that the wind crossed its stern—a maneuver called a "jibe"—was difficult; and if a strong wind caught the sail on one side of the boat and flung it across to the other, it could be downright dangerous. More than one sailor, like a ball hit by a bat, had been knocked right out of a boat. But there wasn't much choice. It was that or lose out altogether. Only the best sailors could accomplish it and still have a shot at finishing among the first three boats, in order to score points for the race. The maneuver was not made easier by the fact that the Lightnings, jockeying for position for their own start five minutes later, began to crowd the line almost as fast as the C-Scows relinquished it.

The Lightnings were the second to race because they were the second-fastest. On the other hand, though slower than the C-Scows, a Lightning could sail through weather that would knock a C-Scow flat. It was the heavy-weather boat of the fleet. Because it had a jibsail—a second sail in front of the mast, which the C-Scow lacked—and often carried that spinnaker for downwind legs (experienced skippers even used them on a reach) a Lightning carried a skipper and two crew members.

Again the cannon bellowed, the flag shot up the staff, and the Lightnings beat off to windward.

Finally, the rest of the fleet came online. Most were Comets that looked like a Lightning's little sister, carrying a skipper and single crew member. The Comets were accompanied by a potpourri of other small boats too few in number to have a "class" of their own—periodic Snipes, Thistles, Highlanders, Flying Scots, and whatever else had come out that day to join the fun. They crossed the line like a Mummer's Parade, everyone wearing a unique uniform.

By the time the Comets and their entourage got under way, the lead C-Scows—like greyhounds chasing a mechanical rabbit—were already bearing down on the first mark. And on days when the wind was really on a howl, the smaller boats were barely out of hailing range when the lead scow barreled across the finish line.

Once again, the mast was determinative. Sighting along the line, I tugged the cannon's firing cord at the instant the mast obscured the buoy, informing the whole north end of Chautauqua lake that the C-Scows had a winner. Then Sally's job got complicated, as she recorded the finishing order of each boat. That wasn't difficult as long as they crossed one at a time; but when three or four boats bunched up, fighting running duels all the way from the second mark in an attempt to blanket and overtake each other, it took both of us to get the thing straight. On occasion, three or four boats crossed in such close company that we had barely more than the diameter of their masts by which to determine their places.

But that wasn't always the worst of it. C-Scows were so fast that they sailed two races each day, but the second couldn't begin until the slowest boat completed the first. Which meant that they might still be jockeying for position at the starting line, maybe thirty seconds short of the gun, when the lead Lightning boomed across the line, spinnaker aloft and yielding to no one. God help us if, in our excitement, we fired a finish gun for that Lightning that some of the C-Scow skippers mistook to be their starting gun. We might not have survived the protest that followed. The Lightning just had to wait for its victory signal; and like as not, by the time we got one off, it was halfway home and the crew no longer cared.

Those days never ended with a whimper. First came the rest of the Lightning fleet, the proud spinnakers prancing by in rank order. But there was always the possibility that the fastest Comet would overtake the slowest Lightning; and the best-handled C-Scows, tearing around the course for the second time, might yet pass half the fleet. I still recall the crass but good-humored amateur whose brand-new and spinnaker-less Lightning lumbered across the finish line in tandem with the winner of the second C-Scow race. Responding to the C-Scow's cannon, he rose to his feet, bowed expansively in *Shadow's* direction, and yelled across the open water: "Thank yew! Thank yew!" I couldn't resist: I shoved another shell into the cannon and gave him a one-gun salute.

PART 10

Coming of Age

CHAPTER 31

Grubbing out a Living

When Cliff answered the knock on the door that spring morning in 1947, George L. Follansbee stood on our front porch. Friends, regardless of age, knew him as Shorty, and few Chautauquans could match his resume of service to the community, including his 1963-64 interim year as president of Chautauqua Institution. Shorty's nickname may have been physically, but never spiritually, appropriate. The victim of polio as a child, he carried the consequences his whole life. But no one who ever watched him coach a ball team—or play the game himself—questioned the grit that was crowded into that abbreviated body. Generations of Chautauquans who knew little about him beyond his faithful service as head usher at Sunday worship in the Amphitheater assumed that he must have been assigned the job by John Vincent, and just never resigned.

The question remained: what was he doing on our front porch? Shorty was not one to meander around an assignment.

"Cliff, we need a counselor at Boys' Club. Will you take the job?"

Cliff was taken aback. He attended club for a month when he was 9, then all season from his 11th to his 14th year. Now, four years later, he was being asked to come on the staff. He was, to put it mildly, nonplussed. Shorty sensed it, and gave him some breathing room.

"You think about it," he concluded, "and let me know. Could you do that by tomorrow?"

"Okay," said Cliff, grateful for the delay. He really wasn't sure he was up to it, or even that he wanted it. It had come so fast.

Mother—who had a way of cutting through the bewilderment in such cases—helped him sort it out. It was, she pointed out, a signal honor. He had not applied; Shorty had come to him. That alone was a fine compliment. And he would help to cover his own cost for being at Chautauqua. (In addition to a modest stipend, Club counselors received season gate tickets.) Besides, she insisted, it would be a wonderful learning experience for him.

Cliff rode his bike down to Club and accepted the job the next morning.

None of us realized, at the moment, that his was just the camel's nose in the tent door. Brother would follow brother, mostly because people assumed (on the basis of conjecture, not evidence) that if one Skinner was good, two would be better, and three outstanding. In any event, over the next few years we were brought on board chronologically until—that remarkable summer of 1951—the Skinner brothers had charge of three of the four boys groups at Club. That was chronological, too: Cliff was senior counselor of Group 4, Frank of Group 3, and me of Group 2. Who knows? Had there been another of us, we could have run the whole place! Absent that, Group 1 remained in the able hands of Andy Landis—who had been counselor to several of us during our own Club days.

Those were heavy summers, rife with as much responsibility as I ever want to carry; but blessed, too, with a run of fine junior counselors, several of whom became enduring friends: George Reed, youngest son of another life-long Chautauqua family and, during our college years, fellow barbershop quartet singer (but that's a story for another chapter); Graham Wightman, companion on a week-long camping trip into Canada the week before we both went off to college; William "Bill" Baldwin, the embodiment of a cooperative spirit.

Indeed, looking back now at the *Chautauquan Daily* report listing the whole Club staff that year is an exercise in emotional recall.

Andy Landis was assisted by Ralph Barlow who, five years later, would be my classmate at Yale Divinity School; Tom Klingensmith, another multi-generational Chautauquan; and Jack Hazlett, McClintock neighborhood pal and grandson of the Chautauqua president. Frank's crew was made up of Pete Peterson—literally a native Chautauquan (he lived there year-round); Texas Kimball; and two of my Clubmates and lifelong friends: Jim Braham, who was also a classmate at Mercersburg Academy, and Bill Karslake, who would one day become an Institution trustee and chairman of the board. Cliff's team included Craig Atwater, yet another of my childhood associates, and Tom Rowe, who was nicknamed "Rowboat" because so few seemed able to understand that his last name rhymed with growl, not grow. Childhood friend Skip Heinz was waterfront associate. And another, Ronnie Barnes (who could pitch a softball so fast underhanded than I dared not blink my eyes as he went into his windup, for fear the ball would smack the catcher's mitt before I got them open again) worked with the newly organized high-school-aged group that evolved into SAC, for Senior Athletic Club.

Reading the roster of the Girls' Club staff makes nearly as great a demand on my memory banks. Serving on the staff in some capacity were all four of the Sample girls, the three Evans sisters, two of the Heinz daughters, one of the Jones girls, and Joan Callahan, a strawberry blond from Alabama with a drawl like magnolia honey who was Frank's steady girl until both of them went off and married someone else.

It would be difficult to imagine a more appealing bunch of young people with whom to work and share so large a responsibility. Most of us had gone through Club together; and suddenly, there we were, making it happen for a new generation of Chautauqua's children. I never quite got over my anxiety about whether or not I was up to doing it right.

Still, the experience was exceptional for me because it was the only time in our lives that my two brothers and I were in the same place at the same time doing the same job. Within the year, Cliff was off to medical school, and time would soon enough pull Frank and me in our own directions. But for one brief shining hour....

On the other hand, I would not want to leave the impression that most of the jobs we had to help our family be at Chautauqua were so elevated. Many weren't. And there was (or so it seems to me) an age-specific deterioration in the level of refinement the jobs possessed.

Ruth Ann's, for instance, were most dignified: she worked several summers waiting table in the Eau Claire dining room.

And Cliff—following his "graduation" from Club—spent a summer as janitor of Smith Memorial Library—a job that, from my perspective, ranked as elevated in spite of its title. At least he got to be in there with all those neat books.

However, his appointment raises a corollary question. How was it that the Skinner children managed to land all those good jobs when so many other Chautauqua youngsters, including a lot of our friends, were also interested? The competition had to be pretty fierce. We concluded, on later reflection, that our several employers—many of them Mother's friends even before she joined the Institution staff—were motivated by something other than our credentials.

Frank was convinced of it, because he was hired on for two summers as the janitor of the CLSC's Alumni Hall, which just happened at the time to be under the supervision of Mother's good friend Myrna Marsteller. This is not to suggest that these were simply patronage appointments. We were good workers. After all, we were trained by an expert. And while we might not know that she had a hand in securing us an assignment, we knew perfectly well that she would not tolerate any of us doing a poor job.

So for two summers, Frank put his home-chore training to work in Alumni Hall. He cleaned all those rooms that dripped with antiques, helped to set up punch-and-cookie receptions several afternoons a week, and was called with some regularity to go up to the girls' dormitory on the third floor because a BAT had gotten in (screech, howl, shriek). None of Chautauqua's older structures (and there were many) escaped a periodic bat invasion because, sooner or later, at least one of the poor critters, nesting innocently in the attic, missed a turn somewhere and ended up indoors rather than out.

Such incidents were more frequent then, because there were so many more bats. And face it: to the chiropteran inhabitants, Chautauqua's old attics must have seemed a cross between heaven and a maternity ward. They were, Mother contended, the reason Chautauqua had no mosquitoes. I cannot attest to the ecological accuracy of her observation, but I can assure you that any mosquito that stuck its proboscis out would not likely last until morning.

I recall, with wonder, standing on the end of our dock on a dead calm evening, unable to find ten square yards of water that did not have at least one of the tiny beasts winging over it, for as far as I could see in every direction. How many tens of thousands must there have been? They flew so low that they sometimes touched the surface, twisting this way and that, over and under each other in an aerial acrobatic so intricate that it was mind-numbing. But not once did I see two of them collide. They were not, as I had been taught as a child, sightless—even though a human being who possessed their acuity of vision would qualify as legally blind. But that didn't matter. In their thousands, they navigated successfully through a blanket of air barely two feet thick but as broad as Chautauqua Lake, all by echolocation—audile radar by which they "saw" everything in their environment. And they saw with split-second accuracy. They knew instantly whether to approach it, like a lake fly or their nesting hole, or to avoid it, like another bat—or a human being.

Which was why the things were so confounded difficult to catch. How do you lasso a winged sprite that can see you better in the dark than you can see it in the light, and can fly for hours through midnight tree-tops and never touch a leaf?

You get Frank to do it!

Actually, Frank's call to the girl's dormitory was neither because of the bats' agility nor his prowess as a bat-trapper. He was sent because most of the girls turned into blobs of petrified jelly in the presence of a bat. Such irrational fear was difficult to account for. It can't have been because of Dracula movies and all that drivel. And never mind the fiction about how bats like to get into your hair. (Could one? Of course. But why would it want to?) More likely, something in the girls' psyches could not deal with anything that went flap in the night, especially in their bedrooms. For them, the monster was no longer under the bed or in the closet; it was right out in the open—and airborne! And they would not likely be persuaded by being reminded that it wasn't even much of a monster—just a minuscule mammal with incredibly soft fur and a web of skin stretched between finger bones so long that if mine were comparable my hands would have dragged on the ground and I'd all the time be tripping over them. No matter, the girls inevitably disintegrated into irrational panic.

In all fairness, bat-management wasn't Frank's most demanding duty, either. Looking back on it now, he remembers being most taxed by taking down all those CLSC banners, hooking them onto their respective poles, and carrying them outdoors to the young boys and girls who showed up on the porch every summer to march in the Recognition Day parade. Even worse, when the parade was over, he had to take them all apart, return them to their hooks on the walls of the stairwell and hallways and rooms, and check to be sure that none had been damaged by being snagged on a low-hanging tree limb or inadvertently dragged on the ground. The whole process consumed almost a week of labor and attention to detail.

Just think: in completing that single assignment, my brother handled—and helped to preserve—more Chautauqua history than most visitors are privileged to witness in half a lifetime.

I may be guilty of selective memory (my siblings would rule <u>that</u> a certainty) but it seems to me that I held a greater variety of jobs as a child than all of them combined. So what I want to know is why I was never given an interesting assignment like cleaning the Library or catching bats in the girls' dormitory in Alumni Hall.

I did have one really cushy job, actually, though I have absolutely no recollection about how I got it. It was around 1946, and I was to stop every afternoon on my way to Boys' Club at one of those substantial cottages along South Lake Drive. The only occupants, as far as I ever discerned, were two women. One was an elderly lady who mostly lived in a wheelchair and, though she never spoke a word to me, appeared to have a sweet and loving disposition. Perhaps she was a stroke victim. I never learned, and upbringing conditioned me not to ask. The other, like Poobah (the governmental functionary in Gilbert and Sullivan's comic Japanese opera *Mikado*, whose official title was "Chief Lord High Everything Else") seemed to be nurse, cook, housekeeper, companion and all-purpose helper.

My job was simple: I was to stop by each day to see whether there were any errands to be run, or a broken hook on the screen door to replace, or something to be lifted that was beyond the helper's strength. That was all. Most days there was nothing. But the job did offer one form of remuneration that I bet my siblings were never paid: one day each week, the helper (in her role as cook) baked brown-sugar buns the size of saucers. Since it would have been rude to decline her invitation to partake of one each day that she made them, I demonstrated my flawless breeding by accepting. No other job I ever held at Chautauqua was so richly compensated.

On the other hand, I'd as soon forget altogether some of the other jobs I had, like the summer that Institution secretary Charlie Pierce hired me as a sign painter. As I recall, I was twelve, and my first duty was to go around to each of the Institution's parking lots, like that behind Norton Hall, and paint numerals on wooden stakes to identify which parking slot belonged to which permit-holder. Only I was given a can of paint that looked like it might have stood on some maintenance department shelf since World War I, and a brush large enough to paint the Hall of Missions. I didn't hang around to find out, but it would not surprise me at all to learn that most drivers simply picked out the number that most resembled the one they were assigned. I had painted them myself, and I could hardly read them. How could anyone expect them to? Halfway through the season, Charlie fired me. He was gentle about it, really. We just agreed that a bit more experience would have been helpful before I took on the assignment. (That and a new brush!)

By far and away my most memorable job was the summer I was hired (it was Charlie again) to be janitor of the bus station and the practice shacks. I never quite figured out the practice shacks. Having been closed up since the previous August, they needed to be aired out, and to have the clutter of cobwebs and dust swept up. After that, though, I never could find much of anything to do. People who came by to blow on a trumpet or oboe or vocalize for half an hour didn't make a lot of dirt.

But then there was the bus station.

> (AUTHOR'S NOTE to relative newcomers and casual readers: the Main Gate Welcome Center through which most Chautauqua visitors enter the grounds today has suffered trough several incarnations over the years, including trolley station, horseless-carriage entry, bus station, and just plain "main gate." This story is set during the era when regular bus service stopped at Chautauqua en route between Jamestown and Westfield, so we often called it the bus station.)
>
> [AUTHOR'S NOTE to squeamish readers: you might prefer to skip the remainder of this chapter and move directly to the next. If, on the other hand, you decide to see it though, don't say I didn't warn you.]

The main task, Charlie let me know right off, was the men's room: "It needs attention." For that comment alone, Charlie should have been nominated to receive the Understatement of the Year Award. I was dealing here with the material embodiment of grubbing out a living. It appeared not to have been touched since the previous summer—and I don't mean to imply late August when the season closed; I mean the entire summer. Under most circumstances, filthy is a perfectly good adjective; but its adequacy in this case was entirely deficient. The place was a county health inspector's worst nightmare.

For a long moment, I stood looking at it, wondering where I could possibly begin. I had the numbing sensation that the place might actually be able to breed filth faster than I was capable of scraping it up.

Well, I hadn't been raised by Ruth Skinner for nothing. And this time, at least, I had been given the proper tools. Everything, that is, except rubber gloves. Aha! I knew that would get you. But never mind. I had never even seen rubber gloves in my life, and wouldn't for a long time to come. But I knew how to clean, and went at it with a vengeance. I started with the sinks. They were easiest; and besides, all the water that I slopped around doing them would simply serve to soften up what was underneath. The same could be said for the commodes, although removing the colorful graffiti from the stall walls—some of which expressed sentiments to which I had not previously been introduced—required me to remove half of the paint as well.

But the real challenge was the urinals. They were the upright kind, pretty much as big as me and looking like eagle-claw bathtubs that had been stood on end and sunk into the wall. It was soon clear that no brush Mr. Fuller ever invented would dent their accumulations. Those things demanded obeisance; so I got down on my knees and went at it barehanded with Dutch Cleanser and a scouring pad. I finally got them sparkling (though that adjective is purely relative in this instance). Finally, I gave my attention to the floor, against which traditional tools proved equally impotent. A mop didn't even dull the surface of dirt that had gotten lacquered onto it, so I employed the cleanser-on-my-knees tactic a second time, scouring a square foot at a time with equally impressive results.

Anything to be at Chautauqua

Leaving the door and windows open to ventilate the place, I went home at noon and bathed for about an hour before I even thought about lunch. And it was dinnertime before my palms and fingertips un-shriveled.

The reaction in the Colonnade was stunning. Charlie went up to the bus station to check things out and returned raving, "I've never seen anything like it! That men's room has never been that clean!" I confess to deriving great pleasure at the prospect of half the Institution staff trekking up to the bus station to stand amazed at the door to the men's room. More gratifying, when Mother got home that afternoon she lavished compliments on me as if I had performed some kind of miracle. She did not dispense praise easily, and never unless she thought it deserved.

I was happy that everyone was so pleased, you understand; but if any of them thought that I had found my life's calling that morning, they had another think coming. I would, in my vocation as a college chaplain, find other reasons to kneel, but adoration of urinals was not one of them. No gate ticket was worth that.

CHAPTER 32

A Posterior of Granite

The bathroom crush was tighter than usual that evening, what with all four Skinner children trying to wedge our ways in to brush teeth and comb hair, sometimes lined up two or three deep craning our necks to see around each other's shoulders and locate our own reflections in a shard of mirror. It did little good to straighten my tie if I was looking at the image of Frank's shirt. But time was short, and the Norton Hall manager had scant patience with doormen and ushers who were late.

The Skinner advantage was geographic. Unlike many of our peers, we didn't need to come half the length of the grounds to reach the blocky, art deco building set thirty yards back from Pratt Avenue behind a terraced brick patio and broad, concrete steps that spanned half the building. Living on McClintock, a short block-and-a-half away, we could walk there in two minutes. As the clock's hands crossed the 7:55 mark, we cascaded out the door, Ruth Ann decked out as if for a prom, we boys already perspiring inside too-warm-for-a-summer-evening slacks, jackets and neckties.

We squirmed at the constraint. Spoiled by Club, where dress was as negligible as modesty allowed, our young bodies had forgotten how uncomfortable propriety could get. But the standard was not negotiable: if we wanted to usher for operas and plays, we would dress as management decreed.

Milling about in Norton Hall's dank lobby, poorly lit by underpowered, lavender-pink chandeliers, we chattered with friends and waited the signal to take out stations, grateful—if only briefly—for the overheated dress code. Even on the cusp of August, Norton Hall's foyer retained a remnant of some sub-zero week last February. Think of it as a natural consequence of Chautauqua's penchant for being in on the ground floor of innovation. Named for the family of Mrs. O. W. Norton, who funded much of its construction, Norton Hall was one of the first poured-concrete edifices in the world. No attempt was made to disguise the fact; the grain of the wooden-board forms erected to hold the fresh concrete in place until it cured was clearly visible on the outside of the building, knotholes and all. It gave new meaning to "heavy construction," and resulted in a ponderous structure in which the air might heat quickly but the building itself changed with glacial sloth. Whenever it stood shut up and empty for more than a few hours, the walls stole whatever warmth the air might have acquired. So we stood there, chilled by last winter's blizzards until the doors, thrown wide, admitted both the public and the day's residual heat to warm things up again. (And warm they did. By intermission, everyone in the building was fused in a vast, communal sweat, and a third of the audience rushed outdoors to mill about on the patio and gasp for fresh air. Paradoxically, half of those neutralized whatever benefit the trip might offer—for themselves and anyone else—by drawing feverishly on cigarettes and exhaling the smoke to tarnish the summer evening. But that was still an hour and a half away.)

"Places!" barked the manager.

Three dozen adolescents bustled into gender-specific position—girls to the heads of main-floor aisles and to the tops of the stairs to the balcony; boys to the exterior doors, each gripping a crash bar in anticipation of the signal to fling it open to admit an audience many of whom already waited outside on the porch. We didn't even glance at our watches. The manager's command was authoritative evidence that it was thirty seconds before the stroke of eight; and by the time we reached our posts, it was eight-o-clock.

"Open!" barked the manager.

"First door to your left, sir."

Nine double doors banged in unison, their attendants barely having time to pull the latches to prop them open before being handed the first ticket by the first patron. Then the foyer filled with coded communication: "First door to your right, ma'am."

"Stairs to your left, sir."

"Last door to your right, folks."

And, rarely, "Stairs to yo.... Oh, I'm sorry, ma'am. This ticket is for Monday night's performance."

That brought a startled response. Few things were more disconcerting (not to mention embarrassing) than getting all gussied up for the opera only to discover that you'd misread your ticket.

Reaching the designated aisle, or arriving atop the balcony stairs, patrons were greeted by smiling girls who again surveyed their tickets, led them down the aisle to the proper row, and pointed out their seats. All went smoothly until it was discovered—as seemed to be the case at least once each evening—that some early and less-attentive patron had taken the wrong seat. Then the girls had to re-check the ticket stubs of those already seated, sort through the confusion, and put everyone where they were supposed to be, smiling patiently as someone already comfortably settled huffed and puffed about having to get up and move. The jurisprudential adage that "possession is nine-tenths of the law" was taken literally by a small coterie of Chautauqua opera and play-goers, even when their own tickets said they were in possession of the wrong seat.

The first time I opened my door (I think it was in 1947), I was in a cold sweat—but not because of Norton Hall's ambivalent climate. Reading section, row, and seat data on a ticket stub, determining where in the hall that seat was, and explaining to the patron how to get there, all in less time that it took to tear the ticket in half, seemed a daunting task. (Besides, I was aware that half the audience didn't need to be told because they'd been sitting in those same seats since before I was born. Who was I to instruct them?) As in most things where poise was the issue, Cliff was my trusted tutor. At eighteen months apart, Frank and I were too close in age for trust: we labored under the illusion that we were competing for something, and wouldn't realize we weren't—and never had been—until years later when we tried, with no greater success, to convince our children that *they* weren't competing for anything. In any event, Cliff's instructions were as precise as ever. My anxiety evaporated in about thirty seconds.

"Stairs to the left, ma'am."

"First door to your right, folks."

Managing Norton Hall's stage had to be a nightmare. The season schedule at the time included six to eight plays and operas each season, all of them staged in Norton Hall. That might not have been so bad, but there was the alternate-night schedule: plays performed on Thursday and Saturday, operas on Friday and Monday. In consequence, a complete breakdown and re-set of the stage occurred at the close of each performance. Sent backstage on some forgotten errand just after the final curtain one evening, I stepped into bedlam. Attendants sorted and arranged period costumes, checking to be sure everything was both there and undamaged. Electricians, gone from their waists up among the overhead border panels, teetered atop immense ladders, readjusting lights. Stagehands knocked down scenery that moments before had transformed Norton Hall's proscenium into an eighteenth century European town square, carried the ungainly flats into the cavernous work room behind the stage, and returned with the facsimile of an early 20th Century urban walk-up. Or maybe the transition was from apartment to square. No matter. Four times each week, entire stage settings were erected and torn down, each able to transport Chautauqua's audiences not just to a different continent, but a different century. And, by the looks of things, it took nearly as much work to accomplish the illusion as it would have the reality.

But that's why we were there. The whole purpose of applying to be on the doorman-usher crew was to get in on the space-time tour: having completed our duties in doorway and aisle, we were admitted to the performance *pro bono*. For Mother, that was serious compensation. Purchasing tickets to twelve performances for a family of five entailed a hefty outlay. But the whole reason for being at Chautauqua was to have a seat at the cultural smorgasbord. Mother would secure for us every advantage that she could afford—and a few she probably couldn't. So, in the years before any of us was old enough to usher or take tickets, she somehow managed to pay the whole freight. It was that important to her.

The location of our seats in the years before we qualified to stand in a doorway or aisle directing traffic was foregone: Mother thought that the second-balcony offered the best view for the money. I don't think she watched a single performance from the orchestra until she and Hutch married. Hutch had long since wearied of climbing balcony stairs (even if not of chasing a golf ball around the links). They would sit on the main floor. But that was after Mother's children had married and moved on. For half a decade before we began to navigate teenager-hood, we owned a controlling share of the second balcony, right section, first row. Then, in serial order, we joined the doorman-usher crew and reduced Mother's outlay one ticket at a time until, finally, she sat alone.

Whenever she came through my door after that, I'd tear her ticket, smile teasingly, and say, "Stairs to your right, ma'am." I got some noteworthy backward glances from <u>those</u> encounters.

Let's not overrate the free-admission benefit, however. Earning our way to the table didn't assure us a chair to sit in. Norton

Hall's managers were content to have us remain for performances; but not at the cost of displacing paying customers. In service to the theater's late arrival rule, we were forbidden to occupy a vacant seat until the end of the first scene. Anyone entering the lobby after the curtain went up (an odd expression: Norton Hall's curtain never went up, it parted at the center like window drapes) was barred from the auditorium until the opening scene ended. Then their scurry down the aisle was obscured by applause. (Whether they progressed without further disruption depended on where in the row their seats were located. If they held tickets to aisle seats, they could almost slip in unnoticed. But if their seats were halfway into a section, patrons already seated were set to muttering as they stood and had their toes trampled during the latecomer's squeeze-by.) Thereafter, unclaimed seats were ours for the sitting.

But if the house was filled before the first curtain—and it often was—we were consigned to the steps of the balcony; and that (recall Norton Hall's concrete constitution) required a posterior of granite. I no longer recall how many performances I endured to the end (or should I say on my end), but it wasn't many. Like as not, by the third act, most of us were lined up around the perimeter, preferring a concrete wall to lean against over a concrete floor to sit on. And on evenings when singers stood about like statues, cluttering the stage with interminable recitative while my butt went numb, I was known to sacrifice the privilege altogether and flee the building. I resisted the notion that cultural enlargement was sufficient reason to endure corporal distress. And though I appreciated Mother's passion for my artistic development, my own agenda was less lofty. I found a walk to the Pergola for a vanilla malted more to my liking; and if I could find a girl to go with me, all the better.

The more serious an opera was, the more likely I was to take the hike. Blame the elevated taste of a Chautauqua audience.

Plays, while generally well attended, seldom filled the house to the bursting point. Norton Hall seemed to be too large a venue for the proportion of Chautauquans desiring to attend plays. So I could almost always find an unclaimed seat. I liked that, because my attention seldom flagged when the professionals of the repertory company of the Cleveland Playhouse took the stage. And the fare mattered little. Whether a comedy such as "The Importance of Being Ernest" or "Harvey," one of the popular murder mysteries like "Ten Little Indians" or "Arsenic and Old Lace;" or a rare performance of one of Shakespeare's unrivaled dramas, I was glued to my seat until the final curtain—and I wanted the seat to be part of Norton Hall's anatomy, not mine.

In part, I confess, my preference was grounded in the freedom of expression that "legitimate theater" brought to the stage. I delighted in the actors' explosive "hells" and "damns" that periodically drove some dowager from the hall without even waiting for the end of the scene, too shocked by such low-brow indignity to remain in its presence. Such words were banned from our household, which was probably why I enjoyed hearing them from the stage; but I was also amused because Mother (she who maintained the domestic gag order) often giggled or laughed right out loud herself. She did not approve of cusswords in social discourse, then or ever; but she knew perfectly well that art mirrors reality, and that the real-world stage harbored a vocabulary far viler than anything ever heard in Norton Hall.

Operas, by contrast, drew large audiences, although some division was still apparent. We children were quick to express delight whenever the Chautauqua Opera Company scheduled lighter fare like "The Tales of Hoffman" or "Die Fledermaus;" and we went plain giddy over comic operas—"Gianni Schicci" or "The Barber of Seville," or Gilbert and Sullivan's classical slapstick. Nothing quite equaled Gil Gallagher's flawless delivery of an alliteration-riddled patter song like "I am the very model of a modern major general" from "H.M.S. Pinafore."

Mother, on the other hand (and for reasons we did not yet comprehend—though we would in time), yearned for the great tragedies—"Madame Butterfly," "La Boheme" or "Faust." Truth be told, had the issue been put to a referendum, Chautauquans would have voted overwhelmingly for heartbreak. Indeed, they already did: on the evening of a comic opera, un-subscribed seats often were available for ushers and doormen desperate to avoid another aching evening on the steps, as many in the orchestra as in the balcony. But when catastrophe stalked the stage, standing room only was the rule, and we young people could lean on the wall or perch on the rocks. Even regulars forced to cancel at the last minute by some misfortune in their own affairs could count on selling their tickets to some late-arriving visitor who came to the terraced steps bordering Pratt Avenue hoping for just such a break. That never happened for comedies.

Withal, we were being treated to larger art than we realized. Early on, Chautauqua became a patron of new talent. Young people seeking to wedge their way into the closed ranks of risk-averse musical organizations that, no credit to themselves, ignored talent until it had already proven itself somewhere else, often found an opening at Chautauqua. So, packed into Norton Hall, we were sometimes graced unaware by greatness in its birth throes. Some among us—those with the requisite experience to know professional potential when they heard it—apprehended where it could lead. The rest of us might not catch on until, several years later, the same voice filled the Met, and we remembered that we heard it first in Norton Hall, before the New York crowd yet knew what it was missing.

I confess to a special fondness for one in particular. When my first wife and I married in Connecticut in 1959, just a week after I graduated from Yale University Divinity School, one of them—because married to my wife's cousin—was in the congregation. Later, few noticed when he quietly whispered into the ear of the pianist of the string trio providing music for the reception. But when the piano broke into "Because," and Charles Kullman almost blew the ceiling off of the room, we all noticed. I thought Mother would come unstitched. It was by far the best wedding present we received—and likely the only one that I will never forget. And he got his "break" at Chautauqua.

There were others—Josephine Antoine, Francis Bible, Clifford Harvout, Julius Huehn, Helen Jepson—whose careers took them way beyond the confines of Norton Hall and Chautauqua's assembly grounds. But they never forgot. They returned, more than once, to sing again for the people who helped to launch their careers and who, time after time, welcomed them back with unabated eagerness.

But Chautauqua could not afford such high-powered stars all the time; so there were the others, our "local favorites," who kept Norton Hall's stage ringing with song and story well-staged and consistently competent: soprano Patricia Bybell, who could capture a young man's fancy all the way to the second balcony; Val Patacchi, his basso so *profundo* that his low E-flat held its own against a whole orchestra; baritone John McCrae, founder of the South Carolina Opera Workshop that developed into the Columbia Lyric Theatre and the Charleston Opera Company; fellow baritone Hugh Thompson, who possessed enough stage presence to command attention when he was neither singing nor moving;

and the talented siblings: soprano Beverly and tenor Donald Dame, who became family friends when Elizabeth Wheeler sent them to Mother to request her services as piano accompanist.

Then there was my personal favorite, because he was a Meadville kid like me, proving that good things can come even from a small Pennsylvania town. Last time we spoke, William Fleck had performed something like forty-seven times on one Chautauqua platform or another. I still recall the way his sonorous baritone filled Norton Hall with sound so dense you could lather icing on slices of it and make an operatic layer cake.

And we were witnesses.

Two Norton Hall footnotes:

In fairness, it should be said that stair-sitting yielded one benefit of which regular ticket-holders were unaware, else the balcony steps might have filled with be-gowned ladies and suited men, all damp: on even a torrid evening (and there were many) the concrete retained its February chill right up to the final curtain. So while my upper half might swelter in discomfort, my lower half was cool—albeit sore. And next to a vanilla malted, that may have been the best I could hope for.

But am I the only child who ever sat in Norton Hall, perplexed by the motto embossed across the top of the proscenium? I read it over and over, but it always came out the same: "ALL ‖ PASSES ‖ ART ‖ ALOPIE ‖ EPIDURES." To read the first three words without the concluding two didn't seem a likely assertion at Chautauqua, where nothing surpassed art. But what could "alopie epidures" possibly mean? Mother explained: "ALL ‖ PASSES [semi-colon] ‖ ART ‖ ALONE ‖ ENDURES" The combination of art deco lettering and a lack of punctuation were what threw me off. But decoding the words did little to reassure me as to their meaning. I wouldn't unravel that one until I attended theological seminar and concluded that the phrase, while earnest, was of dubious theological validity: if art alone endures, what becomes of God? I never pushed the point, however. At Chautauqua—especially in matters artistic—it is best to let sleeping dogs lie.

CHAPTER 33

High School Club

While we are young and not very attentive, places embed themselves in our minds in ways that color a lifetime of memories. Ask any Chautauquan of my generation to list ten things they remember most about their summers there—the ones that brim over with intensity of feeling—and I will give odds that the High School Club will rank among the top five on every list.

It didn't amount to much as a "place," actually, rather like a cross between an old gymnasium and a hay barn. Other than a small, two-room office on one side of the entry, fitted with a window that opened into the hall to control traffic, and a small meeting room on the other side where Club officers met to set policy and plan activities, it was just a single large room with balcony. The balcony was above the offices and meeting room and was fitted out with a hodgepodge of furniture and card tables. It served as our lounge. Otherwise, the main floor was divided in two: one half held three ping-pong tables, a soda cooler, and a few benches, and the other was open for games and dancing. That was about it.

There was one excellent decorative feature: about the time I was old enough to join (grade in school—but nothing else—strictly determined eligibility) some geniuses went around the walls painting life-sized cartoon figures of teenagers engaged in all manner of recreational pursuits. They lent the place a festive air. But the lighting was lousy and the PA system marginal. The ping-pong paddles had been repaired with so many layers of masking tape that a small girl had trouble getting her hand around them (serious players bought their own). And the unpainted floors were in need of constant sweeping because grit and gravel got tracked in from the dirt patch out front where we dumped our bicycles—anywhere from five to fifty of them, depending on the day and time.

Just to get into the High School Club required a degree of stamina. It was upstairs in an old frame structure the main floor of which housed the Boys' and Girls' Club dressing rooms. But the 20-step climb from ground level to the small porch landing was an ascent into kid-haven. Once through the double doors, we were in a teen-agers' world where adults never ventured. Oh, sure, Doc Reed was there. But at heart he was simply a much older version of us—or so we fancied. We just didn't appreciate the skill with which he blended a warm countenance with a firm hand, or carried out his duties in a way that left us thinking we had done it all ourselves.

The High school Club opened at 4:00 p.m. on weekdays, as Boys' and Girls' Club dismissed for the day, adjourned for the dinner hour, then reopened until 10:00 p.m. We came and went at will, and were responsible to entertain ourselves. We were expected to do that most of the time anyway; but self-entertainment at the High School Club led to some of my fondest memories of Chautauqua. That and Linda Baum and Kitty Baldridge.

Kitty and Linda lived in side-by-side cottages, and were inseparable. The surest way to locate one was to find the other. That was fine by Hank Suhr and me who, during those high school summers, were pretty much in synchronous orbits ourselves. The four of us fell into the kind of amity that was never more than friendship, but of a kind that is not eroded by over-exposure. I don't recall how many late afternoons we met at the Club, where we often had the whole cavernous room to ourselves. We played ping-pong until we'd either split the last ball or there were no longer four whole paddles to play with. Then we danced.

"Hey, Doc, put on a record," we'd call through the control desk window.

Soon the room filled with music. It was near the end of the big band era, and the Club owned dozens of scratchy old recordings of songs that were perfect accompaniment for dreamy-headed kids to glide around the dance floor. We danced until Doc threw us out of the building, trading partners between every dance and never running out of things to talk about as we circled the floor, or losing the enchanted feeling of being that close to someone warm and familiar. But it went no further. We were perhaps better prepared than later generations to accept the constraints of innocence. It never occurred to us to toy with each other's feelings, or to pretend that we were owed anything other than the trust that we mutually extended to each other. I have few memories that so fully exemplify what it meant—and how it felt—to be at once intimate and trustworthy.

"Okay, kids, all aboard," Doc announced as we milled around two Institution trucks that idled in the road in front of the High School Club.

It was always an open question what those trucks might smell like. It depended on what they had been used for the day or two previous. If the maintenance crew had been hauling equipment or moving furniture or musical instruments, things were fairly innocuous. But if they had been collecting trash, the aroma could be pretty ripe. In general, the drivers hosed them out well on evenings when they were to transport us on one of our outings.

With a great flurry, we scrambled up the sections of tailgate turned on their ends to serve as ladders, boyfriends reaching down to help girl friends while unattached males, anxious to demonstrate their Tarzan-like qualities, hoisted themselves up the sides and over the rails, and unattended girls were left to fend for themselves. Those who didn't care to be blown to pieces by the wind sat down up front and leaned against the cab, while more robust types lined up along the rails where they could enjoy the wind's full fury. With everyone aboard, the drivers lifted the gates into place and dropped them into their slots with a clatter, and Doc's beaming face appeared between the slats.

"Everyone comfy?"

"Yes!" we roared, anxious to get under way.

"Okay, here we go," Doc chuckled, and walked to the lead truck to take his place in the cab beside the driver. With a grinding of gears, a bellow, and a snort of exhaust, the trucks lurched away, rounded the bend by the bleachers, labored up Hawthorne past the Methodist Deaconess Home and the Thunder Bridge, and onto Massey Avenue.

"Keep your arms in," the driver yelled out his window as he turned into the gate. Good thing, too. Waved on by the gateman, the trucks threaded their way between the brick walls with six inches to spare on either side. Turning up state road 394 to Mayville and around the end of the lake, our boisterous caravan got into high gear, and the fragile bodies of half of Chautauqua's young people, crowded into the open back ends of the trucks, sailed along at highway speeds without so much as a seatbelt. We braced ourselves for the roller-coaster stretch where New York 17 traced the bluff hills that lined the east side of the lake, oblivious to the fact that even a slight mishap could result in unspeakable tragedy—and we loved every minute of it.

On the Road Again...

Coasting down the long slope south of Point Chautauqua, the trucks downshifted on their approach to Midway Park, slowing enough to make the turn into the long entry drive. Excitement reached critical mass as the trucks turned off the highway, and every kid of us lined up at the rails, craning our necks to see ahead into the park. We had barely stopped when the first Tarzans were up and over the sides, and the trucks were half-empty by the time the drivers lifted the gates off the back ends.

"Don't go anywhere!" Doc's voice assumed its no-nonsense tone, the one that meant "Ignore me and you will have cause to regret it." We stopped and waited for marching orders. Not until he had our undivided attention did Doc continue.

"You can go anywhere you want in the park, and do whatever you like. But you may not leave the park for any reason, clear?"

"Clear!" we agreed.

"The trucks will load at 10:30. I expect everyone to be on board by that time. I don't want to have to come find you. Clear?"

"Clear!"

"I'll be around the center of the park here for the next hour or so, if you need me for any thing. After that, I'll be up in the skating rink." Then, smiling broadly, "Okay, everyone. Have a good time!"

We were off with a shout. A few scurried toward the merry-go-round, wanting to get an outside horse so they'd have a chance at the brass ring. Others (apparently finding an hour too long a time to have been separated from the supper table) headed for the snack bar to buy something caloric to put into their faces. Most of us turned in at the penny arcade, an open pavilion equipped with a shooting gallery and a handful of pinball machines and several dozen games of skill that required throwing a ball through a hole or looping a hoop over a peg or knocking something over, all in order to accumulate points toward a cheesy memento or stuffed animal prize. I tried every one of them, and never failed to come away with at least one proud trophy that I took home, showed to Mother, and threw away.

Sundown at Midway had an effect much like the midnight chiming of the clock in the story of Cinderella. Only we didn't turn into pumpkins, we acquired wheels on our feet. As the sun settled into the trees behind Hartfield Bay at the north corner of the lake (spotlighting Miller Bell Tower, now opposite us across the water—an odd perspective for Chautauquans, like seeing a familiar vista turned inside out), more and more of us crossed the tracks of the Jamestown, Westfield and Northwestern Railroad and climbed the broad stairs of the waterfront pavilion to the second-floor skating rink. This was really the main event, the reason we most loved to go there. I suspect that we Skinner kids were not the only High School Club members who seldom got to visit a real honest-to-gosh skating rink (except when Mother agreed to take us to Midway, which we usually were able to persuade her to do about once a summer), and we relished the opportunity.

Laying down our $1.00 admission fees, Hank, George and I stopped at the counter just inside the rink to rent skates.

"Size?" the man behind the counter asked wearily, displaying all the excitement of a tired elevator attendant advising "Watch your step" for the four-hundredth time that day. Maybe he was bored, and who can blame him, being stuck behind that counter while seventy to a hundred people tore around having a splendid time twenty feet away. I could barely hear him above the blare of the Wurlitzer organ that set the pace for the skaters and was so loud that, if the wind was right, we could hear it on the front lawn of the Athenaeum Hotel.

"Ten," said Hank.

A pair of skates came out of one of the compartments that lined the back of his booth, wall to wall and floor to ceiling, each holding a pair of skates with numerals painted on them. He slid them across the counter, so scarred by just that sort of treatment that the rink floor appeared spotless by comparison.

"Give me your shoes," the man commanded. Hank kicked them off, and the attendant put them in the box from which he had taken the skates.

"Next," the monotone continued.

"Nine-and-a-half," responded George. Another pair of skates scraped across a counter in exchange for a second pair of shoes.

"Next."

"Twelve," I said. The man's stone face darkened and his look told me that he didn't really believe me. I clunked my size-twelves on his counter, rendering the issue moot. I was used to people expostulating "*Twelve?!*" when I was asked my shoe size. But hey, I was the third in a row. It was one reason Skinner men were such good swimmers: we were born with swim fins already attached.

I followed Hank and George to a bench set against the rink railing and sat down to put them on. That was the most aromatic part of those outings. It was impossible to know how many feet had worn those skates—though I suppose, being size twelve and all, there were fewer than had worn the ones that Hank and George were lacing onto their feet. Still, I held my breath and tried not to think too much about it.

There were two rinks, really, one encircling the other. An inside oval, comprising perhaps half the skating surface, was used primarily by total novices trying to learn to stay vertical with wheels strapped on their feet for the very first time; and experts who flew and whirled around the room as if they had a go-cart on each foot. We weren't exactly novices, but we weren't experts either. So we took our place among the masses that flowed along a track around the perimeter of the room.

The initial feeling was one of terminal awkwardness. I had to concentrate my full attention on my feet, lest I fall flat on my face. But my kinesthetic sense improved with each round, as if my body remembered, from previous visits, what it ought to feel like to skate, even if my brain didn't. Increasingly, clumsiness yielded to assurance, and I was soon sweeping down the straightaways and crossing my outside skate over the inside one on turns, as if it was the most natural thing in the world and I did it practically every day on my way to school. Yet how I envied the rinkmaster, who positioned himself in the flow of the outer track and skated with us—backwards. He probably could go faster in reverse than most of us could manage going forward; but he dawdled a bit, tracking right up the middle of the lane like a boulder in a river that forces the current to flow around it. Doing so, he moderated the speed and surge of the crowd, and any hotshot who sailed by too fast for safety received an ambulatory word of warning. In a severe case, he was even seen to swerve in front of an offender, poke a finger into his face, and deliver a well-deserved tongue-lashing—all in reverse.

It was around then that time let go. I was mesmerized, and so wholly enthralled that I no longer thought about what I looked like or what I was doing, but simply felt my way through it. I wasn't even conscious of the music, only of the rhythm. I have no idea how many times I circled the building, aware only faintly of the exchange that kept occurring between the cool darkness of the lake side and the glint of several hundred light bulbs in the penny arcade on the landward side. They alternated like lighted station platforms and the dank tunnel voids that came and went through subway-train windows. And I didn't care. I would not again experience so delicious a sensation until years later when I learned how to ski and discovered—under very different circumstances!—the delirium of nearly unfettered motion.

"Don, time to go!" my friends called as I came around the curve nearest the entry. They already had their skates off and were going for their shoes. I looked at my watch as I flew past. 10:20. Where had the time gone? I hardly felt tired. How was it possible to become so absorbed in just flying around a room, body synchronized to the beat of that confounded Wurlitzer, that I could lose two hours without even realizing it?

As I approached the end of the rink on the next sweep, I slipped out the gate, dropped down on the bench to unlace my skates, and retrieved my shoes. Putting them on, I stood up and almost fell on my face.

"Weird, huh?" Hank laughed. It felt like my legs had turned to wood and my shoes to concrete. We were clear down the stairs and halfway to the trucks before I could walk without feeling like I had to concentrate my full attention on my feet.

"Okay, kids, all aboard." Doc announced as we milled around two Institution trucks that idled in the road in front of the High School Club.

It was always an open question what those trucks might smell like. It depended on what they had been used for....

No, the printer didn't make an error and start to reprint the Midway story. It was another week and another trip, to another place that, if anything, we loved even more than Midway. And this trip departed mid-afternoon. Our destination was Panama Rocks, located on the edge of the rural village of Panama, ten miles south of Chautauqua.

If Midway was one hundred percent contrived, Panama Rocks was at least ninety percent natural. Not to wax too esoteric about it: the attraction was a half-mile long ridge of exposed, quartz-conglomerate rock, the residue of Paleozoic-era islands that occupied a river delta on the shore of a vast inland sea that stretched clear to present-day Utah. Compressed by eons of sedimentary buildup, fractured by tectonic uplift, and scoured by glaciers, the rocks emerged as a natural playground of caves and cavernous dens, huge chunks resting atop one another or leaning together to form crevices and passageways, all of it laced by wooded trails.

We knew every feature—"Castle Rock," which stood like a gate at the head of the trail; "Eagle's Claw" and "Crow's Foot"—trees that somehow germinated atop boulders and, against all odds, survived to send roots out to encircle their host stones to find the nurturing soil beneath; "Covered Bridge," where several pancakes of horizontal rock wedged gingerly between vertical slabs; and "Ice Cave Crevice," a deep cleft in which ice could survive long into the summer. None was more popular than "Fat Man's Misery" because the name was not facetious (one of our company, and not a particularly spherical unit at that, actually got stuck and it took us five minutes to un-wedge him). We climbed over, under and through them all, exploring every niche and cranny and regaling each other with "Lookee heres" and "Oh, did you sees."

Ever ravening after the lurid, we wormed our way down through the several levels of "Counterfeiter's Den" (which was no easy feat—there was no real floor) because we had been told that several members of a mid-Nineteenth Century gang that used it as their hide-out to mint bogus specie were trapped by government agents and died in a hail of bullets, leaving their blood to stain the rock walls. Try as we would, searching with flashlights carried along for just that purpose, we never were able to decipher which of the voluminous stains on the rock walls might have been the residue of human blood.

Still, our exploration of the rocks was no more frenzied than our consumption of the picnic supper that followed. It was not just the volume of hot dogs, buns, relishes, chips, cookies and soda that we could consume that still confounds; it was the speed with which we accomplished it, all without the slightest diminution in adolescent jabbering. But there was method both in our gluttony and the speed with which we satiated it. The picnic was prelude to one of the most popular events of the summer: a square dance with a live band in the park's rustic recreation hall.

I have no idea how much prior experience any of my peers may have had, but I had none until my first High School Club trip to Panama Rocks. Standing willing but ignorant on the dance floor, I had first to learn the difference between "bow to your corner" (whatever that might mean) and "do-si-do" (which couldn't possibly mean anything at all). Fortunately, none of that appeared to faze the man who was "calling" the dances. He seemed as accustomed to dealing with blockheads ignorant of square dance nomenclature as he was to directing gangly teenaged feet which, if not carefully tended, could become hazardous to another dancer's health. In five minutes' time, he taught us enough calls and the maneuvers that went with them that we were doing simple squares as smoothly as if we'd been doing them for years.

As the evening progressed, so did the complexity of both vocabulary and dance. Each new square took us one step further into a folk tradition that Americans had practiced for generations, but that most of us hadn't experienced until those nights at Panama Rocks. To say that we loved it would be an understatement. We went at it so hard that everyone in the room got soaked with perspiration and we had to be careful when we put our arms around each other and took hands to promenade that we didn't lose our grip, sending some poor dancer sailing off into the night like the last ice skater in line during a game of "crack the whip."

Indeed, we enjoyed it so much that we brought it home with us, and two squares of us were sent on stage during Youth Night in the Amphitheater to perform before all of Chautauqua. The job of clown fell to me (a character acting assignment, I presume), and I earned special mention in the next day's edition of the *Chautauquan Daily* for executing a promenade in just the fashion we struggled to avoid at Panama Rocks—by sailing away from my partner and orbiting half the stage in an effort to catch up with her.

We never wanted to leave Panama Rocks when the time came to climb back into the trucks. To this day, I still don't. And if I were given the power to turn back the clock, climb that endless flight of steps to the old High School Club, and find my friends of half-a-century ago still there dancing and playing ping-pong and carrying on, I'd be gone even before I finished this sente....

CHAPTER 34

College Club

I wonder: would John Vincent and Lewis Miller have approved of our 1955 College Club fundraising scheme? There we were, right where they first set foot on Fair Point to assess the suitability of the Methodist Episcopal Camp Meeting as the site for their first Chautauqua assembly. And there we were, on the second floor of the pier building erected on that same sacred ground, running "Ye Olde Slave Market." Young women, their faces demurely veiled, stood on a platform where they could be examined like cattle at a livestock auction by young men considering how much of their hard-earned summer income they were prepared to part with in order to have a female slave for an evening.

And if that wasn't bad enough, you should have seen the harem keeper/auctioneer. There I stood, clad in a striped cotton bathrobe held in place by a chain clasp at the throat, one of Mother's large lockets around my neck, calico pajama pants cinched at the waist with a girdle of gold fabric, slipper socks on my feet, and an embroidered turban on my head. Oh...and a long hairy beard, with a four-inch pointed mustache.

"How much am I bid for this fair young lass? Step forward, gentlemen, and consider her qualities. How can you resist that tight curl on her silken forehead? Who will make the first bid? Do I hear five dollars, gentlemen?"

"Two dollars."

"Sir, you do this woman an injustice! A measly two dollars for so priceless a vision? Surely, someone can do better than that!"

As any Chautauquan knew, only one thing would induce otherwise intelligent people to stoop to that level of absurdity just to raise a few bucks: Old First Night. Every summer, Chautauqua organizations vied (to borrow from the Apostle Paul) to "outdo one another in showing zeal," all so that their

...Anything to Raise Money

delegates could step onto the Amphitheater platform on Old First Night in August and thrill the assembled multitude with the generosity of their gifts. So I suspect that Messrs. Vincent and Miller would applaud our motive even as they disparaged our method.

I no longer recall how much the College Club raised that year. Whatever it was, I doubt it was sufficient to put Chautauqua's annual fundraising effort over the top. But of one thing I am certain: it would be a long time before I would again consent to make that big a fool of myself in public—especially since the last woman I handed over to the highest bidder that July evening spun around, grabbed the broken hammer I was using as a gavel out of my hand, and sold me. I suppose I had it coming. The amount bid for me, by the way, is confidential. That's another way of saying that I've forgotten. And I'll bet everyone else has, too.

Louis Wells, who was an educational administrator when he wasn't scurrying around Chautauqua, was director of the College Club. I don't recall what title he held at the college where he was employed, but it had to be in student activities somewhere. The man could rope young people into doing things faster than they could say, "I'd love to, but...." Before they got to "love," they were already committed. The Club's weekly schedule during those summers demanded it. The *Chautauquan Daily* for July 20, 1950 listed the officers for that season. Including a president and secretary, the cabinet of officers was comprised of the coordinators of seven program groups: Saturday Night Party, Wednesday Night Party, Smith-Wilkes Program, House, Old First Night, Discussion Group and Special Activities. What with virtually every college-aged youth at Chautauqua employed, one had to wonder how we ever managed to go to work—or, if we did, how we had enough time left over to keep that program schedule running.

Nor does that list exhaust all the pies in which Louis had at least one finger, among which was one that had me going on Sundays as well as weekdays. Part of his assignment from the Institution was to conduct the Sunday evening Lakeside Service (although I never quite understood how he got pulled into taking responsibility for a Religion Department event). It wasn't as if Chautauquans were short of opportunities to worship on Sundays. Between the 9:00 a.m. services in the denominational houses, the 10:45 union service in the Amphitheater, an afternoon ecumenical Bible study at the Methodist House, the 5:00 p.m. Vesper Service in the Hall of Philosophy, and the 8:00 p.m. Sacred Song Service back in the Amphitheater, one might reasonably assume that, by dinnertime, most folks would be worshipped out. But no, there must be a Lakeside Service at 7:00 p.m., too. It seemed to me evidence that anxiety about an idle mind being the Devil's worship could be carried to extremes. At Chautauqua, the Devil never had a chance to get a word in edgewise!

And once Louis discovered my pre-theological student standing, my doom was sealed. My scrapbooks are spotted with references to Lakeside Services and the parts that I played in them. Don't misunderstand: I'm not really complaining. Of all the services at Chautauqua, those conducted on the shore of the lake Sunday evening, as the sun angled toward the western horizon, were arguably the least pretentious and therefore—to my way of thinking—the most genuine. They exuded an aura of serenity. A few dozen people, mostly older ladies (isn't it always so?) gathered on benches set up in Miller Park at some vantage point overlooking the lake, to end their Sundays in adoration and gratitude.

On the other hand, they were baldly practical exercises for a young wannabe clergyman. I was assigned to read scripture or lead prayer or preach in an outdoor setting where only the bench-sitters cared a fig about what I was saying. Everyone else within shouting distance (it wasn't difficult to tell how far that was: we could hear their shouting, so knew they were within it) went about their business as if we weren't even there. The experience taught me something of inestimable value for the future: that it was possible to generate peace within myself even when I was surrounded by noise and confusion. Indeed, it was essential to be able to do so, because the world (or at least the human beings that inhabit it) were never likely to provide peace willingly. Learning how to generate inner calm, I would come to realize, was the first prerequisite of every spiritual endeavor, be it prayer, meditation or study.

If our sermons were neither as formal nor as lengthy as those delivered in other venues on those Sundays (*that* goes without saying) the speakers at those other events could not lay claim to a more grateful congregation than the one we served. They seemed especially pleased that young people took them seriously; but even more, that young people took seriously what was clearly so important to them. It dawned on us that community was a function of mind and heart, not age or scope of experience.

And if they were a small company, that was good training for an insipient seminarian, too. Few people—especially those privileged to attend large urban or suburban churches—realized that the vast majority of American congregations that gathered for Sunday worship numbered fewer than one hundred souls. (I know—in the intervening years I've preached for at least half of them!)

There may have been only one thing that those faithful folk appreciated more than young worship leaders: and that would be a young barbershop quartet.

Our barbershop quartet survived only a single season. But (and without meaning to sound arrogant) I claim that we made up in academic pedigree what we failed to achieve in longevity. First tenor Fred Parry was enrolled at Yale, where he was a member of the Spizwinks singing group. Baritone George Reed (of Boys' Club junior-counselor fame) was a student at Princeton and sang with the Masoons. Bass Jack Connolly attended Harvard, where he joined the Doozibaars. And while I, as lead, diluted the group's academic purity by attending a non-Ivy institution, I was at least privileged to join the Allegheny Singers—although we sang a classical repertoire. I wouldn't make up for it until graduate school, when I earned my theological degree at Yale.

I suppose it causes no great surprise that, having come together in part because of the College Club, we called ourselves "The Collegians." (Someone did suggest "Three Saints and a Skinner," but it never took.) And since we were never recorded, there is no way any longer to demonstrate how good we might have been—or not. I can report, however, that my brother Cliff, no barbershop slouch himself (he was first tenor in a popular quartet at Allegheny), listened to us one day and ruled, "You guys have terrific blend." But that may be beside the point. We were at Chautauqua, where no earnest musical effort went unrewarded. We were no sooner organized than we were scheduled to sing at a Club function; after which it took Louis a whole three minutes to schedule us to sing at several Lakeside Services. Whatever talent we may have possessed as a musical group, we at least had one appreciative audience at those services.

As is wont to happen at Chautauqua, word got around, and next thing we knew we were signed up for our most prestigious engagement: a performance for the Chautauqua Women's Club at an afternoon social in their lakefront clubhouse. At least 70 women, representing several dozen states and dressed fit for luncheon at the Waldorf-Astoria, gave us a rousing reception. For a fly-by-night outfit like ours, that wasn't bad.

It would have been fun to build on that summer, but it couldn't be. To develop an edge (even more, to keep one), a barbershop quartet had to rehearse often and perform regularly. That was really difficult for a group that could only get together two months out of the year. But it sure was fun while it lasted.

I learned something else useful at the College Club: elevation to public office is less often a result of merit than gullibility—and not on the part of the voters. As the 1950 season got started (it was the first year that I qualified to join) I found myself elected chairman of the Wednesday Night Party group. Truth be told, I detested the job, and was relieved when the end of the season terminated my mandate. The following summer, I thought to escape the political arena by joining the College Club Players drama group, which was preparing to stage a play in the Hall of Christ. It was Channing Pollock's "The Captain and the King," and I was assigned the part of the Leader. That was fine, until I discovered that, in Pollock's metaphorical characterizations, the Leader represented dictatorship.

In 1952, concluding that there was no escaping my political destiny—and despite my day job as a senior counselor at Boys' Club—I accepted nomination as president of the College Club, and was elected. (See? No one else was gullible enough to take the job.) I soon discovered that the position did have one distinct advantage: instead of knocking myself out doing things I didn't really want to do, I could delegate them to someone else.

Then came the strangest twist of all. It may not have been unusual for someone to be elected College Club president twice. But I may have been the only person in history whose terms were three summers apart. It came to that because I was absent during the 1953 and 1954 seasons, having been inducted into a much larger club called the U. S. Army, which did not consider it part of my duty to spend two months at Chautauqua every summer.

(I remember vividly, though, coming home on furlough in August 1953. I had driven non-stop from Camp Gordon, Georgia, where I was stationed at the Military Police Training Center, going by way of D.C. to drop two friends at Washington Station. Knowing my way cross-country, I entered New York on a back road that came north out of Sugar Grove, Pennsylvania. As I cleared the hill behind Lakewood and got my first glimpse of a sun-drenched Chautauqua Lake, my eyes welled up with tears, and I had to pull off the road and dry them before I could drive the last ten miles to home.)

So it was that, when I returned in 1955 with a year to go before graduating from college, gullibility caught up with me again: I accepted the College Club presidency a second time, condemning myself to a summer of doing stuff for people who were smart enough not to burden themselves with it.

PART 11

Closing Up Shop

CHAPTER 35

Ben Hur and Messala on Wicker

"C'mon," Bill said, "we can go up to the lobby and ride the chairs."

Admittedly, Bill Cornell's Chautauqua home was not like anyone else's. His father ran the Athenaeum Hotel, and the family occupied a "garden level" apartment on the uphill side. It was possible to look out their kitchen windows directly at the feet of people walking by on the street.

At the end of August, the hotel sank into hibernation, and would not stir again until nearly time for the gates to close, inaugurating a new season. Furniture was shoved back or stacked up, opening the floors for cleaning. Its removal also created an arena of monumental dimensions, and the sport of choice was wheelchair racing.

But not just any wheelchairs. There were a few of those around, to be sure; but they mostly sat unattended because the lounge chairs—five feet long and looking for all the world like a wicker chaise longues on wheels—were far preferable. Why toot around in Model-Ts when we could ride Duesenbergs? A leftover from earlier times when the Athenaeum catered to wealthy and spoiled summer visitors, the reclining chairs were used to roll elderly patrons right out the door and up the hill to the Amphitheater where they sat, snuggled in hotel blankets, to enjoy the scheduled program. When it was over, they were wheeled back down the hill and into the hotel lobby. To be sure, the whole enterprise demanded a muscular staff. Pushing one of those chairs up the hill, even without a body on it, was not a task for the frail. But holding one back on the downhill return, when gravity threatened to take both chair and frail occupant out of the attendant's hands and deliver them into Chautauqua Lake at high velocity, was at least as demanding.

Rolling four of the pretentious monsters into the center of the lobby and lining them up on an imaginary starting line, Bill, Frank, Lee Delasin and I climbed on board.

Chariot Race

"GO!" Bill shouted, and we were off. Racing around the corner past the dining room door, we swerved into the parlor and crossed its length, careened through the music room and back into the lobby with shouts and laughter that continued to reverberate around the high-ceilinged rooms long after we passed. We were Ben Hur and Messala on wicker, uttering vacuous threats about running each other off the road—though we were more likely to do so by accident than intention, simply because our chariots were nearly impossible to control. So we turned them around and raced in the other direction. Who ultimately won was beside the point. The race was the thing, and it could only happen during the off-season. But it wasn't all that could happen.

It was probably a truism that the majority of Chautauquans only knew the place during high summer, as if three of the year's four seasons didn't really happen there. Some few regulars, particularly those privileged to own cottages, may have come for an October weekend when the grounds burned with the fever of fall's flame; or for an early spring visit when mud and workmen ruled, and those unprepared to cope with streets clogged with carpenter's and plumber's trucks were better advised to stay away. But few, even among them, experienced the place during the abbreviated days of winter when Boreas held the lake in a grip of iron, plowed snow lay three or four feet deep along every street, and it was possible to walk the grounds for an hour without ever seeing another human being.

We, too, were ignorant of all but summer when Mother first brought us there. We drove out the gate at the crack of dawn the day after Labor Day, and did not see Chautauqua again until June. That all changed in 1950, when Mother became registrar of the summer schools. Suddenly, Chautauqua was "home," and we quickly learned that there is, indeed, a great deal of life there between Labor Day and Memorial Day.

It would probably be well to acknowledge up front that there were at least as many opportunities to get into trouble when Chautauqua was abandoned as when it was bustling. The Athenaeum was a case in point. We not only conducted chariot races with impunity, we explored the whole building, examined the kitchen, wandered through upstairs guest rooms and along the fire escapes, and climbed to the roof. Those who never viewed Miller Bell Tower from the Athenaeum roof have missed the most exciting vista that Chautauqua has to offer.

Nor was it the only roof worth climbing. I still own the picture that Mother took of the Amphitheater one winter when so much snow accumulated that a section of roof threatened to collapse, and the entire grounds crew was sent aloft to shovel it off. When they went home, the pile of snow girdling the building was so deep that it nearly touched the eves. I scrambled up the pile opposite the Congregational House, stepped onto the roof, and walked up to the ridge. From that vantage point—with the trees naked of leaves—half of Chautauqua spread out around me.

Then there was my eighteenth winter—the first during which I came home to Chautauqua for Christmas vacation. The grounds lay buried under two feet of snow, but every street and walk was plowed. Public safety demanded that they be kept clear, no matter how bad the weather, so the volunteer fire company's trucks could get through.

(Home on vacation another winter, I stood in amazement before the ashes of a cottage gutted by fire two days earlier. Barely five feet had separated the burned out structure from cottages on either side. Yet the paint on the adjacent houses was not even blistered. That was some serious fire-fighting. Realizing that the burning house could not be saved, fire chief Tom Becker (whose day job was as a teacher and coach at Chautauqua Central School), had divided his force and thrown up a curtain of water between the burning cottage and those next to it until the danger was past. Year-round Chautauquans did not need to be reminded of how much they owed their volunteer fire department. Summer Chautauquans were well-advised to do the same. Every fire had the potential to take half the grounds with it. One never did because of the skill and dedication of those year-round neighbor heroes.)

But I wasn't thinking of fire emergencies that eighteenth winter. I just wanted to climb into Mother's Chevy BelAir sedan and drive it all over the grounds—including the brick walks. Even when the walks were plowed to the curbs, a standard-sized automobile nearly scraped both sides. I suppose that was part of the challenge. I couldn't resist the temptation to drive from the Plaza to the main gate and back on Vincent; then from the Colonnade to the Hall of Christ and back on Clark. That was as far as I got. When I stopped at the Colonnade to pick Mother up for lunch, she got into the car and surveyed me with disgust.

"I'm under orders to tell you that there will be no more driving on the brick walks."

I should have known. All those Institution staff offices on the second floor of the Colonnade had windows the size of billboards looking out over the Plaza. So much for the illusion of private fun. Even before I learned that I had provided unwelcome entertainment for half of Chautauqua's administrative authorities, it was too late.

December 1951 was not a particularly nasty month, weather-wise, but it dumped a pile of wet snow on Chautauqua County; and it was my privilege to be there to take advantage of it. It was the winter Mother rented the home at the corner of Clark and Foster. She was at work that day and I, lately forbidden to motor the brick walks, was looking for something to do. I started toward the Thunder Bridge, wanting to see what the ravine looked like socked in with snow, but stopped in less than a block. The side yard of the cottage at 29 Peck, directly across from the Episcopal Cottage, was layered with 18 inches of damp snow, perfect for packing. It was both challenge and opportunity. I grabbed a fistful of snow and rolled it across the ground. In six feet it had grown in diameter to eighteen inches. Perfect!

I didn't start with a clear idea of what I was going to make. It was a bit like "finding the statue hidden in the marble." I would let the snow build itself—though few artists would willingly have claimed the result. Begun in traditional snow-man fashion, it quickly took on its own personality. Before long, a huge, goofy-looking sailor sat in the yard. His trunk alone was seven feet tall. Had he been standing, he would have reached fifteen. But that was more altitude than I could manage without an extension ladder, so I sculpted him sitting down, legs straight out before him with shoes the size of medicine balls. Behind him, I fashioned a facsimile of a marble monument topped by a model schooner.

Boy, was he homely: ponderous eyelids, bulbous nose, huge lips, and pie-sized ears sticking straight out from his head. I sculpted him a pea jacket and bell-bottom pants. To finish him off, I gave him a hand toy popular at the time: a bladder doll shaped like a bowling pin with eyes, ears and tongue that popped out when the bottom was squeezed. I of course sculpted him in mid-squeeze.

The temperature plunged that night, and my soggy-snow sailor froze hard as rock. I'll bet anyone who walked along Clark that week wondered where in heaven's name the thing came from. He still sat long after I'd returned to school. As I recall, Mother later reported that he didn't finally disappear until spring thaw in mid-March. That was no surprise. He must have weighed a ton and a half.

Two other winter activities required caution. The first was sled-riding. Summer guests who found Chautauqua's hills impressive to drive down, and more so if the trip was on foot or by bicycle, should have tried sledding down one when it was coated with six inches of compressed snow. The favorite among year-round resident children was Miller Avenue; to ride a sled from Roberts to South Lake Drive constituted willful self-endangerment. Getting started was never the problem. All we needed to do was to set our sled's runners on the snow and us onto our sleds. What followed—instantly—was akin to being launched by a catapult. We hit twenty miles per hour by South Terrace; and forty by Simpson. By the Promenade, the whole exercise began to feel suicidal. I doubt that anyone knows how many children's boots had the toes torn out at the bottom of that hill, as children dragged them on the street in an effort to stop before going right on up Mt. Herman and hurtling over the top and onto the frozen lake.

That was the other activity, by the way. By the turn of the year, give or take a few weeks, Chautauqua Lake usually was frozen over. How frozen over it was, however, was a relative value. More than just a freezing night or two were required to build ice sufficient to bear the weight of a human being, and those who ventured onto it short of an extended hard freeze paid for their dim-wittedness, sometimes severely.

Too, the character of the ice varied from one winter to the next. If the temperature first plunged some night when air and lake were calm, dawn might reveal a surface like window glass. That was the best of all options. Once the ice thickened, I could shove back any snow that had fallen and create a fine skating rink. Once, I recall, the lake thickened with little snow accumulation, and we watched ice boats fly up and down the middle of the lake at speeds no fresh-water sailor ever imagined.

But that was the rarest option. More likely, the lake froze piecemeal, as frigid air and plunging water bred ragged ice cubes that soon stuck together and created a granular surface. Then it was ideal for walking—once rigidity went deep enough. How odd it seemed, then, to survey Miller Bell Tower and Fair Point—or the whole shoreline for that matter—while standing a hundred yards out on the surface of the lake.

In neither case was it inevitable that the ice would stay uniform. During extended cold spells, when days were frigid and nights beyond description, the pressure on the ice became unbearable. More than once, usually just before dawn when I was less than soundly asleep and the mercury shrank to its lowest ebb, the unreal stillness of a Chautauqua winter was ruptured by a gunshot crack followed by a long, shimmer sound, as when a handsaw is bent nearly double and then released. The twang threatened to go on 'til lunchtime. That morning, like as not, we looked out the window to see a jagged pressure ridge, birthed like a mountain chain responding to tectonic stress, marring the plane of the ice.

No matter what form it took, however—just so it was frozen deep enough—the lake was always suitable for ice-fishing. When the bottom fell out of the thermometer and the water got rigid enough to trust with your life—usually in early January—it began.

Here and there, a few footprints appeared on the shore, then more, until a well-trodden path stretched across the ice toward deep water. One by one, side trails meandered off the main track. At the end of each, in almost any weather short of a blizzard (though even that did not entirely preclude the possibility), an isolated figure, bundled against the cold, hunched down on a small stool or old kitchen chair missing its back and gazed fixedly into a hole chopped through the ice. A simple line threaded the hole like the eye of a needle, the depth of its baited hook maintained by a bobber that floated on the dead-still water in the hole. The bobber twitched now and again, then was still. The fisherman didn't move. But if the bobber plunged below the surface and vanished, the man sprang to life, jerked the line to set the hook and, assured of success by the taut pulsations of the line, pulled in his catch.

The ice-fisherman I knew best was "Cap" Griffith. When I was small, and before Bill Marsh brought *Gadfly* to Chautauqua, two boats sat at the excursion dock south of the Bell Tower: *Gray Goose* and *Seahorse*. Bill owned them both. Indeed, he built *Gray Goose* himself. But even Bill could only pilot one boat at a time, so he hired Cap to skipper the other.

A slender little man never seen in public without his captain's hat, Cap tipped the scale at about 120 pounds. He and his equally slender little wife lived year-round in a slender little house on North Terrace, downhill behind the Glen Park Cafeteria, which faced onto the Plaza. The Glen Park consisted of two buildings joined by a bridge-room suspended between them, with no foundation of its own. The space beneath formed a low tunnel used by Glen Park staff to go between the cafeteria and the rooming houses they occupied on the downhill side of North Terrace. But the staff didn't invent the route. Cap discovered it, and used it as a shortcut between his house and the Colonnade, in deference to which someone at the Glen Park lettered a sign and hung it on the outside wall of the bridge building. It read, "Cap's Alley."

I went out on the ice with Cap once. Wise in the ways of a lake fed by numerous springs, where upwelling water could thin the ice from beneath and create a concealed hazard, he carried a six-foot pole with which he poked the ice in front of him every step of the way out.

"Once in a while," he instructed, "I poke right through the ice. Then I have to back away and try another route."

He didn't find any thin spots that day. Little wonder. The air had lingered below zero for more than a week. Nor was there enough snow on the ice to form an insulating blanket. We might as well have been treading a concrete sidewalk. Nevertheless, I stayed close to Cap's heels.

Mostly, Cap caught yellow perch, a non-game fish that was legal year-round, at any size and in any number. So he kept them all. I didn't say anything; but it wouldn't have been my choice. I'd caught and eaten perch more than once. Even large ones (they grew to about 10 inches in Chautauqua Lake) were—as one friend put it—108% bones. I was put in mind of Dad's instructions for eating carp: nail the fish to an oak board, boil it four hours, throw away the fish, and eat the board. Cap didn't care. As each perch came through the hole, he removed the hook and threw the fish onto the ice a few feet away. At day's end, he gathered them up—by then as stiff as Dad's carp board—took them home to clean, and stored them in a chest freezer. Several times each week, clear through the next summer, Cap's wife prepared perch for supper. It would have been fun to learn just how many recipes the woman had for perch, but I never thought to ask. About the time she had nearly to stand on her head to reach the last fish in the bottom of the freezer, rime ice was forming at the edges of the lake, Cap got out his poking pole, checked his line, and began to make preparations to sit a half mile out on the frigid lake, alone but never lonely, hunched over his bobber and dreaming of poached perch.

Cap didn't bother with a fishing house, but many fishermen did. When the ice got thick enough to hold a car, they appeared, one or two at first, then half a dozen, finally a whole village, clustered over the deepest water in the lake's north basin, to which the fish migrated during the iron months of winter. It was Mother's favorite scene of the year. During the time that she was working, and living year-round on the lakefront, we could depend on her to notify us, off at school, when the fishing village convened on the lake; and again when it was dismantled, a shack at a time—evidence that vernal spirits were at work thinning the ice.

Soon, then, it would be time to get out the rakes and brooms and mops. A new Chautauqua season was just around the corner.

Afterword

Once engaged with Chautauqua, it is hard to disconnect. But then, no Chautauquan needs to be told that.

When my boyhood ended (some would contend that the process is ongoing) visits to Chautauqua of necessity became less frequent. Even so, though married with children and either in graduate school or attending to newly acquired professional responsibilities, I managed to return with remarkable frequency. Two things conspired to make those returns possible. First, being in campus ministry lent flexibility to my work schedule. There is just so much for a college chaplain to do during the summer when no one's around anyway, and most of that involves planning—which can be done at Chautauqua as well as at home! As a corollary, freed from campus duties, I was at liberty to seek summer employment; and where better than in the place that even my infant children thought was heaven?

In consequence, my resume is rife with references that were recorded only because Chautauqua was there, and I was at Chautauqua.

During the summers of 1960 and '61, for example, I was assistant to the Rev. Dr. Henry Smith Lieper, director of Chautauqua's Religion Department from 1958 to 1967. "Assistant" was a bit pretentious, actually. "Catch-all" would be more accurate. My first responsibility was to direct the Junior Church program that met from 10:30 a.m. to noon on Sundays, freeing the parents of young children to worship in the Amphitheater. So far so good.

The same couldn't be said of my second duty. I was to supervise the Globe Club (which my young charges insisted on calling "Glub-Club") on Sunday evenings. I was comfortable with the assignment. I had been a member as a child, recalled it as a program to acquaint children with the global character of the Christian churches, and remembered that we elected officers from among our own members. I wasn't aware that I was being delusional about it until the opening Sunday. It was like being doused with a bucket of cold water. The person in charge in 1959 had apparently gotten through by showing a series of eight hour-long films on the life of Billy Graham. I arrived at Smith-Wilkes Hall to find a dozen children in an auditorium half-filled with adults waiting for a movie. That took some reorganization.

But the larger share of my time was devoted to clerk-typist duties. Weekday amphitheater services at the time used a revolving set of legal-sized, mimeographed sheets as bulletins. Chaplains of the Week could pick whichever ones they wanted to use. But many of those left over from previous summers were so frayed that they resembled my Grandmother McCafferty's crocheted doilies. And worshippers had carried off a sufficient number that there were no longer enough on some days to supply the congregation. So Hank put me to work in the office at the Hall of Missions, preparing an entirely new set. I spent half the summer laboriously typing one legal-sized mimeograph master after another—just the sort of work that I had prepared for in seminary. I was reminded of a quip by John Oliver Nelson, field work director at Yale and long-time Chautauqua friend: "In most parishes, 'staff meeting' means a conversation between the minister and the sexton." I may not have been Hank's sexton, but I was close.

Against that background, the summer of 1963 appeared to promise something akin to the second coming: I was invited to be director of the High School Club. I confess to some trepidation. To step into the shoes of Doc Reed, who still loomed as a giant in my mind, seemed a step too far. I needn't have worried—but not because my anxiety about doing for that generation of kids what he

"Doc" Wouldn't Recognize the Place

did for mine was unfounded; there simply was no way to accomplish it. While I had been paying attention to graduate school, the world changed, and Chautauqua with it. Trying to revitalize the Sunday morning class was my opening—and monumentally humbling—failure. I knew the old template would no longer appeal, so billed it as a "Rap Session" (remember that vacuous phrase?) during which we'd talk about whatever mattered most to the participants. The first week, ten kids showed up, few of them with anything to contribute. Things never improved. Meantime, the country began its descent into a litigious society, and the mere thought of transporting High School Club members to Midway or Panama Rocks in the backs of Institution trucks made Chautauqua's trustees apoplectic. Our furthest outing was fifteen feet from the Clubhouse: we built a fire on the lakefront and toasted weenies and marshmallows. Be still my heart.

But I assert one thing without fear of contradiction, because so few people have the requisite experience to challenge me: if you want to elevate your stress level, spend four hours of a Friday evening in an overheated and badly-ventilated room with 120 writhing teenagers and a rock band. Doc, you had it sooo good.

No Chautauqua memory, however, brought satisfaction to equal what I experienced when The Rev. Dr. Herbert Gezork, Hank Lieper's successor as director of the Religion Department, tapped me to deliver the 2:30 p.m. Religion Department lectures in the Hall of Philosophy. I felt honored, my children were ecstatic (about getting to Chautauqua, not about my lectures) and Mother was horrified.

She was in the audience on Monday when Herb introduced me and I stepped to the lectern to deliver my first lecture, her hands knitting so furiously that the she almost set the yarn afire.

During the obligatory "Gosh-it's-sure-good-to-be-here" opening remarks, I couldn't resist the temptation to bring her presence—and anxiety—to the audience's attention. It took only this brief anecdote:

Several years earlier, when her minister learned that I would be in town over a weekend, he invited me to preach the Sunday sermon at Hurlbut Church.

"Is your sermon ready?" Mother inquired after dinner Saturday evening.

"Mother," I replied playfully, "I am thirty-two years old and I have a wife and two children. You don't have to worry about me anymore."

"I don't care how old you are," she shot back, "I'm still your mother."

And so she was.

It was 1972. America was in the throes of its environmental awakening. People were curious, troubled, and in search of answers. And people of faith wanted a religious perspective. I had been involved in environmental work for a number of years before Earth Day 1970 sounded the wake-up call that first riveted public attention on the damage we were doing to our world. And I had lectured on the topic, mostly in the upper Midwest. But I had not, in any systematic way, attempted a synthesis of my environmental passion and my theological training. The Chautauqua lectures provided the opportunity to do just that. My topic was "Stewardship and the Environment," with subtitles like "Scientific Evidence vs. Ethical Judgment" and "Standard of Living vs. Quality of Life," and concluded with "Transforming Our Religious Value System."

I don't know just what people who attended the first lecture were expecting. On Monday, however, the hall was perhaps two-thirds filled. It was an average audience at the time, and besides, it was far larger a group than I normally had opportunity to address! On Tuesday, however, only a handful of seats remained empty. And by Thursday people were sitting on the outside wall and overflowed onto the lawn. I admit it: I was thrilled. But not as thrilled as on Friday. We had had difficulty all week getting out of the hall on time to make way for other scheduled events. People were more than a little eager to learn, and there seemed no end to their hunger. So when we again ran out of time on Friday, Herb whispered in my ear, then took the microphone to announce that those desiring to continue were invited to adjourn to the Hall of Missions, where the question-and-answer period would resume. By the time he and I entered the room, the chairs were filled, people were standing around the walls, and we didn't stop until after 5:00 p.m. It was one of the most rewarding experiences of my life.

Every public speaker should be fortunate enough to be questioned by a Chautauqua audience. Their reputation is well-deserved.

The biggest surprise in my post-adolescent experience (though the one I would rank as positing the most predictable outcome) was in 1983 when I was nominated to become president of Chautauqua Institution. I was dean at Allegheny College when the call came: could I set aside an hour to be interviewed by two representatives of Chautauqua's board of trustees? Of course I would. The call was not entirely unexpected. My well-meaning but naïve benefactor had told me that he had thrown my hat into the ring. At the appointed hour, Kay Logan and David Carnahan—two people for whom I had great respect—arrived for the interview. It was all very flattering, and they were faultlessly gracious. It was also a subterfuge, and we all knew it. The board had determined to give every "regular" Chautauquan nominated the courtesy of an interview, and it was my turn. We had a wonderful conversation, and the board had the good sense to elect my friend and Allegheny classmate Dan Bratton as Chautauqua's next president.

Unknown to Chautauqua's trustees, Ruth Williams Knights and I had twice nominated Dan to be president of Allegheny College. (Ruth was my associate dean, a position she had held since before Dan and I enrolled!) In further proof that prophets indeed lack honor only in their own countries, Dan was never seriously considered. When his Chautauqua election was announced, my response was immediate and convicted—and I later wrote and told him so: "As usual, God's judgment in these matters was superior to mine, and Allegheny's loss became Chautauqua's gain. As one who loves both places with something bordering on fanaticism, how can I complain about that?"

Dan never disappointed us. And when he died shortly after retiring, I fully understood Chautauqua's palpable community grief. Seldom in my life has the death of someone outside my own family left me with such a stubborn feeling of empty-heartedness.

My most recent Chautauqua reincarnation occurred in 1985. Patricia and I were early into a nine-year sojourn in her native Oregon. Sitting at my computer one February morning working on the manuscript for a book, my attention was diverted to Pat's hand as it crossed my field of vision holding a classified ad she had just cut from *United Church News*. It seemed that the Chautauqua United Church of Christ Society, Inc. was seeking a chaplain-administrator. I glanced quickly at the bill of particulars, smiled into her inquiring eyes, and responded with just the words she was longing to hear.

"Hey, we're retired. We can do this."

So we applied, and were chosen. Commuting from Oregon admittedly had its disadvantages. But we did so four times before concluding that we had done our share. We concluded prematurely, as it turned out. It wasn't long following our return to Pennsylvania in 2002 that the nominating committee fingered me for the Society's board of directors. What they say is true, you see: there really is no rest for the wicked.

Among the responses I received from my siblings when I contacted them to ask for their help in resurrecting memories that might enrich this book, one in particular struck home. It wasn't a memory so much as an observation offered by my brother Frank, who captured in a single sentence the enduring nature of Lewis Miller and John Vincent's dream: "Maybe a book about Chautauqua," he wrote, "has to end with the fact that there isn't an ending."

That says it all.

Printed in the United States
78519LV00004B/127-174